Student Learning Styles and Brain Behavior

PROGRAMS • INSTRUMENTATION • RESEARCH

National Association of Secondary School Principals

National Association of Secondary School Principals
1904 Association Drive, Reston, Virginia 22091

Contents

Part Three: Brain Behavior Research and Application

Part Four: Next Steps *Scott D. Thomson*

Appendix

Foreword

The Learning Styles Network of the National Association of Secondary School Principals and St. John's University, New York cosponsored this first major conference for practitioners and researchers on student learning styles and brain behavior. The conference was designed to bring together leading persons in these related fields for a unique exchange of information and discussion of mutual concerns. Conference participants shared in a rich program of general sessions, clinics, workshops, and swap shops. Featured speakers included many of the key leaders in the learning styles and brain research fields.

The format of this volume emulates the threefold thrust of the conference—programs, instrumentation, and research. Part One reports representative attempts to implement learning styles analysis and diagnostic-prescriptive education in schools and classrooms. Part Two presents selected learning style assessment models and related research. Part Three explores the developments in brain behavior research and application. Part Four suggests some next steps. The Appendix includes the NASSP Student Learning Styles Model (1979), an annotated bibliography of selected learning styles instrumentation, and information about the Learning Styles Network.

Learning styles are cognitive, affective, and physiological traits that characterize how learners typically best learn. Brain behavior research explores the microcosmic world of brain development and learning—brain growth and functioning, cognitive processing, hemispheric differences and integration, and sex-related learning differences. Together the two fields constitute a significant cutting edge of contemporary efforts to create a more personalized and effective system of education.

School programs and research in learning styles and brain behavior have mushroomed in the past decade. Concepts discussed only by clinical psychologists and neuroscientists a few years ago are now the focus of major efforts to better understand learning and to improve schools.

Knowledge about learning styles and brain behavior is a fundamental new tool at the service of teachers and schools. It is clearly not the latest educational fad. It provides a deeper and more profound view of the learner than previously perceived, and is part of a basic framework upon which a sounder theory and practice of learning and instruction may be built.

The key question explored by many of the presentations in this volume is "What do we do about individual differences among learners?" If we wish individual students to have optimum learning experiences in our schools, we must make some changes in the educational delivery system. But do we change the learning environment or do we try to change the learner? Some believe that we need more responsive instructional environments based on stylistic and skill differences among learners. Most of the individualized instruction and learning styles efforts to date have concentrated on this approach.

Others feel that we should help the student become more responsive to the *existing* learning environment. If a youngster is not very adaptable or cannot cope well in a conventional classroom setting, or if he or she is more right-brain oriented, some say that we should and can enhance his or her learning styles to allow for more successful school achievement.

The decision is value-laden but surely not irreconcilable. A program-person continuum is implied. Will our approach be innovative or therapeutic? Most learners will require some skills or style therapy as well as a more personalized program of instruction. The presentations in this report suggest some of the appropriate ways to do both.

A special word of thanks to NASSP Executive Director Scott Thomson and Professor Rita Dunn of the Learning Styles Network for proposing that there be such a conference, and to Anne Smith Gray, NASSP's Director of Professional Development, for coordination and arrangements.

NASSP sincerely hopes that the concepts, theories, research, and programs appearing in this publication will stimulate even more productive activity on behalf of American education.

James W. Keefe
NASSP Director of Research

Contributors

Robert Ballinger, French teacher, Worthington High School, Worthington, Ohio

Virginia Ballinger, Spanish teacher, Upper Arlington High School, Upper Arlington, Ohio

Walter B. Barbe, editor-in-chief, Zaner-Bloser, Inc., Honesdale, Pennsylvania

Thomas R. Blakeslee, president, Orion Instruments, Woodside, California

Patricia K. Brennan, math teacher, St. Joseph's Junior High School, Long Island City, New York

Angela Bruno, associate professor, College of Education, University of Akron, Akron, Ohio

Kathleen A. Butler, adjunct lecturer, University of Connecticut, Storrs, Connecticut

Marie Carbo, Director of Research and Staff Development, Learning Research Associates, New York City

Kenneth J. Dunn, Professor, Graduate Programs in Educational Services, Queens College, City University of New York

Rita Dunn, professor, School of Education and Human Services, St. John's University, Jamaica, New York

Anthony F. Grasha, professor of psychology, McMicken College of Arts and Sciences, University of Cincinnati, Cincinnati, Ohio

Anthony F. Gregorc, associate professor, Department of Curriculum and Instruction, University of Connecticut, Storrs, Connecticut

Shirley A. Griggs, coordinator of counselor education, St. John's University, Jamaica, New York

Leslie A. Hart, author, New Rochelle, New York

Helene Hodges, administrator/teacher, Junior High School 22, New York, New York

Sheryl (Riechmann) Hruska, professor, Department of Human Services, University of Massachusetts, Amherst, Massachusetts

David E. Hunt, professor, Department of Applied Psychology, Ontario Institute for Studies in Education, Toronto, Ontario

James W. Keefe, director of research, National Association of Secondary School Principals, Reston, Virginia

Gerald E. Kusler, director of instructional and professional development, East Lansing Public Schools, East Lansing, Michigan

Gordon Lawrence, professor, Department of Instructional Leadership and Support, University of Florida, Gainesville, Florida

Charles A. Letteri, director, Center for Cognitive Studies, University of Vermont, Burlington, Vermont

Jerre Levy, associate professor of behavioral sciences, Department of Biopsychology, University of Chicago, Chicago, Illinois

Michael K. Martin, English language arts facilitator, Bishop Carroll High School, Calgary, Alberta, Canada

Michael N. Milone, Jr., director of research and learner verification, Zaner-Bloser, Inc., Honesdale, Pennsylvania

Philip K. Oltman, research psychologist, Educational Testing Service, Princeton, New Jersey

Janet Perrin, executive secretary, National Network for the Study of Learning and Teaching Styles, St. John's University, Jamaica, New York

Gary E. Price, associate professor, Department of Counseling, University of Kansas, Lawrence, Kansas

Richard M. Restak, neurologist; instructor, Georgetown University Medical School, and the Washington School of Psychiatry

Ronald R. Schmeck, professor, Department of Psychology, Southern Illinois University, Carbondale, Illinois

Bruce M. Shore, associate professor of education, McGill University, Montreal, Quebec

Richard Sinatra, director of reading, School of Education and Human Services, St. John's University, Jamaica, New York

Seldon D. Strother, director, School of Curriculum and Instruction, College of Education, Ohio University, Athens, Ohio

Scott D. Thomson, executive director, National Association of Secondary School Principals, Reston, Virginia

Ralph A. Vigna, principal, Bishop Carroll High School, Calgary, Alberta, Canada

William Warner, director of instruction, 916 Area Vo-Tech Institute, White Bear Lake, Minnesota

Robert Zenhausern, associate professor, Graduate School of Arts and Sciences, St. John's University, Jamaica, New York

Part One

Student Learning Styles Programs

CHAPTER 1

Learning Style/Brain Research: Harbinger of an Emerging Psychology

Anthony F. Gregorc

Education today is making an insufficient impact on the human potential for learning. A primary contributing factor is our fragmented view of instruction. Twenty-two years of teaching and administrative experience, including 12 years of research into how people learn and teach, have left me with two deep concerns.

First, we, as professional educators, lack an aggregate of agreed-upon facts and principles which serve as a basis for our labors. This concern is captured in John Goodlad's statement:

> In spite of some self-congratulatory rhetoric to the contrary, education is still a relatively weak profession, badly divided within itself and not yet embodying the core of professional values and knowledge required to resist fads, special interest groups, and—perhaps most serious of all—funding influences.[1]

Second, we lack a coherent psychology which permits us to investigate, classify, and understand the phenomena of learning and teaching. Instead of a holistic, broadly-based psychology, we, as individuals, appear to subscribe to separate "schools"—behaviorist, psychoanalytic, humanistic, existential, transpersonal, Eastern, esoteric, cognitive, developmental, medical intervention (drugs and electrical), etc. Each of these schools has its founders, disciples, interpreters, truths, facts, and methods of investigation and classification. Each also has its strategies and technologies for normalizing people and for improving learning and teaching. Unfortunately, some of these schools are at odds with one another. As a result, we continue to run in educational circles.

My experience tells me that learning style and brain research has the potential to serve as a framework that could put the various facts and psychologies into a perspective and thereby lead us toward becoming a united profession.

Five *general* points could affect the formation of that framework: (1) What learning style research is teaching us; (2) What brain research is

---

1. John I. Goodlad, "Can Our Schools Get Better?" *Phi Delta Kappan,* January 1979, p. 342.

teaching us; (3) What potentials lie before us; (4) How the potential of this research could be snuffed out; and (5) Why I believe we must persist in our efforts in the learning style/brain research arena.

What Style Research Is Teaching Us

One of the greatest findings emerging from learning style research is a reaffirmation of the theory of relativity. Succinctly expressed by Bentov:

> The theory of relativity emphasizes the notion that no matter what we observe, we always do so relative to a frame of reference that may differ from someone else's, that we must compare our frames of reference in order to get meaningful measurements and results about the events we observe.[2]

This finding is profound! It means that there is not just one view of reality and one school of thought. Empirical, phenomenological, and scientific research have revealed that people perceive both the physical, concrete world and the nonphysical, abstract world. Some individuals, however, are more "at home" with one world than with the other. This predilection affects what they see and don't see and what they experience and don't experience despite equal opportunities to interact with the so-called "same environment."

Researchers have found that people organize their thoughts in a linear, step-by-step order *and* in a nonlinear, leaping, "chunk-like" or holistic manner. Again, some people show decided tendencies toward one or the other. Such partiality affects their use and scheduling of time, the physical arrangements of their environments, their daily planning, their view of change, and their view of the future.

The linear-oriented person sees tomorrow as the direct result of yesterday's and today's careful planning, efficient use of time, and task-related efforts. This individual expects to receive the fruits of his labors—not surprises.

For the nonlinear person, tomorrow contains the past, the present, and it could contain a modifying element which is absent today. This individual develops general plans, lives for surprises (sometimes called miracles), and celebrates each day as "the first day of his life."

Learning style research also teaches us that people think in different ways. This view is highlighted by Hannah Arendt's definition of thinking. She states: "Thinking is an activity of examining whatever happens to pass or to attract attention regardless of results and specific content."[3] Some people think with their sensory apparatus; others think with their hearts. A few think with their intuition; and, of course, some think with their intellect. If these are differentiated forms of thinking, then the plea to develop higher level thinking among students takes on broad and exciting connotations.

---

2. Itzhak Bentov, *Stalking the Wild Pendulum* (New York: Bantam Books, 1979), p. 4.
3. Hannah Arendt, *The Life of the Mind* (New York: Harcourt Brace Jovanovich, 1978), p. 5.

Learning style research indicates that people's styles reveal how they identify, judge, substantiate, confirm, and validate *truth*. To some people, seeing is believing. To others, truth comes through "feeling it in one's bones," through "chills," or through "gut" reaction. Some know truth through insight, hunches, and intuitive flashes; others only accept truths which fit their intellectual formulae and are backed by statistical studies or are replicable on demand. This multiplicity of truth-testing approaches challenges those of us who want people to accept our truths and believe as we believe.

Learning style research has also shown that we, as human beings, can separate ourselves physically and mentally from our environments. We can also associate with environments in varying ways. Again, however, predilections appear. Some of us demonstrate separative, independent, individual "me-oriented" behaviors and appear to learn and produce best in environments which support such behavior. Others, however, reveal a natural affinity toward collective, interdependent, group "we-oriented" activities. Such natural orientations toward and away from specific environments should prompt an analysis of the types of behaviors which are "programed" into our classroom expectations.

These are but a few of the findings about individual styles that appear in the research. They are, however, representative samples of similarities and differences among people. When we turn our attention away from an individual's style, we are immediately confronted with an environment which consists of people, objects, and processes. And, from style research, we quickly come to realize that each of these has stylistic elements built into them too.

For instance, a teacher may present a lesson by using a style that requires high abstraction ability to decode a lecture, linear organization of thought to follow the teacher's logic, a tacit acceptance of the teacher's truths or the truths of cited authorities, a willingness to learn on one's own without discussion, and the ability to sit quietly on hard chairs in a dimly lit auditorium which has a history of heating problems.

The teacher, as both a medium for the content of the lesson and an environmental engineer, places demands upon the student for adaptation through his or her decisions. Some students will and can adapt. Some, however, won't and can't (to the degree needed) for a variety of reasons.

The teacher is, however, not the only medium in the classroom. When we analyze classroom products, activities, and organizational designs, we find that each of these has built-in stylistic demands. Books, computers, programed instruction, and movies all make particular stylistic demands. The same is true for simulations, guided fantasy activities, brainstorming, and silent reading. And, anyone who has experienced both open-classroom and .traditional classroom organization structures has certainly experienced variable stylistic demands. This research strongly supports Marshall McLuhan's position that the "medium is a message and a massage." And it causes me to pause and reflect upon how haphazard, naïve, and selfish some educators are in their selection of instructional means, methods, and environmental conditions.

What Brain Research Is Teaching Us

As I review the data coming to us from brain research, I sense a serious, scientific approach to understanding how the brain functions. I also sense that the major research is moving in two directions: pure research into how the brain works, and physical experimentation designed to remedy certain neurophysiological problems so that a patient can live a more productive life.

These research motivations are not quite the same as those prompting the efforts of learning style researchers. The pure research and medical application thrusts of the brain researchers can benefit us; however, we must be very careful when adapting tentative brain hypotheses or special case training techniques into our everyday classroom strategies. Brain researchers have much to teach us, but we have much to learn before we run amok with homemade conclusions and consequent activities built on our interpretation of their data.

These are, of course, cautionary words. They should not, however, be construed to mean that brain research is not applicable to learning style research. Indeed the two are compatible in certain ways. When the physical efforts of the brain researchers are combined with the psychological efforts of the learning style researchers, several parallels emerge:

1. The brain is differentiated in function: the two halves process different kinds of information in different ways. The hemispheres appear to "house" specific functions like analytical and synthetic processes, imagery and verbal responses, and simultaneous and successive processes in different sections. This supposition supports empirical evidence about the differences in stylistic responses to stimuli.
2. The two halves of the brain are connected and therefore function holistically. Despite reasonable specialization of the hemispheres, they indeed work together. This, in part, accounts for empirical evidence that people can register at least some information to varying degrees irrespective of the instructional technique. This fact also accounts for the generalized impression that we all learn the same way.
3. Certain environmental stimuli and cultural activities stimulate specific functions more than others. If these functions are well developed in an individual, the responses will be refined and clear. This, however, points to the biases in some of our teaching techniques and raises questions regarding the balancing of our approaches.
4. Brain growth periods may occur in which certain data can be gathered and reinforced better than at other times in human growth and development. This lends credence to the empirical and psychological positions regarding cycles, ages and stages, periods of absorption and reflection, transitions, and crisis periods in human life.

These are only a few findings. They are, however, important core findings which provide physical correlations to empirical, phenomenological, and psychological research discoveries. Such parallels provide strong evidence that individual differences do indeed exist and that some of our instructional approaches are inappropriate for many individuals.

What Potentials Stand Before Us

Marvelous opportunities stand before us. Learning style/brain research can provide the impetus toward a framework built on a sound knowledge base and toward an emerging psychology which will help us promote the development of the holistic human being.

These combined efforts can also serve as a launching pad for more thought-provoking questions such as those now being raised regarding mind/brain differences. Is there a difference between the mind and brain as neurosurgeon Wilder Penfield believes? He states:

> . . . one cannot assign to the mind a position in space and yet it is easy to see what it does and where it does it. . . . The brain is the vastly complicated master organ within the body that makes thought and consciousness possible. In its integrative and coordinating action, it resembles, in many ways, an electrical computer.[4]

If there are differences between the mind and the brain, what are they?

We can begin to examine our beliefs and presuppositions about thoughts which limit us. If nonlinear, holistic grasping of information is a natural ability anchored in the brain, can we now expand our view of change which, to date, has been built upon the idea of gradualism? Can we seriously begin to consider concepts like synchronicity, eurekas, and the idea of time/no time and infinity? Can we open ourselves to appreciate people who "march to a different drummer"?

Can we openly begin to study such subjects as clairvoyance, mental telepathy, precognition, and telekinesis as we learn more about the electromagnetic fields of the brain and how they interrelate with the environment?

Can we look with renewed vision and hope at some of the people presently labeled "learning disabled"? Are they all truly disabled in a neurological sense or is their disability, in some cases, symptomatic of their inability to align and adapt to style expectations or the demands of the environment(s)? Could we, as a profession, be creating "learning disabled children" through our own ignorance of how the brain functions and how people learn?

And finally, as more and more links between mind/brain and the physical body are uncovered, can we ask questions such as: Does the body have signal systems that alert us to alignment and misalignment between our own abilities and the demands being placed upon us? Is the syndrome called "burnout" in some measure due to misalignment, overcompensation, and overachievement in style? And, can misalignment be remedied through pain killers, drugs, alcohol, and get-away weekends?

---

4. Wilder Penfield, *The Mystery of the Mind* (New Jersey: Princeton University Press, 1975), pp. 10–11.

These and many more questions need to be addressed. Style and brain research offer serious responses.

How Styles Could Become a Fad

Despite all the positive potential and the results that can emerge from learning style/brain research, there is an equally negative potential for the misuse, abuse, and diminution of the information and research data. Such negativity can result in styles becoming another educational fad.

Five *in-house forces* could mitigate against the success of our labors.

FORCE 1: THE NATURE OF THE PRESENT SYSTEM

The present system that undergirds the schools has a long history and a strong presence. Schools, as systems, represent coordinated sets of facts, assumptions, doctrines, programs, and procedures. The word "coordinated" is especially noteworthy when we consider that a fundamental idea guiding the programing and procedures in most schools is the Average Children Concept. This concept:

> . . . is essentially the belief that all children, except for a rare few born with severe neurological defects, are basically very much alike in their mental development and capabilities, and that their apparent differences in these characteristics as manifested in school are due to rather superficial differences in children's upbringing at home, their preschool and out-of-school experiences, motivations and interests, and the educational influences of their family background. All children are viewed as basically more or less homogeneous, but are seen to differ in school performance because when they are out of school they learn or fail to learn certain things that may either help them or hinder them in their school work. If all children could be treated more alike early enough, long before they come to school, then they could all learn from the teacher's instruction at about the same pace and would all achieve at much the same level, presumably at the 'average' or above on the usual grade norms.[5]

If the Average Children Concept is a hidden "fact" undergirding a given school's curricular programs, instructional procedures, and organizational designs, the "facts" of basic universal abilities *and* individual predilection differences emerging from learning style/brain research will not fit the system. The integrity of the system cannot tolerate such dissonant facts except in non-mainstream activities such as alternative schools and special education programs.

FORCE 2: SUPERFICIAL AND EXCESSIVELY COMPLEX PRESENTATIONS

The study and use of learning style research can be thwarted by the ways in which we convey our ideas. By making inservice presentations too brief

---

5. Arthur R. Jensen, "How Much Can We Boost IQ and Scholastic Achievement?" *Environment, Heredity, and Intelligence.* Cambridge: Harvard Educational Review, 1969, p. 4.

and by making applications sound too easy, we can jeopardize the integrity of the concepts and invite all types of abuses. A one-hour inservice session on learning styles and brain research, if not handled carefully, can result in misunderstanding, reflected in phrases such as: "I know all about it now," "Oh, I already do that," "Is that all there is to it," "It's just a new name for using a variety of approaches," or "Now I know how to teach to the right side of the brain." Each of these responses conveys superficial awareness rather than the understandings which can emerge from such research.

Superficiality is, however, only one half of the coin. The other half is excessive depth and complexity. The ideas and research data can be clothed in esoteric jargon and in complex, intellectual constructions that cause people to avoid or choose to remain ignorant of them. People may claim that they "don't have the time or the background to study it," or may ask, "Why do they make such a simple thing sound so complicated?"

FORCE 3: THE EMERGENCE OF SNAKE OIL PEDDLERS

We have recently witnessed a tremendous growth in the number of educational consultants specializing in learning style/brain research. Many of these consultants are knowledgeable, insightful, and excellent presenters. They have validated the content of the messages they are conveying and some have done their own research. Such individuals play a vital role by broadening learning style concepts and by training teachers in the use of specific techniques.

There is, however, a second type of consultant that I choose to call "the itinerant snake oil peddler" or collectively speaking, the "Saturday Night Specials." These individuals have no original equipment; they often steal and modify materials beyond recognition and original intent. They "borrow" handouts from sessions they have attended, perform their research at the kitchen table on a Saturday night, and fashion a dog-and-pony show which they plan to market on Monday. These individuals often go off half-cocked, sell their product cheaply, and take the position, "You pay your money and take your chances."

These consultants have a low commitment to the study of learning style and brain research. Such research is, in their eyes, the current bandwagon for them to ride until something new comes along. Because of their motivation and shallowness, they can do a great disservice to years of research, theorists' reputations, the integrity of other consultants in the field, and to the acceptance of learning style ideas.

FORCE 4: THE ILLUSION OF A PANACEA

A claim such as, "Matching learning styles with teaching styles will save education!" is so global and sublime that it can trigger natural suspicion of the whole topic.

Theorists, researchers, and consultants must be careful not to convey the idea that addressing learning styles is a panacea. Learning style research can provide us with the tools needed to understand the psychologies of learning and to improve teaching. However, there are many other elements which affect the learning process. Among these are goals, content, curriculum, ages and stages, adaptation abilities, and the employment of human will power to decide and be motivated toward and away from various wants, desires, and aspirations. In other words, researchers, theorists, and consultants must be careful not to promise more than can actually be delivered.

FORCE 5: SCHOLASTIC ARROGANCE

The fifth force that could discourage use of the data emerging from learning style/brain research is the most subtle and the most potent: the conscious or unconscious need or desire of an individual to cast the world in only one image—his own.

The fact of individual human differences in learning is not going to be easily accepted by educators who firmly believe in the primacy of the human intellect. These educators may appear enthusiastic about the data but they will never use them. They place the intellect on a pedestal. They relegate such things as hands-on experiences, emotions, and intuitive flashes to second-class status which should be experienced either at home or out of school. They perceive instructional and testing techniques associated with differentiated approaches as being "soft," lacking in academic integrity, and as contributing to the lowering of standards.

A desire to maintain control over one's personal image of the learning process can also manifest itself in another way—keeping the data secret. These individuals will not talk about learning styles because they fear that knowledge of learning style concepts could lead students to question their educational rights and responsibilities or request self-discovery and self-directed learning opportunities. Students might even challenge the system and eventually probe a teacher's competency. All of these potential activities could spell trouble and seriously challenge the professional "priesthood."

Conclusion

Learning style/brain research activities hold extraordinary potential to significantly and positively alter the professional behavior and student learning process in our classrooms. The five forces cited represent elements of inertia that can hamper learning style research and application in our schools. Researchers and educators must be aware of these resisting forces and not fall prey to glamour and naivete.

A cry for recognition and acceptance is being heard throughout the world today. People want to be acknowledged as unique unto themselves: physically, mentally, and emotionally. Learning styles and brain behavior research is revealing the psychological source of each person's inherent need to say, "I, a unique human being, exist!"

CHAPTER 2

Getting To Know You

Gerald E. Kusler

We *do* lust after easy answers to big problems. Apparently that desire inflames people in all professions; at times it seems almost to *define* educators. Usually we learn—thousands of dollars, hours, and promises later—that the answer is perhaps part of an answer, perhaps no answer at all. Those of us who have tasted the ashes a few times have come to stand back a bit from the fire: perhaps we can use some of the warmth without abandoning ourselves to the flames.

With that caution, I address the subject of "individualizing,"—"diagnostic and prescriptive" education. Neither the term nor the ideas it cloaks is the answer to the problems of teaching and learning, but the essential good sense in both can make teaching and learning more successful.

No special educational mumbo jumbo was performed over the word "individual" when we added the omnipotent verb-maker "-ize." Most teachers are smart enough to realize that the kids they're sharing space with are real. So they treat them in an "individualizing" way. If "individualizing" could stop there, most of us would say, "OK. It's a chilly word for a warm thought, but, OK."

"Diagnosing and prescribing" is a metaphor perhaps as harmful as it is useful. Its utility lies in the fact that it asks us to see each learner and his or her condition separately; its disservice is that it can suggest that learners are sick and that teachers are healers. In fact, if teachers really begin to see themselves as healers or rescuers, they'll require an ever-fresh supply of flawed beings needing their service!

A substitute for the medical metaphor would describe teachers as discoverers and nurturers. Rather than "diagnose" a problem and its causes, the teacher would use all possible methods to discover the combinations of qualities that best define a person as a learner. The teacher no longer cries, "I see what your problem is," but rather, "how much you can do!" And in the process, the teacher helps the student to better know himself or herself, especially as a whole and healthy being.

In that context, we can help teachers know and do something about "individualizing, diagnosing, and prescribing."

Cognitive Style Mapping

To begin, we might consider what help teachers really need. Most secondary teachers want to know the students they teach. But, two factors tend to block even the most committed. First, teachers don't really know what they need to know about learners. Consequently, teachers accumulate a Fibber McGee's closet full of personal anecdotes, family histories, test scores, and the imprecise recollections of other teachers. If their energy level doesn't droop, they find ways to be with the kids extra hours, enabling them to infer more. Second, the typical secondary teacher spends about 90 hours in class with between 125 and 150 youngsters. "Getting to know you" can become "putting the name with the face (or the seat)."

Clearly, teachers need a way of locking in what they need to know about learners. And they need quick and efficient ways to get that information. That's what the various learning styles instruments offer—focus and speed.

The step beyond knowing the student as a learner now takes on form and direction. Now the teacher can select methods and materials that fit the learning style. Choices do not have to be based on hunches, good intentions, or the vogue.

One procedure for determining learning style is cognitive style mapping, a method developed by Joe Hill for community college use, then modified with his help for elementary and secondary schools. At East Lansing we have used the inventory for more than 10 years and have trained many people in its use.

The inventory will not be presented here. Out own convictions and our commitment to Hill dictate that we share the inventory without cost, but only after the recipient has been trained in both the theory and uses of cognitive style mapping. We normally require about two-and-a-half days for that training to:

- Review 28 elements
- Review structure of inventory and scoring
- Present and discuss some representative profiles.

What happens in a school when people begin to understand cognitive or learning style will vary broadly. Some educators will respond structurally, systematically. The classroom will be rearranged. Multi-media equipment will be introduced. Teachers will downplay certain methods and elevate others. Contract learning, small group work, and self-paced instruction will emerge as the most approved approaches. The effort to match methods and materials to learner styles will lead to more or less sophisticated computer-aided management systems. Student style will be matched with teacher style as classes are formed. The idea of schools-within-a-school will grow again. Sometimes entire schools will be restructured to make the most of these new understandings about learners and learning.

Some Significant Outcomes

The various school "plans" represented at this conference reflect, at least in part, structural changes emerging from cognitive or learning style knowledge.

These, too, will pass. A few years from now the structures will have eroded; the systems will have been switched off. But in cognitive or learning style (and brain development studies, as well), there are some vital, if not revolutionary insights—and those will last.

Among the most significant insights is that we are coming to know the real meaning of the unassailable cliché about individual difference. For the first time, we can know which of the many differences affect a person's learning.

- Instead of "Sally, you just have to work harder," we'll hear, "Sally, I think you probably spend too much time going over the text. Let's find a way to shortcut that for you."
- Instead of, "Here's the assignment due in four weeks," we'll hear, "Mark, that long-term assignment might be tough for you to set up. Why don't you stop by after class and we'll figure out a way for you to break it down into shorter periods."
- Instead of, "She never has done well on standardized tests," we'll hear, "When we talked about her reflective style, we picked up part of the reason for poor test results. She did much better last time." The examples are infinite.

Our thinking about how people learn has given us an information framework consistent with another cliché about human potential. Although educators have voiced poetically our belief in the great growth and capabilities of youth, our behavior has often denied these very words. One reason for this inconsistency is that most of our carefully collected information about learners tells us only what they *cannot* do or gives us some easy-to-use explanation for their failure to achieve.

Information about family problems, socioeconomic status, bed wetting, and low test scores is generally useless to the teacher trying to unlock a learner's potential. Worse, that information can often cause the teacher to believe there is very little potential to unlock. On the other hand, both learning and cognitive style assume no limits. The question is never, "Can he learn?" or "How much can he learn?" It is only, "How will he most readily learn?" You cannot "fail" a student's cognitive style inventory; you can't even get it into the lower quartile!

Especially in secondary schools, lasting change will affect learners. They will begin to know something about their learning styles, be able to talk about how they learn, and even be able to help their teachers teach. Though we sometimes speak dreamily of teaching-learning as a partnership, the fact is that our professional imagery most often has us doing something *to* learners. Already, in schools where learning or cognitive styles are assessed and shared with learners, students are taking a bigger hand in structuring how they will learn what is taught. Another of the cliché goals of education is "creating the independent learner." Teaching them how they learn and what to do about it seems like a very worthy start.

One additional lasting outcome deserves mention. Right now, at least in some schools, the short-range consequence for teachers seems to be a strong push toward either of two models: matching student to teacher styles, or the multi-method classroom. In time, however, we will remember that teachers are learners, too. We will acknowledge that they, too, have unique style traits and we will realize that teachers can perform best in ways consistent with their own styles. In short, teacher difference, like learner difference, will be legitimate.

We will also understand that grouping by teaching-learning style is an exercise in administrative symmetry. Styles are not incompatible: learners can adjust to teaching styles and teachers can adjust to learning styles—without loss of learning. Concrete awareness of each person's uniqueness will modify behavior and results for teachers and learners.

The vision I am presenting must seem modest at best to those whose "school of the future" will be a marvel of planned and managed learning. What I can see, however, is determined by where I stand. And the tallest rock I can find to stand on is the realization that the teacher counts most. Whether one speaks of personal recollections, controlled observation, or tightly managed studies, if the question is, "What most affects students' learning in schools?" the answer is *teachers.* And those teachers whose students do learn, project two qualities:

1) They are *authentic,* a term to define someone who understands himself and what he believes, and acts like it.
2) They have *expectations*—expectations growing out of knowing about and believing in students; expectations that students can achieve, not that they'll fail; and expectations of themselves.

Even the curriculum itself is significant only as it is translated into teacher expectations. Given that teachers make the big difference, the results of recent studies of school and instructional effectiveness should seem almost obvious:

- Time-on-task has a heavy impact on student learning.
- Direct teacher-student interaction is a key element in successful classrooms.
- Teachers have to "own" the curriculum and the system.
- Teacher expectations are enhanced when supported by a school climate of positive expectations.
- Whole group and small group instruction could turn out to be more beneficial than more individualized work and student-student group work.

Nor are these and related findings in any way antithetical to cognitive style and development. Great chunks of the research support a simple dictum: *know* yourself; *know* your students; believe in what both can do. Because of cognitive and learning style work, we can *know* ourselves and our students in a way that counts—as learners and thinkers.

CHAPTER 3

Cognitive Style Mapping By the Hill Model

William Warner

In an era when retention, accountability, and efficiency are the passwords, educational institutions are searching for a new means to continue their existence into the '80s and beyond. In the past, techniques and approaches have been experimented with and tossed aside only to see a new "kid on the block" take its place. The experimentation of the '70s is history, but it has not been wasted or lost because educators have come to realize two important, distinguishing characteristics from their experiments: The specific diagnosis and treatment of individual learner differences and the management of the learning environment.

These characteristics highlight a movement toward a more scientific approach to the learning-teaching process which has forced educators out of the traditional role of information-giving into a model patterned after the medical profession.

An emerging technique that seems prepared to step into this role is cognitive style mapping. Developed in the late '60s by Dr. Joseph Hill, this diagnostic prescriptive technique has been refined and catalyzed with space age computer technology at institutions like Wisconsin's Fox Valley Technical Institute and Minnesota's 916 Vo-Tech Institute in Bear Lake. The resultant program is one that can be implemented and administered at institutions irrespective of size and resources.

Cognitive mapping is an inventory process used to identify and describe an individual's preferred learning style. Based on the original Hill model, this system references preferred types of media, instructional strategies, and environment structure that are determined from individual differential analysis. The program is designed to analyze 28 distinguishing characteristics of learning and relate them, through prescription development, to daily instruction.

The development, implementation, and administration of a system of cognitive mapping, while desirable, has been shunned by some institutions as an impossible innovation because of its complexity. If properly planned, however, this need not be the case and mapping can become a basis for managing any institution's learning environment.

Planning Phases

The cognitive style mapping process involves four basic phases: (1) inventory of student learning style differences, (2) validation, (3) prescription development, (4) curriculum adaptation. The institution must confront all four phases in the planning stage; the absence of any one of the phases can sabotage the entire program. A staff member should be delegated to spearhead the implementation and overall direction for the program, but need not be tied to either instructional or student services. This individual should be at liberty to select a committee of instructional and support staff to develop an institutional plan for the implementation and utilization of cognitive style mapping. This plan should address the following:

1. *Inventory Phase.* The inventory process is the battery of questions that is given to students to determine the 27 components of their style. Several forms are available and institutions may choose to tailor-make their own. Processing can be done through other institutions or devised locally. Potential agenda items for this phase include:
   a. Which students are to be involved—all incoming students or students from certain programs?
   b. When should the inventory be administered—prior to matriculation or after?
   c. What inventory should be used—a locally developed inventory or one of the original Hill inventories?
   d. Where should data be processed—locally or at another institution already set up for processing?
   e. Who is responsible for administration of the inventory?

Most institutions prefer to pilot a sample group (several programs) using existing inventories and processing centers and then expand if the pilot proves successful.

2. *Validation Phase.* This process involves the empirical observations of inventory results to affirm construct validity (is the inventory measuring what it is intended to measure). It involves assessing students through observation, one-to-one sessions, or group discussions of the inventory results. The feedback also may be used to update each individual's learning style. The institution must place responsibility for the map validation process with the appropriate person and provide a mechanism (either computer or mechanical) for it to occur. Individuals to be involved could include (but are not limited to) teachers, counselors, advisers, and homeroom teachers.

3. *Prescription Development.* This phase includes the development of learning prescriptions and the ultimate channeling of this information to instructional staff. Institutions must determine:
   a. Who gets the information—counselors, teachers?
   b. How is the prescription written—by computer or manually?
   c. How does the information reach the receivers—hard copy, computer hard copy, or cathode-ray terminal?

One of the major steps in the implementation of cognitive style mapping is the development of prescriptions based on the maps of the individual learners. The prescriptions provide alternative paths for students to move through the program.

4. *Curriculum Adaptation Phase.* The alternatives provided from prescriptions are normally in the form of alternative learning resources. This requires the development of curriculum using a multi-modality approach. Curriculum development based on student learning styles need not be a costly and time-consuming process. The administrative role is to provide a framework in which instructors can use multi-modality approaches that are effective and efficient. Instructors can share materials, resources, and ideas. Most schools have a wide variety of resources (AV, books, other print materials, activities, etc.) that are in storage or can be shared from one program to another. Administrators need to make people aware of what resources are available so the resources can be properly utilized.

Another more costly approach is to provide time for instructors to develop alternative approaches to instruction. Information from cognitive mapping can be utilized to provide guidance in developing these materials. The types of resources appropriate to different learning styles can be accommodated in the resources that are developed or purchased.

The planning stage involves a great deal of effort in the form of learning, research, and inservice. Remember, this process will be the basis for the ongoing administration and development of the program and should not be limited in scope or creativity. It is also important to utilize personnel from all aspects of the institution to allow the program to involve all of the potential services of the institution.

Implementation and Maintenance of Cognitive Style Mapping

Cognitive style mapping can be implemented to varying degrees using a variety of strategies. The strategies must be based on the situation in the local institution, and must take into account the local resources, personnel, attitudes, and politics of the institution. The degree of implementation can range from individual instructors to districtwide involvement. The amount of involvement affects the overall implementation plan. The involvement of staff in cognitive style mapping on a voluntary basis appears to be the most effective implementation strategy. Instructors must be personally committed to cognitive style mapping as a philosophy and as an approach to teaching. This commitment can only be made by the individual instructor and not through administrative directive.

School personnel must be trained to properly implement cognitive style mapping. Once the initial implementation is accomplished there is a need for ongoing inservice. However, the initial inservice is critical. Instructors must feel they have enough knowledge to work effectively with students. The ongoing inservice is important to orient new staff as well as to update original staff on new applications and uses of mapping.

The administrator must budget for the expenses of inservice activities, but there are few other budgetary considerations. Other costs can usually be absorbed into the existing program operating budgets.

The 916 Vo-Tech Program

916 Vocational Technical Institute has utilized cognitive style mapping since June of 1977. The instructional system is personalized, competency-based for all instructional programs. The system operates 12 months a year and is an open entry and time variable system. Initially, a pilot project was developed to determine the appropriateness of mapping. The pilot project indicated cognitive style mapping could be beneficial to both students and staff. The program was expanded, on a voluntary basis, to all interested students and instructors. Currently about 80 percent of the programs are utilizing mapping to some extent. About 50 percent or 1,000 of the students are mapped annually.

Cognitive style mapping can be an effective tool for both instructors and students to gain more from the learning process. Administration must create the atmosphere that will allow instructors to implement the program. The result will be more appropriate instruction and student self knowledge essential to direct the student toward realistic career goals.

CHAPTER 4

Counseling Middle School Students For Their Individual Learning Styles

Shirley A. Griggs

The role of the school counselor is a comprehensive one: aiding students with both their educational, career, and personal development, and helping them plan for and progress toward educational and vocational goals. School counselors work primarily with students, both individually and in groups. They also work in a consultative role with teachers, administrators, parents, and community agency personnel, as school records and testing results are used extensively to help students develop their individual plans.

In order to implement this complex role, counselors rely on a variety of counseling approaches. The growing numbers of theories and techniques in counseling differ in terms of philosophy, major personality constructs, counseling goals, the relative importance of diagnosis, counseling techniques and strategies, and targeted clientele. Frequently, school counselors employ the philosophic orientations of the counselor education programs in which they were prepared or certified.

Hollis and Wantz (1980) surveyed 475 counselor preparation institutions in the United States. Overall, they identified the philosophic orientations of counselor education programs as follows:

1. Eclectic—24.1 percent
2. Phenomenological—22.2 percent
3. Behavioral—13.8 percent
4. Cognitive—10.5 percent
5. Existential—5.6 percent
6. Field—5.4 percent
7. Psychosocial Dynamics—4.1 percent
8. Psychoanalytic—4.0 percent
9. Trait-Factor—3.9 percent
10. Transactional Analysis—2.6 percent
11. Others—3.8 percent

Thus, school counselors are exposed to a variety of counseling theories, with some theories and techniques more emphasized than others. The fundamental question in evaluating counseling effectiveness is: Which *counseling approaches* (behavioral, existential, field) are most appropriate with which *types of clients* (background variables, individual learning styles, personality characteristics) with what *kind of problem* (educational, vocational, personal, social) in what *kind of setting* (individual counseling, group counseling, classroom, peer helping), using what *kinds of techniques/interventions/methods* (cognitive techniques, auditory versus visual versus tactual-kinesthetic approaches, structured versus unstructured modalities)?

Traditionally, diagnosis has been viewed as an important counseling function and is defined as a summary of an individual's problems and their causes, a description and understanding of that person's personality dynamics (Shertzer and Stone, 1980). A thorough knowledge of the student's individual learning style can facilitate the diagnostic process in counseling. The Learning Style Inventory (Dunn, Dunn, and Price, 1975; Dunn and Dunn, 1978) has been used extensively in diagnosing individual learning styles and prescribing curricular learning interventions to respond to individual needs.

The Dunns and Price view learning style as the manner in which different elements from five basic stimuli affect a person's ability to perceive, interact with, and respond to the learning environment. The LSI learning style elements include the following:

1. *Environmental Stimuli:* light, sound, temperature, design
2. *Emotional Stimuli:* structure, persistence, motivation, responsibility
3. *Sociological Stimuli:* pairs, peers, adults, self, group, varied
4. *Physical Stimuli:* perceptual strengths (auditory, visual, tactual, kinesthetic), mobility, intake, time of day.
5. *Psychological Stimuli:* global/analytic, impulsive/reflective, cerebral dominance.

A number of research studies indicate that matching teachers' teaching styles to students' learning styles results in improved student achievement and attitudes. Martin (1977) found that among high school students, those high in independence (self-learners) functioned better in an alternative instructional environment, resulting in higher grades and increased satisfaction with school. Conversely, dependent students (teacher-oriented) fared better in a traditional environment. Copenhaver (1979) found that students have significantly more positive attitudes toward a subject when their learning styles are congruent with their teacher's teaching style. Cafferty (1980) determined that the greater the degree of congruence between the teachers' style and the students' style, the higher the grade point average of the students.

This same paradigm can be applied to counseling interventions; that is, the individual's learning style should determine the counseling techniques and strategies utilized. Learning style elements that seem to be particularly important to the counseling process are:

- High versus low need for structure
- Global versus analytic mode of processing
- Group versus individual sociological preference
- Auditory versus visual versus tactual/kinesthetic perceptual strengths
- High versus low level of motivation.

A number of counseling theorists are recognizing the importance of matching counselor style and type of counseling intervention to the style of the person being counseled. The field of neuro-linguistic programing (NLP) has developed around this concept. NLP is "a new model of human communication and behavior that has been developed during the past four years by Richard Bandler, John Grindler, Leslie Cameron-Bandler, and Judith DeLozier. NLP was developed initially through the systematic study of Virginia Satir, Milton Erickson, Fritz Perls and other therapeutic wizards" (Bandler and Grindler, 1979).

The NLP model stresses the importance of the counselor responding to an individual's representational system, which is predominantly auditory, visual, or tactual/kinesthetic. Once the counselor has identified the student's favored system and responded out of that system, feelings of trust and rapport increase. On the other hand, if the counselor responds in a different system, the student experiences difficulty and oftentimes appears resistant to counseling (Harman and O'Neill, 1981).

For example, if the student's representational system or perceptual strength is *visual,* the counselor might ask:

"Do you have *visual images* in your head as you are talking and listening to me?"

"Can you *see* what I am saying?"

If *tactual/kinesthetic,* the counselor might ask:

"Do you *feel* good about what you did?"

"Are you *in touch* with what I am saying?"

If *auditory,* the counselor might respond:

"I *hear* what you are saying."

"As you recall the conversation with your teacher, what do you *hear* her saying to you?"

A graphic illustration of students' varied representational systems is outlined by Grindler and Bandler (1976) as follows:

Meaning	Tactual/ Kinesthetic	Visual	Auditory
"I understand you."	"What you are saying *feels* right to me."	"I *see* what you are saying."	"I *hear* you clearly."
"I want to communicate something to you."	"I want you to be in *touch* with something."	"I want to *show* you something."	"I want you to *listen* carefully to what I say."
"Describe more of your present experience to me."	"Put me in *touch* with what you are *feeling* at this point."	"*Show* me a clear picture of what you *see* at this point."	"*Tell* me in more detail what you are *saying* at this point."

The counselor's role is to:

1. Respond adequately to a broad range of students' representational systems or perceptual strengths
2. Deal with incongruity of messages. For example, the students says one thing but it is not consistent with body language
3. Help the student expand his or her representational system through the varied counseling techniques.

Responding to a variety of perceptual strengths assumes that the counselor is skilled in the use of imagery, puppetry, simulated counseling games, bibliotherapy (to respond to the visually-oriented student), relaxation techniques, and art therapy (to respond to the tactual/kinesthetic student), as well as verbally-oriented techniques such as rational-emotional therapy, client-centered therapy, and behavioral counseling.

Elements of learning style that are compatible with selected counseling objectives and interventions for students at the middle school level are presented in Table 1. These objectives of counseling are related to the developmental tasks of middle childhood listed by Havighurst (1952):

- Learning physical skills necessary for ordinary games
- Building wholesome attitudes toward oneself as a growing organism
- Learning to get along with peers
- Learning an appropriate sex role
- Developing fundamental skills in reading, writing, and arithmetic
- Developing concepts necessary for everyday living.
- Developing conscience, morality, and a set of values.
- Developing a responsibility for an independent self.
- Developing attitudes toward social groups and institutions.

The counseling interventions may extend to individual or group counseling or group guidance settings including the use of programed counseling materials and simulated games involving play media, story-telling, etc., that are compatible with students' learning styles.

Longitudinal data on the Learning Style Inventory suggest some counseling applications. The majority (80 percent) of gifted youth prefer learning alone, while the majority (75 percent) of culturally different youth prefer learning with peers (Griggs and Price, 1980). Girls tend to have stronger auditory preferences while boys have stronger visual preferences. The counseling program must be responsive to these individual learning styles.

The school counselor should function as a consultant to teachers, parents, and administrators regarding learning styles. The counselor works with teachers to assess learning styles and to interpret student needs, based on style differences. The counselor can help teachers develop strategies in addition to the predominant lecture-discussion model of instruction.

Increasingly, school counselors are involving the parents of elementary and middle school children in the counseling program. Through child-study groups, the counselor can help parents understand the individual learning style of their child and make provisions for learning style by creating a home study environment that is supportive.

Table 1
Learning Style Elements Compatible with Selected Counseling Objectives and Interventions

Objective in Counseling	Counseling Intervention	Compatible Learning Style Elements
1. To help students become aware of careers and more knowledgeable concerning career choice.	Conduct group counseling sessions using value clarification games and career exploration games with 7th grade students.	*Physical elements:* high need for visual, tactual/kinesthetic sensory perception and low need for auditory. *Sociological elements:* peer-oriented.
2. To help students who are experiencing adjustment problems express feelings and communicate more effectively.	Conduct individual counseling sessions using play media (dolls, puppets, clay, drawing materials) to help the student express self.	*Physical elements:* tactual/kinesthetic perceptual strengths. *Emotional elements:* low need for structure. *Sociological elements:* self or adult-oriented.
3. To help students develop social skills, i.e., understanding, friendship, and cooperation.	Conduct group guidance sessions in a 6th grade classroom utilizing the DUSO (Dinkmeyer, 1970) kit containing a problem, a story, role-playing activity, and puppetry.	*Emotional elements:* high need for structure, low on motivation and responsibility. *Psychological elements:* global orientation, right hemispheric dominance.
4. To help students develop conscience, morality, and a set of values.	Through the mutual storytelling technique (Gardner, 1971) a tape recorder is used in individual counseling in which the student is guided to create a story and a moral. The counselor follows up with a story that reflects a healthier resolution or a more mature approach to the situation.	*Sociological elements:* self and adult. *Physical elements:* individual counseling can be scheduled during the time of day preferred by the student. Predominantly auditory approach.
5. To help students build wholesome attitudes toward self and others.	Through "self-enhancing educational" techniques (Randolph and Howe, 1973) focus on how to relate and interact with self and others effectively. Developed particularly for underachieving and alienated youth.	*Sociological elements:* self-learned processes of problem solving, self control, and self direction. *Emotional elements:* designed for the unmotivated, irresponsible, and youth with short attention spans.

Finally, the school counselor works with school administrators to develop counseling programs that are responsive to individual learning styles. This implies that instructional and counseling interventions will be designed that are compatible with the various learning styles.

A thorough knowledge of individual learning styles can help counselors in consultation with teachers, parents, and administrators develop strategies, techniques, and programs that are responsive to individual needs.

References

Bandler, Richard, and Grindler, John. *Frogs into Princes.* Moab, Utah: Real People Press, 1979.

Cafferty, Elsie. "An Analysis of Student Performance Based upon the Degree of Match Between the Educational Cognitive Style of the Teacher and the Educational Cognitive Style of the Students." Doctoral dissertation, University of Nebraska, 1980.

Copenhaver, Ronnie W. "The Consistency of Student Learning Styles as Students Move from English to Mathematics." Doctoral dissertation, Indiana University, 1979.

Dinkmeyer, Donald C. *Manual: Developing an Understanding of Self and Others.* Circle Pines, Minn.: American Guidance Services, 1970.

Dunn, Rita, and Dunn, Kenneth. *Teaching Students Through Their Individual Learning Styles: A Practical Approach.* Reston, Va.: Reston Publishing Co., 1978.

Dunn, Rita S.; Dunn, Kenneth; and Price, Gary E. *Manual: Learning Style Inventory.* Lawrence, Kans.: Price Systems, 1975.

Gardner, Richard A. *Therapeutic Communication with Children: The Mutual Storytelling Technique.* New York: Science House, 1971.

Griggs, Shirley A., and Price, Gary E. "A Comparison of Learning Styles of Gifted Versus Average Suburban Junior High School Students." *Roeper Review* 3(1980): 7–9.

Grindler, John, and Bandler, Richard. *The Structure of Magic II.* Palo Alto, Calif.: Science and Behavior Books, 1976.

Harman, Robert L., and O'Neill, Charles. "Neuro-Linguistic Programming for Counselors." *Personnel and Guidance Journal* 59(1981): 449–53.

Havighurst, Robert. *Human Development and Education.* New York: David McKay Co., 1952.

Hollis, Joseph, and Wantz, Richard A. *Counselor Preparation 1980.* 4th ed. Muncie, Ind.: Accelerated Development, 1980.

Martin, Michael K. "Effects of the Interaction Between Students' Learning Styles and High School Instructional Environments." Doctoral dissertation, University of Oregon, 1977.

Randolph, N., and Howe, William. "Self-Enhancing Education: Its Focus." Symposium on Group Procedures and Human Relations Training for Educators. Athens, Ga.: University of Georgia, 1973.

Shertzer, Bruce, and Stone, Shelley C. *Fundamentals of Counseling.* 3d ed. Boston: Houghton Mifflin Co., 1980.

CHAPTER 5

Learning Activities for the Tactual Learner

Angela Bruno

Many students do not do well in school because the specific instructional method used to teach them does not complement their individual learning style. Extensive research verifies that not all students learn best through their visual and auditory senses; such students are usually highly tactual and tend to both gain and retain information when they become involved with the actual use of hands-on materials.[1]

Selected examples of resources that respond to a student's need for tactual involvement in the learning process are called learning circles, task cards, and innovative electroboards.[2] These game-like resources are naturally motivating, and, because they are also self-corrective,[3] a student who has difficulty using them nevertheless is able to successfully identify the correct answers through inductive or deductive learning.

Directions for the construction of learning circles, task cards, and innovative electroboards are shown respectively in Figures 2, 3, and 4. The students themselves can be encouraged to produce these materials once samples are available to them. By the time they are in the second or third grade, they can be motivated to seek the information on their own for the needed content. Students should be further encouraged to translate that information to all or any of the three tactual resources using the "Basic Tools and Materials" pictured in Figure 1.

Although secondary science and mathematics examples are featured in all the figures, the three self-corrective resources can easily complement both elementary and secondary curricula by simply varying the difficulty of selected content.

Generally, the highest percentage of our elementary students are tactual.[4] When these youngsters manipulate hands-on materials, they tend to

1. Rita Dunn and Kenneth Dunn, *Teaching Students Through Their Individual Learning Styles: A Practical Approach* (Reston, Va.: Reston Publishing Co., 1978); Anthony F. Gregorc, "Learning/Teaching Styles: Their Nature and Effects," In *Student Learning Styles: Diagnosing and Prescribing Programs* (Reston, Va.: National Association of Secondary School Principals, 1979).

2. Angela Bruno and Karen Jessie, *Hands-On Activities for Student's Writing: Innovative Learning Style Resources* (Englewood Cliffs, N.J.: Prentice-Hall, 1982).

3. Cecil D. Mercer and Ann R. Mercer, "The Development and Use of Self-Correcting Materials with Exceptional Children," *Teaching Exceptional Children,* Fall 1978, pp. 6–11.

4. Rita S. Dunn and Kenneth J. Dunn, "Learning Styles/Teaching Styles: Should They . . . Can They . . . Be Matched?" *Educational Leadership,* January 1979, pp. 238–44.

remember more of the required information than when they use any other sense.[5]

Because tactual resources are naturally responsive to students' tactual senses, and because they are different from general class discussions or the lecture method, learning circles, task cards, and innovative electroboards will be appreciated and used. More important, students will learn from them!

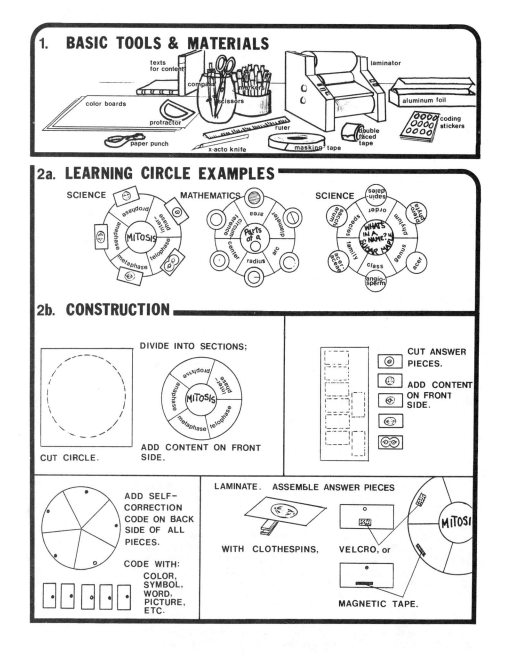

---

5. Roberta Wheeler, "Teaching Reading According to Students' Perceptual Strengths," *Phi Delta Kappan,* December 1980, pp. 59–62.

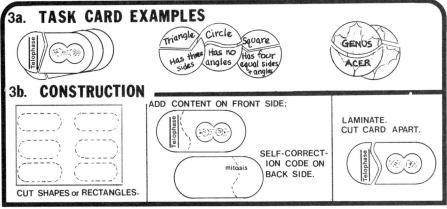

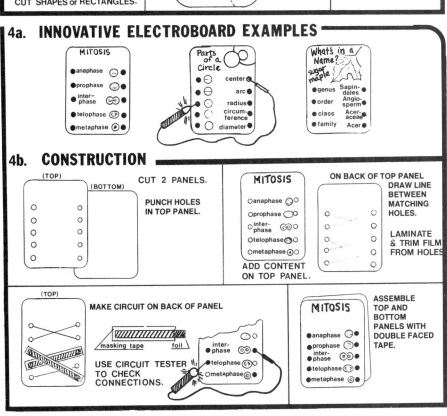

Illustrations by Pat Nauss

CHAPTER 6

Madison Prep—Alternatives Through Learning Styles

Helene Hodges

Madison Prep developed as a community-based, alternative junior high school designed completely around the diagnosis and prescription of individual learning styles. It is situated in the Lower East Side of New York City, an area of deteriorating neighborhoods, substandard housing, high population density, and low-cost tenements and public housing. While there are pockets of middle class housing in the area, the neighborhood is characterized generally by abandoned, dilapidated, crumbling, and burned-out houses. Madison Prep closed its doors last year. Therein lies a story.

District #1 has a large percentage of Hispanic, black, and Chinese children with learning patterns typical of disadvantaged areas throughout the country—gradual achievement and growth until the third grade and a steady decline from the fourth grade on. That condition is referred to as "progressive retardation."

Madison Prep's program served seventh, eighth, and ninth grade students who displayed high rates of academic underachievement and/or nonachievement, low reading and math scores, negative attitudes toward school, and rejection of a traditional educational environment. Many of its students had a history of criminal activity including arrests, drug addiction, gang activities, and assaults.

The primary goal of Madison Prep was to help its students develop and implement a realistic learning and behavior program which would keep them in school. Primary consideration was given to students whose emotional handicaps, behavioral disorders, or developmental disabilities interfered with their learning progress and self-control.

Program Model

The program model, illustrated in Figure 1, consisted of three major components: an informally designed, highly structured, tactual/kinesthetic *cognitive* environment; a secure and highly supportive *affective* environment offering "in-house" clinical services; and a *social interaction* component providing community interaction and practical work skills developed to prepare students for part-time and summer employment.

Objectives, stated behaviorally and contained in contracts, were negotiated between students and teachers who set short and long-term goals

Figure 1

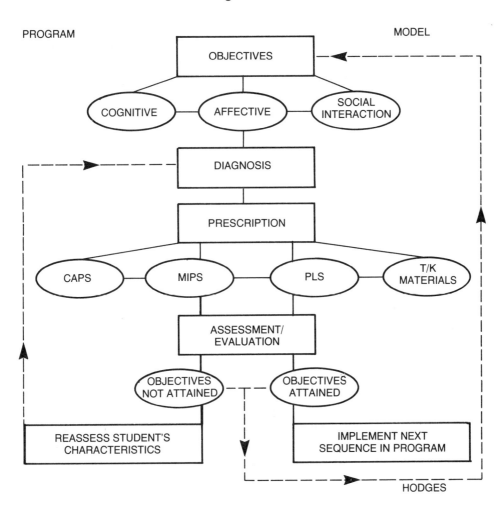

relative to academic progress, behavior in and out of school, personal de-velopment, and peer relationships. Students were diagnosed, prescribed for, and evaluated on the basis of an analysis of their interests, level of achieve-ment prior to instruction, and learning style preferences.

Cognitive Component

The instructional or cognitive component of Madison Prep offered an interest-centered, individualized curriculum. Entering students were ques-tioned about their interests and the curriculum was developed based on the responses of the youngsters. In addition, the results of the Dunn, Dunn, and Price Learning Style Inventory (LSI), informal teacher-made questionnaires, and standardized achievement tests assisted us in devising and implementing an individualized instructional plan for each student. This continuing diag-nosis and evaluation enabled the staff to determine the appropriate academic contract for each student.

Importance of Learning Styles

Observation and testing of student learning styles, as well as experimentation with innovative strategies at Madison Prep, revealed that our
students displayed distinct learning style preferences. Specifically, they were
not motivated, persistent, or responsible; they required an informal, but
highly structured environment which provided for intake and mobility; and
they preferred to work with an adult or peer and to learn tactually (by
touching or manipulating materials) and kinesthetically (through "real life"
experiences such as trips or making and building things).

Because our students were not persistent, not responsible, and did not
achieve via conformity, we offered them many alternatives. Methods of
instruction included opportunities for small and large group instruction,
one-on-one interaction, and peer tutoring with appropriate tasks and assignments. Our individualized instructional materials presented our students
with alternate ways of learning information, skills, and abilities. Those materials included contract activity packages, multisensory instructional packages, task cards, programed learning sequences, games, puzzles, and other
manipulative materials. Those resources were housed in different sections of
the school called interest centers, learning stations, and media centers.

Contracts were designed to accommodate the wide variety of academic
levels and abilities found among our student population and were geared to
perceptual strengths. Contracts allowed our staff to provide varying amounts
of structure as needed by individual students. Comfortable, yet specific time
limits enabled our students to progress at their own pace.

Of all the elements of learning style, perceptual strengths and structure
appeared to have the highest priorities in formulating appropriate prescriptions. In accordance with Dunn and Dunn, new material was presented
through the strongest modality and reinforced through the second strongest
modality. For example:

- Our *auditory* students learned best when they *listened* to the information, *read* about the subject, and then *took notes* on important items.
- Our *visual* youngsters learned best when they *read* about the subject
  before the teacher discussed it; *looked* at illustrations, charts, and
  other visual aids; *took notes* on important items; and then *listened* to
  an explanation of the new materials.
- Most of our students who were *tactual* learners required manipulative
  materials to *feel* or *touch* and materials to *construct* "educational
  games." They were then guided to *write* and *read* about the subject
  and then to *listen* to an explanation of the new material.
- Our kinesthetic learners needed to become *totally involved* in "real-
  life" situations like taking field trips or building things. They *felt* or
  touched manipulatives, *wrote* and *read* about the subject and, finally,
  listened to an explanation of the new material.

In most cases, approximately 90 percent of traditional classroom instruction is geared to the auditory learner. Teachers *talk* to their students, *ask*

questions, and *discuss* facts. However, we found that only 20 to 30 percent of any large group could remember as much as 75 percent of what was presented through discussions. By utilizing a multisensory approach to teaching, we assisted our students to overcome the difficulties with perception they had experienced in the traditional program that emphasized lecture and discussion.

Core Curriculum

Our thematic core curriculum offered an interdisciplinary approach to instruction. Based on students' interest and the director's experience, aerospace and aviation were used as a vehicle for teaching the major disciplines—math, science, social studies, and language arts/reading. Basic aeronautics, principles of flight, meteorology, navigation, history of flight, and basic aircraft and rocket construction techniques each had a place in an appropriate discipline.

Teacher-pupil conferences were arranged informally on a weekly basis to give both teachers and students a chance to evaluate progress. The student's independent reading was the focus of those conferences.

Weekly group sessions and individual student-teacher conferences allowed students to take part in setting their goals and school regulations. Contracts were designed so that each step in the process was outlined. For example, time limits were defined, degrees of mastery and proficiency were stated, and so forth. Contracts were prominently posted on bulletin boards, and pupils maintained folders with their work and recorded their progress.

Affective Component

The affective component of our program was a treatment community in which all staff members, to some degree, were part of a therapeutic team. Everything that happened in and around the facility was intended to accrue to the well-being of the student.

Frequent family contact to enlist parental cooperation and participation helped to ease family tensions when problems affected student performance. Clinical services were also made available to parents and other family members. Weekly individual and group counseling sessions were conducted. Results of admission procedures and testing were used to develop behavioral prescriptions based on prevention, counseling, and advocacy services.

Because delinquent behavior can be exacerbated by unemployment and lack of work skills, work performance and appropriate behaviors were stressed.

Our students worked and earned money. More important, they learned and began to develop socialized work habits. Workshop experiences helped students to acquire skills and habits in such areas as concentration, self-control, dexterity, interpersonal relations, and self-direction. Successful training in acceptable, useful, and potentially marketable work skills produced greater feelings of self-esteem, confidence, and social acceptability.

The students' work hours were determined on an individual basis, with consideration given to age, interests, and motivation. Permission to work additional hours and earn more money was based on academic, behavioral, and social gains.

Specific educational and public relations activities were planned to gain and maintain the public's understanding and support for the program.

The End of the Story

At Madison Prep, we attempted to meet the needs of students who were not responding to conventional strategies and administrative structures. Our program model allowed us to confront the problems of low achievers and to serve a population of students whose learning styles were mismatched with traditional school practices.

Approximately 85 percent of our students substantially increased their achievement levels in both reading and mathematics compared with their previous performance in their formal school settings. Many students were able to reverse failure syndromes and reduce anti-social behavior. Our data revealed that, when taught through methods that complemented their learning style preferences, our students became increasingly motivated and achieved better academically.

The results also showed significant improvement in student attendance and attitudes toward school. Attendance at Madison Prep averaged 80 percent among a group of students who, in the past, were truant for weeks at a time.

Madison Prep was located in the basement of a New York City housing project. Its students participated in designing, painting, and decorating their environment, and it was *their* school. Its staff and students were proud. When New York City's budget crisis required that Madison Prep personnel return to Junior High School 22 where they originally had been assigned, its students protested and boycotted. That behavior in and of itself was remarkable; imagine secondary delinquent nonachievers challenging the demise of an educational institution! They actually *wanted* to attend school! Teaching through their learning styles had made a dramatic difference in their achievement, attitudes, and behaviors—words synonymous with their "lives."

References

Dunn, Kenneth. "Madison Prep: Alternative to Teenage Disaster." *Educational Leadership,* February 1981, pp. 386–87.

Dunn, Rita, and Dunn, Kenneth. *Teaching Students Through Their Individual Learning Styles: A Practical Approach.* Reston, Va.: Reston Publishing Co., 1978.

Steps in Managing the Diagnostic-Prescriptive Process in The Foreign Language Classroom

Robert and Virginia Ballinger

Our involvement in the diagnostic-prescriptive process is a direct result of our desire to meet the individual needs of the students we teach. As experienced teachers of French and Spanish, we have used many approaches to help students learn a foreign language. It did not take many weeks in the classroom to realize that no one method of instruction, whether it be the audio-lingual approach, a form of individualized instruction, or a more traditional teacher-centered approach was going to meet the needs of all our students. Many students were succeeding but many were having difficulties. We intuitively knew that a more varied approach would help meet the needs of every student and we began a search to find a way. This paper is an explanation of how we are managing to meet the individual needs of our students through a diagnostic-prescriptive approach.

Step I: Written Objectives

The first step in the diagnostic-prescriptive approach is to list the objectives for each lesson in order to clarify the direction of the lessons. Students need to know the objectives so they can understand clearly what needs to be learned. Post the list of objectives on a bulletin board so that students can refer to them when the need arises. Also, anyone coming into the classroom can see what the students are striving toward.

Step II: Diagnosing Students' Learning Styles

To diagnose the learning styles of our students, we use the Learning Style Inventory (LSI) developed by Kenneth and Rita Dunn and Gary Price. Each student's answer sheet is computer scored and the results are forwarded to the teacher. The teacher receives a printout that shows the elements which are factors in a student's ability to learn and a class composite listing the percentage of students exhibiting each learning style characteristic.

Time is taken to discuss the results of the LSI with each student—an important step in the process because it lets the student know that the teacher really cares about how he or she learns. In addition, students become aware of their own learning style. Students who know how they learn can begin to have control over their own learning. They also realize that there are legitimate differences in learning style and begin to develop a tolerance for those differences.

Step III: The Prescriptive Process

Creating materials to meet the individual learning styles of the students is exciting, challenging, and rewarding.

The information received from the LSI indicates that a large percentage of our French III students need structure. These students receive a copy of the objectives for the lesson (Fig. 1), an explanation of how they will be evaluated, and a calendar which lists the daily activities for class and for homework.

Figure 1
Leçon 2
Le Début de l'Histoire de la France

Les Objectifs

Objectif 1: Histoire—La France à l'époque de Grecs et des Romains
    a: les Grecs et les Romains viennent en France
    b: Jules César et l'influence romaine en France

Objectif 2: Histoire—Le commencement de l'ère chrétienne en France
    a: l'Eglise chrétienne en France
    b: Clovis, le premier roi chrétien des Francs

Objectif 3: Littérature—Jules César décrit les Gaulois
    a: la religion des Gaulois (les druides)
    b: la religion des Gaulois (le Nouvel An)
    c: un portrait de Vercingétorix
    d: Astérix

Objectif 4: Littérature—Grégoire de Tours raconte l'histoire de Clovis et du vase de Soissons

Objectif 5: Grammaire—Les verbes
    a: les verbes de la Seconde Série au présent
    b: les verbes suivis d'un infinitif sans prépositions, ou avec *à* ou *de*

L'Évaluation

Objectif 1	=	20 pts.
Objectifs 2+4	=	20 pts.
Objectif 3	=	20 pts.
Objectif 5a	=	20 pts.
Examen sur Leçon 2	=	100 pts.
Leçon 2	=	180 pts.

Deux Projets

Projet A: pour deux personnes (10 pts.)
    Ecrivez et jouez une pièce basée sur "les Druides et le Nouvel An" (*Trésors du Temps*, p. 25).

Projet B: pour deux personnes (10 pts.)
    Ecrivez et jouez une pièce basée sur "Clovis et le Vase de Soissons" (*Trésors du Temps*, p. 28).

Students needing less structure work on the same objectives but are allowed to make decisions about the kinds of projects they will pursue and the work schedule they will follow within a given timeframe to accomplish the objectives (Fig. 2). The projects created by these students are used as resources by other students.

A variation on this process is employed for the Spanish students. Two sets of assignments are given for a selected objective: one set for the students

---

Figure 2

Explications des Projets—Leçon 4

There are three types of projects:
1. *Cognitive:* in which you demonstrate some factual knowledge you have learned.
2. *Affective:* in which you express your feelings or impressions on a topic.
3. *Creative:* in which you make your own production based on what you have learned.

Project #1 is to be based on either Objective 1 or Objective 4. Here are some examples you may choose from.

Activity **Reporting Alternative**

Objective 1: Cognitive

Draw a poster explaining the Crusades. Use pictures and graphics to illustrate various facts about the Crusades.

Show your poster to 3–4 classmates and to your teacher, and display it in the room.

Objective 4: Creative

Write a horoscope for a friend in which you use at least 10 verbs in the future tense. Record your horoscope on tape.

Play your tape for 3–4 students and your teacher. Display your tape and script in the room so others may listen to it.

Objective 4: Affective

Make a set of flash cards with at least 10 different activities which you *would* do if you had a million dollars.

Show your cards to 3–4 students and your teacher and explain to them what you *would* do.

Project #2 is to be based on either Objective 2 or Objective 3. Here are some examples you may choose from.

Activity **Reporting Alternative**

Objective 2: Affective

Write what your personal reaction would be to at least 5 events during the Guerre de Cent Ans and/or facts about Jeanne d'Arc. Record your reactions on tape.

Play your tape for 3–4 students and your teacher. Display your tape and script so others can listen to it.

Objective 3: Cognitive

Make 2 sets of flash cards, one for the important quotations and another with the important vocabulary from the play.

Show 3–4 classmates and your teacher how you used these cards to learn the important quotations and vocabulary from the play. Display your cards in the room so others can use them.

---

who need structure, and another for those requiring less structure. All students work on the same objective, but the methods vary according to learner needs.

Materials have also been designed for learning in small groups of three to five students. Allowing students to work in small groups encourages them to assume responsibility for their own learning. Many students who otherwise would not be involved during regular class instruction seem to come alive when they are allowed to work with their peers. Two small-group techniques which we have found to be very successful are Team Learning and Circle of Knowledge.[1]

Team Learning is a good way to present new material, and has been very successful for assignments that ask students to read a passage in the foreign language and then answer a series of questions about the content. The first several questions are generally factual and the answers are easy to find. Interpretive and creative questions are included to help the students begin to structure their own learning. When students are given the opportunity to work together, they help each other to understand the meaning of the selection. Each group then shares its answers with the entire class.

The Circle of Knowledge is a small-group technique for reviewing material. Groups of four or five students work together to review material already learned. In vocabulary drill, for example, an element of competition is added when, at the end of a specified length of time, each group in turn must repeat a word from their list. Points are given for the number of words accredited to each group. Since words can be used only once, students must listen carefully to each other to avoid repeating a word already given.

Students who prefer to work alone, are persistent, responsible, and need less structure, do well with a Contract Activity Packet (CAP). The CAP contains a list of objectives and suggests ways in which a student can meet them. The student is encouraged to make choices and set a timeframe.

Some students seem to learn better when they are given tasks that can be accomplished in a relatively short period of time. A Programed Learning Sequence, covering one objective, is ideal for this type of learner. The students feel successful because the objective is learned and they are ready to proceed to the next objective.

It has been a challenge to create materials for those students who have a tactile preference. Learning circles, task cards, flash cards, verb boards, and crossword puzzles have been used.

Conclusion

Managing the diagnostic-prescriptive process is challenging, but the results are exciting. Students learn to work more efficiently, achieve more,

---

1. Rita Dunn and Kenneth Dunn, *Teaching Students Through Their Individual Learning Styles: A Practical Approach* (Reston, Va.: Reston Publishing Co., 1978), pp. 2–17. Specific directions for designing these two types of small group activities are given as well as several examples.

and take on increasing amounts of responsibility for their own learning. Teachers have greater success with students and learning becomes exciting. In the classroom, where efforts are made to meet individual learner needs, students and teachers work together to create a climate for both productivity and satisfaction.

CHAPTER 8

Learning Styles at Bishop Carroll High School

Ralph A. Vigna
Michael K. Martin

Bishop Carroll High School, located in Calgary, Alberta, Canada, is an academic-industrial arts high school which accommodates 1,200 students in grades 10 through 12, 49 faculty members, 22 instructional aides, 10 clerical aides, and 21 general aides.

The alternative high school was built and designed to encompass the philosophy and teaching-learning strategies of the Model Schools Project. When the project terminated in June, 1974, several of the schools formed the Learning Environments Consortium (LEC), whose primary goal is personalized education.

Bishop Carroll High School and the LEC are committed to focus on a diagnostic-prescriptive model of education formulated in 1979 by James Keefe with research and application of student learning style.

Educators have long accepted the premise that different students have different learning styles and abilities. Research also has suggested that one single instructional method or program is not suitable for all students. Improvements in education can result from efforts to match instructional methods, programs, and environments with students who are best able to learn from them. This contention has been supported by the work of Domino,[1] Martin,[2] Dunn and Dunn,[3] and others.

What Is a Learning Style?

The question that has plagued educators and researchers is how do youngsters learn? What elements and/or factors affect learning? What is a learning style?

Learning style is a hypothetical construct. Gregorc states that "Learning style consists of distinctive behaviors which serve as indicators of how a person learns from and adapts to his environment. It also gives clues as to how a person's mind operates."[4] Keefe defines learning styles as "characteristic

1. George Domino, "Interactive Effects of Achievement Orientation and Teaching Style on Academic Achievement," *Journal of Educational Psychology* 62(1971): 427–31.
2. Michael Kenneth Martin, "Effects of the Interaction Between Students' Learning Styles and High School Instructional Environments," doctoral dissertation, University of Oregon, 1977.
3. Rita Dunn and Kenneth Dunn, *Educator's Self-Teaching Guide to Individualizing Instructional Programs* (West Nyack, N.Y.: Parker Publishing Co., 1975).
4. Anthony F. Gregorc, "Learning and Teaching Styles. Potent Forces Behind Them," *Educational Leadership,* January 1979.

cognitive, affective, and physiological behaviors that serve as relatively stable indicators of how learners perceive, interact with, and respond to the learning environment."[5]

How has Bishop Carroll High School approached this recent educational focus? In 1978, after examining a variety of instruments, the school elected to use the cognitive/learning style instruments by Joseph Hill and Dunn, Dunn, and Price as part of a pilot study. East Lansing, Michigan was using the Hill instrument, Cognitive Style Mapping, and had computer scoring. Price Systems in Kansas computer-scored the Dunn Learning Style Inventory (1978). A budget was established, a timeline designated, arrangements made for scoring, and the faculty was informed of a proposal to examine these inventories. Teacher-Advisers (T-As) were asked to volunteer themselves and their Grade 10 and Grade 11 advisees. Seven T-As volunteered. Fifty students were administered the Hill instrument, 50 the Dunn instrument, and 50 were administered both instruments. A total of 106 students actually completed the Dunn instrument and 112 completed the Hill instrument.

After the computer results were obtained, three meetings were arranged. Participating T-As were asked to review the results of each instrument with students whom they knew very well and check the instrument for validity. Another meeting was spent reviewing each instrument, and a third meeting focused on the implications for curriculum development, instructional techniques, and learning environments. A summary of the conclusions would be too lengthy to elaborate on here, but the participants were extremely positive and indicated that the information gained would assist them in their T-A roles. In addition, it was verified that the results would have far-reaching effects for the total school.

As a result of these meetings and our commitment to the LEC model, it was decided that the Dunn instrument would be used in the fall of 1979 by all faculty members.

Results of the LSI

The results of the LSI have had major implications for Resource Center learning environments, the development of learning guides, and instructional techniques. Let us first examine the changes that the faculty implemented in their various resource centers. Some students can work well with noise while others (41 percent) need quiet when they study. Each of the nine resource centers designated part of their area as a quiet area. A large number of students (84 percent) prefer to work alone. Resource centers have arranged for individual seating with some grouping of students (usually in couples). Acoustical dividers are extensively used in many resource centers. These dividers not only allow for various groupings but are sound and sight barriers. Their design and coverings tastefully decorate areas as well. Certain students need mobility and require food intake. Students can be observed moving freely and eating within resource centers. Students frequently sit in hallways

5. James W. Keefe, "Learning Style: An Overview," *in Student Learning Styles: Diagnosing and Prescribing Programs.* (Reston, Va.: National Association of Secondary School Principals. Reston, Virginia, 1979).

and on the stairwells to do their schoolwork. A significantly high number of students (37 percent) indicate that they prefer an informal design. To accommodate some of these students, English Language Arts purchased comfortable padded bean bags and chairs for the leisure reading and in-depth area of the resource center. Efforts to accommodate various learning styles have been made by each of the nine resource centers.

Effects on Curriculum

How has the awareness of different learning styles affected the curriculum? The learning guide is the primary instructional mode at Bishop Carroll High School; these guides were primarily visual. Today serious efforts are directed at developing a curriculum which allows students to achieve the course objectives by means of their learning preference. An extraordinary number of audiovisual aids are now incorporated into the subject area curriculum. The number of media programs used in a six month period in 1978-79 increased from 4,339 to 10,236 in 1980-81. The number of students who used media programs increased from 7,128 in 1978-79 to 13,831 in 1980-81 during the same six month period. Conscious efforts have been made to include tactual and kinesthetic assignments as well as the usual paper-and-pencil assignments. A significant increase in assignment choices has occurred.

The methods of imparting instruction have also undergone significant changes. The curriculum goal is to have each student progress through a program to which he or she is best suited and in which he or she can be successful. Diagnosis of previous learning is essential. To work with each individual student to maximize potential is the ultimate goal. Improved learning can result from attempts to identify student learning styles and to match these styles with instructional methods, programs, and environment. At one time, the mathematics subject area team used the paper-and-pencil approach exclusively, with individual assistance. Now math uses a variety of approaches in an attempt to match instructional methods with learning style preferences. Complementing the usual learning guides are multi-text references, videotape productions, small-group seminars or lessons, large-group instruction, and, of course, individual assistance. Business Education has developed introductory videotapes for its typing program. English Language Arts makes available feature films and cassette recordings as well as the printed texts.

Important changes in curriculum, instructional strategies, and environments have and will continue to take place. New understandings of the learning process are on the horizon. These understandings will have a greater impact on education than previous educational innovations.

Bishop Carroll High School will continue to collect data, administer new learning style instruments as they become available, keep informed of current research, and continue to adapt its learning environments, curriculum guides, and teaching strategies to the needs of the individual student. We are part of an essential process to personalize education. Learning is our first priority!

Part Two

Student Learning Styles Instrumentation and Research

CHAPTER 1

Assessing Student Learning Styles: An Overview

James W. Keefe

For thousands of years, educators have sought to define education's role in meeting the needs of the individual. Socrates, in utilizing what is known today as the Socratic method, sought to foster individual development. Rousseau, in *Emile,* addressed the needs of the individual. John Dewey, in his monumental work at the beginning of the twentieth century, focused on the learner as an individual. In recent decades, considerable research and experimentation have been devoted to developing what is known variously as "individualized" or "personalized" instruction.

Ultimately, education must come to grips with the different learning needs of the individual learner. These learning differences flow from variations in individual intelligence, drive, skills, and accomplishment as well as personal and family predispositions and the cultural influences of the wider society. In spite of considerable dialog, there is still substantial discontinuity between theory and practice in identifying and meeting these needs.

The educational profession has helped perpetuate a kind of "fictitious individualization" by equating lower pupil-teacher ratios with meeting student needs. The theory of individualization has been with us for many years, but there has been little application of the concepts in the majority of school systems. Individualization is a "creed without substance."

Today, some educators have intentionally departed from the traditional discussion of classroom materials and pupil-teacher ratios and are raising critical questions about the ways in which students learn. These efforts and related research focus on student learning skills and "learning styles." Much has been written about basic learning skills and we do not intend to treat this important issue at this time. Until recently, however, information and research on the *ways* that pupils learn have seldom been a part of proposals to individualize education. Yet, as society changes and costs increase, research on learning becomes increasingly significant.

Publications such as NASSP's *Student Learning Styles: Diagnosing and Prescribing Programs* point to new directions that school systems must examine as they review their effectiveness. The key to effective schooling is to understand the *range* of student learning styles and to design instruction and materials that respond directly to individual learning needs.

Student Learning Styles

I would like to share with you a model for conceptualizing learning styles that may be helpful in thinking about the various instruments available for its assessment.

Learning styles are cognitive, affective, and physiological traits that serve as relatively stable indicators of how learners perceive, interact with, and respond to the learning environment.

Learning is an internal process; we know that it has taken place only when we observe a more or less permanent change in learner behavior resulting from what has been experienced. The learner behaves differently than before. Similarly, we can recognize individual learning style only by observing a student's overt behavior. Learning style is a moderating variable that links underlying causes with learning behavior. Gregorc (1979) suggests that "style appears to be both nature/nurture in its roots." Styles reflect genetic coding, personality development, and environmental adaptation. Styles are hypothetical constructs that help to explain the learning (and teaching) process. They are relatively persistent qualities in the behavior of individual learners.

Most learning styles are bipolar, representing a continuum from one extreme of a trait to the other. Frequently, no greater value is placed on either extreme. It is acceptable, for example, to be a kinesthetic or an audiovisual learner, to reason abstractly or concretely. The value-neutral quality of many learning styles makes the approach particularly attractive for assessing instructional applications in populations with strong cultural or ethnic variations.

Elements of learning style appeared in the literature as early as 1892, but the findings were plagued with methodological problems and a preoccupation with determining the *one* perceptual mode that would best improve student learning. Specific research on *cognitive* styles was greatly expanded in the United States after World War II at Brooklyn College, the Menninger Foundation, and the Fels Institute. Current efforts to explain the underlying processes of learning and teaching reflect two lines of research. One group retains dominant interest in the cognitive dimensions of style. The other is concerned with *applied* models of learning and teaching and multidimensional analysis of styles.

Learning style analysis in school-based programs would seem to demand both approaches. Accordingly, we will categorize learning styles in cognitive, affective, and physiological domains. We will give brief examples of each of these domains and the types of psychometric measures that are available to assess them. Examples have been selected for their representativeness and diversity.

COGNITIVE STYLES

Cognitive styles are "information processing habits representing the learner's typical mode of perceiving, thinking, problem solving, and remem-

bering" (Messick, 1976). The vast majority of research on personality-related learning variables has dealt with cognitive style. Each learner has preferred ways of perception, organization, and retention that are distinctive and consistent. These characteristic differences are called cognitive styles.

Messick (1976) lists more than 20 dimensions of cognitive style that are derived from experimental research. Some of these elements are straightforward, others are very complex. Some of the newest styles founded on brain behavior research are cognitive (i.e., hemispheric dominance). It is possible to organize the style dimensions in a general way as they touch on either reception, concept formation, or retention. (See Appendix 1 for Student Learning Styles Chart)

The following styles and assessment devices illustrate the cognitive domain of learning style.

Perceptual modality preferences/strengths describe learner tendency to use the different sensory modes to understand experience. Strengths and preferences are not synonymous; indeed, a preference may be weaker than a true strength. The conventional modes are kinesthetic or psychomotor, visual or spatial, and auditory or verbal. Preference seems to evolve from kinesthetic in childhood to visual and eventually verbal in later years. In adults, all three modes function cooperatively with a preference/strength in one or the other. All students ultimately need to learn to use all modalities with some effectiveness.

▶ The *Edmonds Learning Style Identification Exercise* (ELSIE) is a simple but effective method of detecting perceptual modes (See Appendix 2 for more information on this and other instruments cited in the paper). ELSIE is concerned with the ways students internalize individual words. It provides a profile of perceptual style based on the individual's pattern of response to 50 common English words that are read once at five-second intervals. Students are asked, upon hearing a word, to indicate which of the following responses occur to them most spontaneously:

1. *Visualization*—a mental picture of some object or activity
2. *Written Word*—a mental picture of the word spelled out
3. *Listening*—no mental picture but the sound of the word carries meaning
4. *Activity*—physical or emotional feeling about the word.

The learner's scores in all four categories are important to the profile which is charted on a stanine scale arranged as bands above and below the median of a pilot group.

Field independence vs. dependence measures a continuum of an analytic as opposed to a global way of experiencing the environment. Independents perceive things clearly from the background field, but dependents are influenced by the overall organization of the background and see parts of the field as "fused." Independents differentiate among experiences while dependents see them as integrated. The field independent learner will tend to be highly analytic and systematic; the field dependent learner, holistic. This style has been the subject of much research.

▶ The *Group Embedded Figures Test* (GEFT) is one of several embedded figures tests developed by Herman Witkin and his colleagues at Brooklyn College. The EFT was originally designed to assess cognitive functioning, social behavior, body concepts, etc. The group version of the test utilizes picture mazes (optical illusions) to assess analytical vs. global styles of information processing. Test subjects are asked to discover and trace a number of simple forms hidden within more complex figures. The following illustrates this technique. The simple figure is located at the bottom right of the complex figure.

Simple Form

Complex Figure

The GEFT is short and easy to administer. It has been widely used in research and, more recently, in classrooms. It actually measures analytical ability; global ability is derived by inference.

Transaction Ability Profile. A number of researchers have developed bi-dimensional models of cognitive style, combining two information processing dimensions. Anthony Gregorc's Style Delineator model looks at concrete vs. abstract and random vs. sequential styles. The resulting matrix profiles learners on four distinct learning patterns: Concrete Sequential (CS), Concrete Random (CR), Abstract Sequential (AS), and Abstract Random (AR).

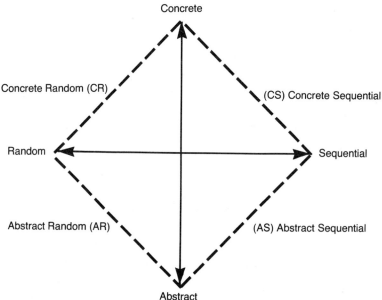

The Style Delineator model has emerged from classroom research in diagnostic-prescriptive education as a means of exploring the match and mismatch implications of teaching and learning styles.

▶ The *Gregorc Style Delineator* assesses Gregorc's four bi-dimensional learning patterns. The inventory is a short, self-report instrument consisting of 40 words in 10 sets of 4 each. The student ranks personal impressions of the words in each set, identifying his or her spontaneous, natural ways of transacting with the learning environment. The resulting scores are visually profiled on a bi-dimensional matrix that shows the various style proclivities. Ninety percent of those tested have a definite preference in one or two of the four categories.

Cognitive Profile—Charles Letteri of the University of Vermont has taken assessment of the information processing domain a step further by combining several existing cognitive style dimensions in a profile that predicts student achievement on standardized achievement tests. This multi-dimensional Cognitive Profile charts the student's position across seven cognitive style continuums. Research projects dating back to 1977 have revealed three types of profiles:

- *Type I* is associated with high achievement levels in academic performance on standardized tests. This type of learner scores strongly on the majority of the following dimensions: analytical, focuser, narrow, complex, reflective, sharpener, and tolerant.
- *Type II* is descriptive of average performance on standardized tests and reflects an intermediate range on the style continuums, or a mixed profile—an inconsistent pattern of styles.
- *Type III* is characterized by low academic performance on standardized tests and by style proclivities in the majority of these dimensions: global, nonfocuser, broad, simple, impulsive, leveler, intolerant.

No instructional value judgments are inherent in assigning these profiles, but they do assume the presence of a *traditional* school setting. Students with varying sets of characteristics score differently on standardized tests of school achievement. Letteri's continuing "augmentation" research indicates that style dimensions are modifiable and that cognitive profiles can be altered. Schools that already incorporate alternative learning environments may facilitate augmentation by providing conditions better suited to individual learners.

▶ The *Cognitive Profile* is derived from a battery of single bi-polar style tests that, in combination, predict student achievement on standardized tests. The test instruments are administered in their original clinical forms or in slightly modified versions. The styles and related continuums are the following:

1. Field independence vs. field dependence—see above for definition.
   Analytical ⟷ *Global*

2. Scanning—the degree of attention to task and susceptibility to distraction.

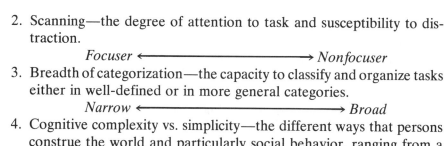

       Focuser ⟵————————————⟶ *Nonfocuser*

3. Breadth of categorization—the capacity to classify and organize tasks either in well-defined or in more general categories.

       Narrow ⟵————————————⟶ *Broad*

4. Cognitive complexity vs. simplicity—the different ways that persons construe the world and particularly social behavior, ranging from a multi-dimensional to a uni-dimensional perspective.

       Complex ⟵————————————⟶ *Simple*

5. Reflectiveness vs. impulsivity—the consistency in the speed and accuracy of hypothesis formation and information gathering. Reflectives are slower and more accurate, impulsives faster and less accurate.

       Reflective ⟵————————————⟶ *Impulsive*

6. Leveling vs. sharpening—variations in memory processing. Sharpeners rely heavily on visual (rote) memory and recall data as distinct and different; levelers tend to blur memories and to merge associated but distinct concepts.

       Sharpener ⟵————————————⟶ *Leveler*

7. Tolerance for incongruous or unrealistic experiences—the differences in willingness to accept perceptions and experiences at variance with the conventional. Low tolerance implies a preference for more conventional, more predictable ideas and approaches.

       Tolerant ⟵————————————⟶ *Intolerant*

AFFECTIVE STYLES

The second domain of learning style encompasses personality traits that have to do with attention, emotion, and valuing—with the processes of motivation. Motivation is the end-product of attention, activity, and interest. *Affective learning styles are these same motivational processes viewed as the learner's typical mode of arousing, directing, and sustaining behavior.* Affective styles are the products of a wide variety of influences: the cultural environment, parental and peer pressures, school practices, and personality factors. Values are involved. Not every student can be successful in every learning environment because family or ethnic customs may be at odds with school practices. There is a large subjective component here. Most teachers think of students as motivated if they do what the teacher wants done, as unmotivated if they do not. For this reason, careful diagnosis of affective style is necessary, indeed, fundamental to the success of a diagnostic-prescriptive approach to schooling.

Several characteristic affective styles and their supporting instrumentation are discussed in the following paragraphs.

Conceptual Level is a motivational trait developed by David Hunt at the Ontario Institute for the Study of Education. Conceptual Level (CL) describes the *degree of structure* a person needs to learn effectively. Low conceptual level signifies a need for high structure, high CL means that the learner needs less structure. Students typically develop through unsocialized, dependent, and independent stages, requiring successively less structure and increasing self-expression and autonomy.

▶ The *Paragraph Completion Method* (PCM) is a semi-projective method to assess Conceptual Level. Students are given six incomplete statements and are asked to write at least three sentences about each, reflecting how they really feel about the topic. The topics are:

1. What I think about rules . . .
2. When I am criticized . . .
3. What I think about parents . . .
4. When someone does not agree with me . . .
5. When I am not sure . . .
6. When I am told what to do . . .

The topics were chosen to reveal how students handle conflict. Completion responses are considered to be "thought samples" and are scored on a scale of 0-3 in terms of their conceptual complexity and personal maturity. Scoring the PCM demands a cultivated clinical judgment based on training and practice.

Locus of Control characterizes the forces within an individual's personality that direct or stimulate action. These perceptions of causality may be internal or external. The internal individuals think of themselves as responsible for their own behavior, deserving praise for successes and blame for failures. The external individuals see outer forces, circumstances beyond their control, luck, or other people, as responsible for what happens. There is some evidence that a greater sense of internality can be developed. Internality is a highly desirable school-rated trait.

▶ The *I /E Scale* by Julian Rotter is one of several instruments available for the assessment of locus of control. The Rotter questionnaire presents a series of 29 paired alternatives that describe the ways certain important events in society affect different people. Test subjects are directed to select the one statement of each pair that they actually believe to be true. The statements present choices like the following:

a. Most of the problems in people's lives are a result of bad luck.
b. People's problems come from the mistakes they make.

The scale is quickly and easily hand scored.

PHYSIOLOGICAL STYLES

The third domain of learning style describes the characteristic learning-related behaviors of the human body. *Physiological styles are biologically based modes of response that are founded on sex-related differences, personal nutrition and health, and reaction to the physical environment.* Physiological factors are among the most obvious influences on school learning. The student who is hungry, ill, or malnourished behaves differently than the youngster who is healthy. Boys and girls learn differently in certain situations. All learners are affected by the physical environment of the school.

Two elements illustrate the range of styles within this domain.

The *Environmental Elements* that influence learning are light, sound, and temperature. The related physiological learning styles are the individual learner's varying reactions to these elements. Few learners are bothered by light variations but many find it hard to work under distracting noise conditions. Extreme temperatures affect almost everyone. Imagine the plight of the light-sensitive, shy, cold-blooded youngster who is forced to sit next to the window in a chilly, open-style classroom.

▶ No specialized instrument is available to measure environmental styles but the *Learning Style Inventory* by Dunn, Dunn, and Price incorporates environmental elements as a major area of assessment. Teachers who are sensitive to the physiological implications of the learning environment can readily assess these elements by *observation* and provide appropriate options for students differently affected (NASSP, 1979).

Time Rhythms are personal variations in learning readiness related to the time of the day. Some learners perform best in the early morning, others in the afternoon or even late at night. These differences likely reflect early childhood sleeping and waking patterns but may also derive from the more fundamental circadian rhythms of the body (the culprit in "jet lag").

▶ Rita and Kenneth Dunn have developed a simple *Time Questionnaire* to chart this element of style. The instrument is a short checklist that enables the learner to analyze preferred working times during the day. Scores are derived for early morning, late morning, afternoon, and evening. The questionnaire asks respondents to choose among such items as:

- I usually hate to get up in the morning.
- I usually feel a "low" after lunch.

Comprehensive Instruments

A few researchers have formulated learning style instruments that assess more than one style domain and several of the dimensions. No existing instrument measures all major elements of the three domains of style; some of these devices primarily measure the cognitive and affective domains, others the affective and physiological. Some examples follow.

Cognitive and Affective

▶ The *Myers-Briggs Type Indicator* (MBTI) is a measure of personality dispositions and preferences based on Carl Jung's theory of psychological "types." Jung postulated two basic bi-polar mental processes (sensing-intuition and thinking-feeling) and two fundamental orientations to life (extraversion and introversion). The MBTI adds a fourth dimension (judgment-perception) to identify the dominant mental process. The resulting matrix categorizes individuals into 16 types. The following diagram illustrates the relationships.

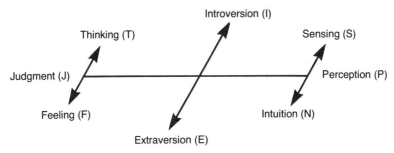

The MBTI provides information about the ways learners prefer to perceive meaning (sensing vs. intuition—a cognitive dimension), to express values and commitment (thinking vs. feeling), and to interact with the world (extraversion vs. introversion). The latter preferences are affective elements of learning style. The judging vs. perceiving dimension simply identifies the dominant preference in approaching reality (affective or cognitive).

MBTI theory is sophisticated and the typology elaborate. Research is coordinated by the Center for Applications of Psychological Type (CAPT) in Gainesville, Florida.

▶ *Cognitive Style Mapping* is the brain child of Joseph Hill, former president of Oakland Community College in East Lansing, Michigan. Hill developed mapping as a component of his conceptual framework for education which he called the "educational sciences." He expressed cognitive style in terms of mathematical set theory. In much simplified form, his framework would translate as follows:

5		1		2		3		4
Cognitive Style	=	Symbols and Meanings	×	Cultural Determinants	×	Modalities of Inference	×	Memory Functions

The fourth set, neurological, electrochemical, and biological aspects of memory functioning, has never been completed for lack of appropriate data. The present theory and practice of cognitive style mapping is based on the interrelationship of the first three "sciences." Each of these dimensions is composed of various elements that interact to formulate an individual's cognitive style.

- *Symbols* include words, numbers, sensory data, and psychomotor representations (games, sports, dance).
- *Cultural determinants* are family and peer influences, and personal style preferences.
- *Modalities of influence* are the inductive and deductive reasoning processes.

Two assessment techniques have been used in Cognitive Style Mapping.

1. Empirical Mapping involves the systematic *observation* and the re-

cording of information on the various style elements. It is ordinarily used with younger children.

2. Mapping Inventories consisting of statements keyed to the style elements have been developed at East Lansing High School (Michigan), Ohio University (Athens, Ohio), and Mountain View Community College (Dallas, Texas). These instruments are self-report inventories that ask test subjects to indicate whether they usually, sometimes, or rarely engage in the stated cognitive style behaviors.

The following are representative items.

- I prefer spoken directions instead of written ones.
- I can tell when someone is bluffing.
- I consult with my family before making decisions.
- I work best in an organized setting.

In some places, graphic profiles are charted to represent each student's cognitive style.

Mapping presents an elegant theory of learning style and excellent item coverage of the perceptual, conceptualizing, and social motivation dimensions. Unfortunately, it suffers from a limited application in secondary schools and needs a current research base.

Cognitive, Affective, Physiological

▶ The *Learning Style Inventory* (LSI) developed by Rita Dunn, Kenneth Dunn, and Gary Price is the most widely used assessment instrument in elementary and secondary schools. The LSI incorporates many useful affective and physiological elements of learning style but only touches on the cognitive (in the area of perceptual modalities). The authors are currently working to expand the model in the psychological (cognitive) domain.

The Dunns and Price define learning style in terms of four pervasive learning conditions and 18 elements. Students complete a 104-item self-report questionnaire that identifies learning preferences with regard to immediate environmental conditions and their own emotional, sociological, and physical needs. The inventory is designed to support alternative approaches to instruction by profiling the elements of each individual's learning style. The current version of the LSI assesses these 18 elements:

Environmental	Emotional	Sociological	Physical
Sound	Motivation	Self-oriented	Perceptual
Light	Persistence	Colleague-oriented	Intake
Temperature	Responsibility	Authority-oriented	Time
Design	Structure	Pair-oriented	Mobility
		Team-oriented	
		Varied	

Computerized scoring is available with individual and group profiles. Printouts indicate learning preferences on 36 subscales.

The Learning Style Inventory is a practitioner-oriented instrument with commendable validation and widespread application, particularly in elementary and middle-level schools. It lacks a clearly defined cognitive domain and may be more ideosyncratic than practical in some of its elements.

State of the Assessment Art

No current learning style instrument provides a truly comprehensive assessment of the cognitive, affective, and physiological domains of learning style. To say this is not to criticize the many excellent first generation instruments presently available. Many of these devices intend to measure only a single element or domain and do so admirably. Others attempt to be broader but focus in practice on two of the domains. The time is ripe for researchers and psychometricians to collaborate in identifying those elements of style that are most important to the teaching-learning environment and to develop a workable second generation instrument. NASSP stands ready to vigorously support and sustain such an effort.

Learning styles diagnosis is unquestionably a primary component of the teaching-learning cycle, one that opens the door to a personalized approach to education. Style diagnosis gives a powerful new tool to educators who want to improve student learning. Viewed apart from a personalized philosophy of education, learning style analysis is merely an interesting new assessment technique. In the context of a systematic diagnostic-prescriptive approach, however, it is the base on which an edifice of personalized schooling can be built—a truly *modern approach* to education.

Selected References

Ball, Samuel, ed. *Motivation in Education.* New York: Academic Press, 1977.

Dunn, Rita, and Dunn, Kenneth. *Teaching Students Through Their Individual Learning Styles: A Practical Approach.* Reston, Va.: Reston Publishing Co., 1978.

Gregorc, Anthony F. "Learning/Teaching Styles: Potent Forces Behind Them." *Educational Leadership,* January 1979, pp. 234–36.

Hill, Joseph E., *The Educational Sciences,* rev. ed. Bloomfield Hills, Mich.: Oakland Community College, 1976.

Hunt, David E.; Butler, L. F.; Noy, J. E.; and Rosser, M. E. *Assessing Conceptual Level by the Paragraph Completion Method.* Toronto: Ontario Institute for Studies in Education, 1978.

Lawrence, Gordon. *People Types and Tiger Stripes.* Gainesville, Fla.: Center for Application of Psychological Type, 1979.

Letteri, Charles A. "Cognitive Profile: Basic Determinant of Academic Achievement." *Journal of Educational Research,* March/April 1980, pp. 195–99.

Messick, Samuel, ed. *Individuality in Learning.* San Francisco: Jossey-Bass, 1976.

NASSP. *Student Learning Styles: Diagnosing and Prescribing Programs.* Reston, Va: National Association of Secondary School Principals, 1979.

Reinert, Harry. "One Picture Is Worth a Thousand Words? Not Necessarily!" *Modern Language Journal,* April 1976, pp. 160–68.

Rotter, Julian B. "Generalized Expectancies for Internal Versus External Control of Requirements." *Psychological Monographs*, Vol. 80, No. 10, 1966, pp. 1–28.

Sperry, Len. *Learning Performance and Individual Differences.* Glenview, Ill.: Scott, Foresman & Co., 1972.

Witkin, Herman A. *Cognitive Style and the Teaching-Learning Process.* American Educational Research Association Audiotape, 1974.

CHAPTER 2

Teaching Through Modality Strengths: Look Before You Leap

Walter B. Barbe
Michael N. Milone, Jr.

The basic tenet of the learning styles movement is that instructional methods and materials should, whenever possible, be consistent with students' learning styles. In other words, before leaping to conclusions about instruction, we should first look at how students learn best.

As fundamental as this principle appears, it is occasionally violated by even the strongest advocates of the learning styles philosophy, who in their enthusiasm sometimes make decisions about instructional practices without actually assessing student learning styles. These well-meaning professionals base their curriculum choices on traditional beliefs about student learning styles rather than on information gathered through systematic observation or the use of standardized assessment procedures. Our research, and that conducted by others, has shown that what we think is true is not always the case, and that assessing student learning styles is a necessary prelude to designing an appropriate curriculum.

The findings presented in this paper were obtained through the use of the Swassing-Barbe Modality Index (Barbe and Swassing, 1981). The SBMI is a matching-to-sample task that involves four basic shapes: square, circle, heart, and triangle. A sequence of shapes is presented and the person tested is expected to reproduce the sequence using a pool of loose shapes. The results of the SBMI are reported in percentage scores for the visual, auditory, and kinesthetic modalities, providing a measure of the relative strength of the major modalities. The SBMI has proven useful with students and adults, and is easily administered and scored by classroom teachers.

The standardization research for the SBMI and other material pertaining to modality-based instruction are available from the authors (Barbe and Milone, 1981; Barbe, Swassing, and Milone, 1979). A filmstrip describing the SBMI and other aspects of modality-based instruction can be obtained at no cost on a loan basis from the Zaner-Bloser Co., 2500 W. Fifth Ave., Columbus, Ohio 43216.

Girls Are as Kinesthetic as Boys

One of the first surprises we encountered was that the females we tested were just as kinesthetic as the males (Barbe, Swassing, and Milone, 1979). Our discussions with teachers and parents, as well as our review of the literature, led us to believe that males would learn better kinesthetically than females. This was not the case for young children, adolescents, or adults.

We did, however, find that few females knew they were kinesthetic learners. When the results of the test were shared with many kinesthetic females, they were at first surprised to learn about their modality strength. After a few questions about how they preferred to learn, however, these subjects recognized that they managed to add a kinesthetic element to many of their learning experiences.

The success of our questioning effort leads us to believe that self-report instruments such as the Learning Style Inventory (Dunn, Dunn, and Price, 1975) have great potential with many students. Although there is no guarantee that modality strength and modality preference coincide (Barbe, Swassing, and Milone, 1979), the use of multiple questions, as in the Learning Style Inventory, increases the likelihood of obtaining a reliable response.

Kinesthetic Learners Are Surprisingly Successful

One of the long-standing beliefs in education is that kinesthetic learners are underachievers. We found that, contrary to our expectations and those of most other researchers, the kinesthetic learners we identified had achievement scores that were on a par with those of other groups of students (Barbe and Milone, 1981).

When we began our research, we went on the assumption that kinesthetic students could not achieve well academically. When research proved otherwise, we were forced to rethink our position, and to reflect on some circumstances that most other researchers had overlooked: surgeons and dentists do quite well academically and are probably kinesthetic learners (at least we hope they are). Rhodes Scholars, chosen on the basis of academic and athletic excellence, are likely to be kinesthetic. There does, after all, seem to be hope for students who learn by doing.

Despite our finding that kinesthetic learners seemed to do well academically, we suspected that some basis in fact must exist for the contention that kinesthetic students have learning problems. We examined our data carefully for some relationship we may have overlooked and found that students whose dominant modalities were a combination of auditory and kinesthetic had relatively low reading achievement scores. We believe that these students enjoy active learning but, in seeking kinesthetic stimulation, create "noise" that interferes with their auditory processing. Because much of what is learned in school is auditory, these students may have been generating interference that contributed to their own learning difficulties.

Visual Learners Are Not Always Good Readers

Hugh McCammon (1981) used the SBMI to compare the modality strengths of good and poor readers at the high school level. His groups were matched according to sex, age, grade, and intelligence, and differed only in their reading achievement as measured by the Metropolitan Achievement Test. Unexpectedly, the poor readers were much more visual than the good readers, an outcome that neither McCammon nor we anticipated.

Two factors seemed to contribute to the poor reading ability of these students who had well-developed visual skills. First of all, their modalities were not so well integrated as those of the good readers. Even though the poor readers had visual skills capable of undertaking the reading task, they were probably not able to transfer information efficiently from the visual to the auditory modality, a capacity that is essential to successful reading. Oexle and Zenhausern (1981) derived a similar conclusion from their research on hemispheric activation and reading. They stated that:

> At least one type of disabled reader seems to depend strongly on the right hemisphere and has difficulty activating the left hemisphere for the auditory encoding of visual stimuli, a central task required for competent reading (p. 36).

The second factor reflected the fact that these same students had been taught to read using a phonics-based approach. Nothing is inherently wrong with this type of reading instruction; for many students, it is probably correct. But students who are very visual may experience difficulty learning to read if their initial instruction is aimed at the auditory modality. McCammon's poor readers may have done well with a sight-word approach that was geared to their modality strength; instead, they were forced to rely on their weaker modality, with the end result that they never learned to read well.

Conclusion

These three brief examples suggest that we should "look before we leap" when developing curriculum that is intended to reflect student learning styles. Certainly, the learning style movement has great potential for improving the education offered to students in today's schools. This potential will be realized, however, only if we identify student learning styles before attempting to modify how we teach.

References

Barbe, W. B., and Milone, M. N., Jr. "Modality Characteristics of Gifted Students." Paper presented at the Council for Exceptional Children, New York City, April 1981.

———. "What We Know About Modality Strengths." *Educational Leadership*. 38(1981): 378–80.

Barbe, W. B., and Swassing, R. H. *The Swassing-Barbe Modality Index*. Columbus, Ohio: Zaner-Bloser, 1979.

Barbe, W. B.; Swassing, R. H.; and Milone, M. N., Jr. *Teaching Through Modality Strengths: Concepts and Practices*. Columbus, Ohio: Zaner-Bloser, 1979.

Dunn, R.; Dunn, K.; and Price, G. *Learning Style Inventory.* Lawrence, Kans.: Price Systems, 1975.

McCammon, H. "Modality Integration in Remedial and Nonremedial Readers." Master's thesis, Marywood College, 1981.

Oexle, J. E., and Zenhausern, R. "Differential Hemispheric Activation in Good and Poor Readers." *International Journal of Neuroscience* 15(1981): 31–36.

CHAPTER 3

Development of the Group Embedded Figures Test

Philip K. Oltman

Cognitive styles research has a history of more than three decades, and because of their pervasiveness in the individual's functioning, cognitive styles have been studied in many subfields of psychology. In recent years, research has turned toward issues relevant for the educational process.

Cognitive styles are a person's typical ways of processing information. This very general definition indicates that cognitive styles will enter into a person's behavior in a very wide range of activities. Although styles have consequences for a person's pattern of abilities, they are not abilities themselves. Although there are many kinds of cognitive styles, this discussion will focus on a dimension known as field dependence-field independence.

Field Dependence/Field Independence

The field-dependent and field-independent cognitive styles are contrasting modes of processing information. In general, a person with a relatively field-independent cognitive style tends to use internal sources of information in perception and problem solving, while relatively field-dependent people tend to refer more to external sources of information. I will make this distinction clearer with some specific examples in a moment, but I want to point out here that this is a continuous dimension, not two dichotomous types. People vary continuously along the dimension just as they do in height, weight, or hair color. The two extreme ends of the dimension, field dependence and field independence, are used in discussion for convenience, with no implication that there are two types of people. Field dependence-independence is a continuum, not a typology.

To make the discussion more concrete, we can turn to some examples of the ways in which the field dependence-independence dimension can be assessed. This line of research had its origins in laboratory studies of perception initiated by Herman A. Witkin. The question was, how do we know which way is up? One source of information is from the visual field. Another is from sensations within the body stemming from the pull of gravity. Ordinarily, these two sources of information about the "upright" coincide; either serves as a valid cue. In the laboratory, however, they can be separated to determine which source of information is more influential.

In one approach, the entire visual field is tilted by seating the observer in a tilted room. When this is done, and the individual is asked to adjust the body to an upright position in a tilting chair, a wide range of individual differences is observed. Some individuals adjust their bodies to a tilt close to that of the tilted room; others adjust to the true vertical regardless of room tilt. The first group of people are called "field dependent," because their judgments of body tilt are strongly influenced by the tilted visual field provided by the room. Those who make their settings upright regardless of room tilt are called "field independent," because they rely on their internal perception of the force of gravity rather than on the visual field.

In a variation of this situation, called a Rod-and-Frame Test, a tilted square frame is substituted for the tilted room. A tilting rod (rather than the body) must be adjusted to the vertical. Again, a wide range of differences is observed, with those who are field dependent in this task also showing field dependence in the tilting room situation.

The original research on field dependence-independence was based on tasks such as the tilting room and Rod-and-Frame Test, but later it was found that another type of visual task with no involvement of perception of the upright was correlated with performance on those tasks—the Embedded Figures Test. In the Embedded Figures Test, the observer is asked to find a simple geometric form which is hidden within a complex pattern. Relatively field-dependent people tend to take the perceptual organization of the complex pattern as it is given and have some difficulty breaking it up to find the embedded figure within it. Relatively field-independent people, on the other hand, can restructure the visual field, break up the complex pattern into simpler components, and more readily find the simple figure which is hidden.

Performance on these tasks is viewed as a style because of the consistency shown from one task to another in the way information is processed—specifically in whether responses are primarily determined by the external field or by internal frames of reference. Aspects of this style can be seen in personality, interpersonal behavior, learning and teaching, choice of careers and interests, and in many other facets of an individual's behavior.

The Group Embedded Figures Test

The Group Embedded Figures Test (GEFT) was developed to meet the need for group testing using the Embedded Figures Test format. The original form of the Embedded Figures Test (EFT) was individually administered. While individual administration is ideal from the point of view of control over the conditions of the test and for score reliability, it is of course not practical when large groups of study participants must be tested. Since we wished the GEFT to mirror the EFT in every respect possible (excepting only the group-administered format) we used almost all the EFT items in the GEFT.

As in the EFT, the test taker cannot see the simple figure and the complex figure at the same time. The simple figures are printed on the back of the booklet, and can be looked at whenever the test taker wishes, but they are not visible at the same time as the complex figure. While the individually administered EFT utilized various colors to help hide the simple figure, printing costs made this approach prohibitive in the GEFT. Rather, we achieved the same effect by shading parts of the complex figures.

It may seem unimportant that the GEFT is printed in blue ink, but there is a very practical reason for that. We originally printed the tests in black ink but we found that pencil lines drawn by the test takers were very difficult to see, making the job of scoring more taxing than it should be. By changing to blue ink, we were better able to score the tests.

In the initial development of the GEFT, we prepared 32 trial items—24 from the original EFT and 8 similar ones. We then made up two 16-item forms, and administered them to groups of students in a large metropolitan college. Each form had the items arranged in four different orders, so that any given item sometimes came earlier in the test and sometimes later. If we had used only one order, items at the end would have only been attempted by those few students who finished the entire test. We also administered the Rod-and-Frame Test, an individually-administered EFT containing items the students had not seen in the group form they took, and a human figure drawing test scored on the Articulation of Body Concept scale which is related to this same cognitive style.

We selected items from the total set of 32 by examining correlations between pass-fail scores on each item and total score on the group form, the score on the individual EFT, and Rod-and-Frame Test scores. The 20 items with the highest correlations were incorporated into a single composite form and administered to yet another group of students, using varying time limits with different subgroups to arrive at an optimum for the test. Finally, we constructed the final form of the test using the 18 best items, divided into two 9-item subtests so that reliabilities could be computed. The subtests were matched for difficulty, correlations with the criteria, and use of simple figures.

We also added a short set of practice items at the beginning of the test. These items are very simple so that almost anyone can do them readily. They give test takers some practice on the mechanics of the test, including drawing in the simple figures, flipping back and forth between simple and complex figures, and working rapidly. These items are not scored, but they can be inspected if an individual has a remarkably low score to determine whether the instructions were understood.

Finally, I will mention an often-asked question for which I have no answer. What is a field-dependent score and what is a field-independent score? There are no generally agreed upon cutpoints. Since the dimension is a continuous one and not a dichotomy, the definition of extreme groups is arbitrary. One could also ask at what height individuals will be considered tall? In many cases, there is no reason to think of clearcut subgroups. Correlations can be computed between GEFT scores and the other variables of interest so that all the data are used, rather than reduce a continuous variable to a dichotomy and thereby throw away information.

CHAPTER 4

Learning Style Across Content Areas

Kathleen A. Butler

Every classroom operates on the energy created by the interaction between the teacher and the students. This interactive process is influenced by a strong and vital, yet sensitive and subtle force—the style of learning of the teacher and the student. The teacher's style, often a neglected factor in analyzing classroom dynamics, is as vital a consideration as the student's style, regardless of content area or grade level.

Teacher and student styles act and react together to permit student learning to be more, or less, successful. The implications of these styles for classroom learning will be addressed in this paper, based on this author's interpretation of the Gregorc Style Delineator.

Gregorc Style Delineator

Anthony F. Gregorc has defined learning style as "the distinctive behaviors which serve as indicators of a person's mediation abilities and capacities." Using a phenomenological research methodology—an approach which considers the individual's reality reflected through the person's awareness, consciousness, and perception—Gregorc found that stylistic traits were best defined as external attributes that reflected the mind's natural abilities, capacities, and preferences for channeling data. Learning style, then, signaled the natural means by which a person most easily, efficiently, and effectively understood self, the world, and the relationship of the two. Albert Einstein aptly summarized the meaning of phenomenological style for the individual by stating, "Man tries to make for himself in the fashion that suits him best, a simplified and intelligible picture of the world."

Gregorc's research on style led to the discovery of five sets of dualities—those of perception, order, processing, relationship, and decision making—and to the development of the Gregorc Style Delineator. In this paper, only two dualities will be considered: the Concrete/Abstract Perception Duality and the Sequential/Random Ordering Duality. Four sets of learning style patterns emerged from the combination of these two dualities: Concrete Sequential (CS), Abstract Random (AR), Abstract Sequential (AS), Concrete Random (CR).

Under phenomenological analysis, Gregorc found that the behavioral characteristics of individuals in each of these stylistic patterns reflected highly discerned attitudes, motivations, and reasoned thought. From this research, the *Gregorc Style Delineator* was developed to permit individuals to self-assess their learning style pattern and preferences.

Most people used one or two styles naturally well, according to Gregorc's research. He also found that some people operated from their natural style almost exclusively while others attempted to operate from a non-natural style when it was necessary to accommodate or adapt to the needs of others or the environment. These people had "style flex."

Interviews and observations also indicated that some individuals could adjust easily to another style when necessary, while others had difficulty. Some people, moreover, would not adjust their style and others *could not* adjust their style. The many reasons for these differences in style flex ability should be explored before considering whether to match or mismatch learning and teaching style in the classroom.

Stylistic Differences

For the purposes of this article, a limited number of descriptions from among the four learning style patterns have been selected from the Style Delineator characteristics, and some examples from this author's research and work with teachers have been selected to reflect the differences in teaching and student style.

The Concrete Sequential style (CS) reflected a preference for order; precision; schedules; physical, hands-on experiences; and a product-based effort. Teachers with this predominant style provided a highly structured classroom with hands-on projects for students, relied on worksheets to reinforce content, stressed practical lessons, worked under strict time limitations, and were oriented to results. A strong CS-style second-grade teacher observed that she would provide already-organized materials to her students—such as pre-cut hearts to decorate—because it was important to her that the students have a "realistic" product to take home to parents. A dominant CS sophomore lamented to his parents that he never knew how to do his English assignment because the teacher's directions were "too loose." He was an honor-roll student, but could not tolerate the general directions of the teacher. He needed the specific, procedural directions required by the CS mind.

By contrast, the Abstract Random (AR) style reflected a preference for emotional sensitivity, psychically pleasing environments, strong relationships with others and flexibility in time, activities, and demands. AR teachers offered a personalized class; stressed high morale, humor, and self-expression; tended to use a thematic approach to address content; and liked to use media and discussion as their primary teaching tools.

A secondary-level biology teacher revealed his AR style by focusing in class on the themes of life on earth: the ecological systems and the beauty of nature. He used facts and data to support his themes rather than teaching the facts and data for themselves. In his classroom, poetry and literature that reflected biological themes were as important as charts and classifications.

Films about the meaning of biological life were apt to take precedence over a dissection table. Mike, an AR student, had a similar thematic tendency. He had no difficulty designing a colorful symbolic cover for the class yearbook yet could not succeed in certain classes with highly sequential teachers.

The Abstract Sequential style (AS) reflected yet another view of the world. The AS style preferred intellectual and vicarious experiences and valued logical, rational, theoretical, and analytical approaches to the world. As teachers, they often appeared at the high school and college level where they taught from a base of content expertise and enjoyed a forum for intellectual debate. They relied almost exclusively on lecture format and extensive reading assignments, documented evidence, and evaluation by formal testing. A dominant AS history professor used his style to debate the merits of all of the theories within an historical period, whereas the CS person might have concentrated on the course of events, or the AR teacher might have launched into the personalities of historical figures.

Finally, the Concrete Random (CR) style looked to the physical world as the opportunity to develop and utilize creative and original problem-solving talents. This person looked for and gave out options, demanded independence, and wanted to invent new ideas or products—to create the unexpected. As teachers, the CRs used a problem-solving approach to the curriculum that often included games, simulations, critical issues, discovery, and experiments. They stressed the need for students to challenge, to probe, to ask "why." They insisted that students "think for themselves" and often replied to a student's question by saying, "what do you think?" or "what do you want to do?"

A CR elementary level teacher mirrored her CR dominance in a thank-you note to a student for the student's self-designed holiday present. She wrote, "I will keep it always to remind me that it is a wonderful thing to be creative." The CR student (prone to ask the question, "I wonder what would happen if . . . ") delights in open-ended, self-designed work that interests him or her. John, a middle school student, thought it quite easy to design a working model of the human circulatory system—and win first prize in the science fair.

Natural mind qualities, teacher style, and student style, are intact and in place long before either enters school. One can begin to imagine the complex turn of events and attitudes as styles of students and teachers begin to interact, or interfere, with each other.

Differing Roles of Style

Once in the classroom, three stylistic roles must be addressed if the role of style is to be taken seriously:

1. Style must be considered as a reflection of the mind, as an instrument of thought. Before a book is opened or an assignment is given, the teacher's being and the student's being cause energic vibrations to color, direct, excite, control, or abuse one another. Some students report that they can tell

whether or not they will learn or enjoy a class after the first 10 minutes of class on opening day! The teacher's being is that powerful. Other students thrive on the presence of one teacher but dismiss others. Still other students work all year to please the teacher but never seem to be on his or her wavelength.

Likewise, some teachers report that they are immediately "attracted" to and favor certain students while completely missing the magic trigger to another's mind. Some teachers believe that they treat the individual needs of all their students, but are shocked when a parent confides that the child is "scared to death" of the teacher. At times, the power of the individual presence is wielded simply by tone of voice or manner of dress.

If the individual's being influences the class, certainly the atmosphere, ambience, and social tone of the class style must also be considered. Everyone has heard the phrase, "this is a great group," or "this year's class is very immature." The class style, as a whole, influences the course of the year.

2. Curricular style is a determiner of teacher effectiveness as well as of student success. Marshall McLuhan captured the potency of curricular style when he stated that "the medium is the message." Indeed, the medium— workbooks, movies, texts, experiments—can help or hinder students' learning. The curricular choices made by teachers, accepted by them, or imposed on them, can be crucial elements in school success. The strong CR-oriented teacher, for example, would have greater enthusiasm and ability to direct a science curriculum that emphasized a problem-solving, experimental approach to science than one that was controlled by pre/post assessment tests. A student with a creative writing ability would find little expression in a sequential, skills-building curriculum that was not creatively supplemented by a sensitive teacher.

By contrast, an AS teacher may use a film to supplement a history assignment. But the film may offer little assistance to the Abstract Random student if the teacher's attitude indicates that movies are only for fun, or that movies are not important enough to discuss. One may ask how often teachers evaluate their students' film experiences on tests. Some children garner exceptional learning experiences from media never tapped by textbooks, workbooks, group discussions, or tests. Without doubt, curricular style matters to the mental health of both the teacher and the student.

Every class starts with a given curriculum—formal, or informal, the teacher's, the student's, or the textbook publisher's. Can adjustments be made to accommodate many styles? Yes, there are strategies and techniques that help match student style to curricular style. This is accomplished by directly matching the student's style to the style of the content, or by providing bridging techniques that help the student learn the material or the material's style. These strategies and techniques can be used at any level or in any content area.

Illustrations of a bridging technique, a multiple approach, and a matching strategy are given below. These examples, however, represent only one of many possible choices. For demonstration purposes, strategies for use with the novel *Red Badge of Courage* have been chosen.

The first example illustrates *bridging techniques* to help learners understand material presented in one style only. In this illustration, all students must read the novel—an Abstract Sequential learning style demand. All students must also complete one assignment from among the four learning style category choices. Students may choose which "bridge" they prefer, or the teacher may assist students in choosing the bridge most appropriate for them. Bridging techniques may be used whether or not students have knowledge about their own stylistic preferences.

Bridging Techniques

CS	AR
Teacher provides a series of self-check questions for each chapter.	Teacher asks students to prepare a list of questions dealing with the characters' feelings based on chapters, events, or themes.
AS	**CR**
Teacher asks students to read a critical essay and provides the class with a summary of the critic's position.	After they have read each chapter, teacher asks students to brainstorm a list of optional events which could occur in the next chapter.

A second illustration shows the use of a *multiple approach* to the curriculum. All students complete the activity in each learning style category. Under these conditions, students will be matched to their own style at some point, but stretched to engage the approach and the content of another style at other points. The key factor in the success of this strategy is offering four *different types* of approaches to the content. Teachers should note the ease or difficulty with which students work in the different styles and offer individualized assistance wherever necessary.

Multiple Approach

CS	AR
Students prepare three flow charts: • events • character developments • themes.	In groups of three, students discuss one teacher-prepared question, one group-prepared question.
AS	**CR**
Students write an interpretive essay on one quote from the novel.	Students describe how they would have solved a problem found in the novel, and state why they would have taken that approach.

A third illustration presents a *matching strategy*. In this approach, each student chooses one learning style activity that matches his or her learning style. Students make the selection themselves, or request teacher assistance in finding the activity most appropriate for him or her. In the example, only one activity is offered for each style. In practice, several options should be available in each category. The reader should note that this example of a matching strategy goes beyond the text and content of the novel. Matching strategies may stay within the bounds of the content, as demonstrated in the multiple approach example, or may allow the students to extend the content.

Matching Strategy

CS	AR
Students collect or design a replica of an original artifact of the historical period of the novel by contacting museums, friends, collectors, or historical societies. Demonstrate use and development of the artifact.	Students interview someone who was in a war zone. Find out the meaning of his/her "courage." Write a poem, song, essay, short story, or journalism article about the person. Supplement with slides, photos, collage, if desired.
AS	**CR**
Students read several critical reviews of the novel. Prepare an analysis of the scholars' interpretations.	Students write and enact a simulation which reflects major themes in the novel.

Any product that reflects outstanding ability might be channeled to an appropriate outlet. A perfect replica, for example, might go to a library or museum. A poem could be submitted to a publisher, a paper to a journal, a simulation to a teacher magazine.

3. The third stylistic consideration concerns the environment. Environmental style influences the potential for classroom learning. Environmental style includes the administrator's style which directly and indirectly regulates classroom function. The very random administrator may "drop in" to a class at any time, distressing the very sequential teacher who would like to be perfectly prepared to do his or her best.

Environmental style is influenced by parental style, the formality and sequence of the official curriculum, as well as the physical setting of the school, classroom, and surroundings.

Options for Action

Options are available for assessing and addressing these stylistic differences. First, teachers and students can reflect on the nature and meaning of mind qualities. This is an *attitudinal* option. Teachers and students can understand the strengths and limitations of their own personal style.

Many adults have well-formed learning styles, but others have styles that are still "hiding in the closet." Who is the real person? Some teachers possess a well-defined style that is not appreciated or allowed to be used in the classroom.

This author has identified five levels of development of student style as a result of interviews, observations, checklists, and student essays. These are:

- Overt style—easily and clearly recognized
- Emergent style—not clearly defined
- Experimental style—unsure which style is natural
- Masking style—pretending to be a style
- Hidden style—untapped by environment or personal experience

Both students and teachers must have the option to consider the potential and accuracy of identified style through personal questioning, testing, and modification of instrument results.

A second option for assessing and addressing stylistic differences can be exercised by providing choices within the curriculum. This is a *technical* option. Under these circumstances, the learner may be matched to the curricular demands, or the curriculum and teacher may be matched to the learner's needs. By matching learner, teacher, and curricular style, the learner is usually able to achieve higher test scores, to consider him or herself a successful learner, and to feel validated as a person. The price of always matching learning style, however, may be that the student does not learn how to flex, how to meet another's needs, how to adjust to conditions that cannot be changed, or how to stretch into a difficult area as a potential avenue for growth. For these reasons, students can benefit from some mismatch.

When properly guided and controlled, mismatch can provide appreciation for others, foster growth experiences, untap hidden talents, and teach the art of flexibility. Under less controlled conditions, mismatch can lead to lowered self-concept, poor learning, and a host of physical and mental problems. Within our schools, there is a role for matching and mismatching student learning styles. Neither should be done by chance. Both are necessary; both require serious attention.

A third option for addressing stylistic differences is through synergy—an *interactional* approach. Under this condition, administration, faculty, and students work to assess style, its impact, and its effect. They learn to appreciate each other, but to be themselves. They learn how to respect others, to style flex, and to keep individual integrity.

The implications of an interactional approach are twofold. First, an individual can learn to understand how another thinks, but also to appreciate that he or she may not think the same way. Second, a person can learn to be like another, but must understand that he or she cannot be another. The individual must be true to self.

Schools and teachers can address stylistic differences. They can achieve the goal of meeting individual differences. Accepting the challenge is the first step.

CHAPTER 5

Cognitive Profile: Relationship To Achievement and Development

Charles A. Letteri

The question of how to improve the academic achievement of students has been at the center of most educational research efforts.

In the last 20 years there has been an almost exponential increase in both the type and amount of research directed toward the resolution of this question. These efforts generally have been divided into four areas related to learning: environment, affective domain, behavioral studies, and cognitive factors.

The first three approaches have been tried alone or in some combination with varying degrees of limited success, probably because they only indirectly address the question of learning itself. They attempt to manipulate or direct those external factors that might prove conducive to learning but are not directed at the learning (cognitive) process itself. Only cognition directly addresses the problem of learning and provides a link to remediation and improvement of learning procedures that are significantly related to academic achievement.

The environment, general behavior patterns, and affective elements are important, but researchers must move beyond these elements and address the learner and how he or she learns before they can significantly improve achievement for all children.

Our research efforts during the past several years have been conducted in the area of cognition—in particular, cognitive controls. These efforts have been concerned with three primary questions:

- What cognitive factors can reliably measure and describe the differences in levels of academic achievement between various individuals?
- Is it possible to remediate, through training, certain of these cognitive differences found to be associated with below-grade-level achievement?
- Can these remediated controls be transferred and generalized to certain areas of academic achievement?

The research, to date, has provided satisfying answers to these questions.

Cognitive Controls

Cognitive controls are information-processing habits that function across a variety of content areas (Messick, 1970). They are ways of achieving intellectual goals which are general enough to be characteristic of a large segment of one's individual activity and to distinguish that individual from other individuals in search of the same goals (Bourne, 1971). The various dimensions of cognitive control constitute the unique mode of intellectual operation that an individual employs when attempting to learn; that is, these controls are descriptive of how an individual learns.

The majority of recent research efforts have been concerned with the correlations between one dimension of cognitive control and other variables such as personality traits, subtests, or standardized tests. This unidimensional approach, however, does not furnish the investigator with a complete picture of the cognitive processes being employed in a given intellectual task (Letteri, 1976). Moreover, this prevailing research strategy fails to provide the organizing principle (Santostefano, 1978) necessary to understand the relationships that might exist among various cognitive dimensions. Nor can it provide information relating the combined impact of a configuration of cognitive dimensions (a Cognitive Profile) on various criterion variables. An emphasis on studies employing measures of several controls related to academic variables has provided new resolution to these issues.

Cognitive Profiles

Reviews of the literature and instrumentation led to the selection of seven Cognitive Controls: Reflective/Impulsive; Scanning; Analytic/Global; Breadth of Category; Tolerance for Ambiguity; Leveling/Sharpening; Complexity. The selection was based on validity, reliability, and correlations with various areas of academic achievement. Individually, the measure lacked good generalizability across all areas of academic achievement. Research needed a battery of instruments that would reliably and validly describe and predict levels of achievement across all areas of academics for all children in all grades. The seven bipolar dimensions of the Cognitive Profile provide such a battery.

COGNITIVE PROFILES: ACADEMIC ACHIEVEMENT

Three specific types of Cognitive Profiles were discovered by employing the seven bipolar dimensions in several research projects (n=525, grades K to 16+). When applied to a sample of seventh and eighth grade children, for example, the cognitive profile significantly ($p < .01$ or better) differentiated subjects into superior academic achievers (as much as four grade levels above peers), a Type 1 Cognitive Profile; average academic achievers (within one grade level of peers), a Type 2 Cognitive Profile; and those who fail to meet grade level achievement (as much as five grade levels below peers), a Type 3 Cognitive Profile.

In addition, these profiles can predict academic achievement across all subject areas at a level of $p < .05$ or better and can account for between .62 and .87 of achievement score variance in all areas of standardized testing (Letteri, 1980).

Cross-sectional data (n=250, grades one to eight) reveal that while there is a difference between Type 1 and Type 3 children beginning in the first grade (about one grade level), the magnitude of the difference does not reach serious proportions until the fourth grade when it is approximately two grade levels. This magnitude of difference continues to grow until the eighth grade when the difference between a Type 1 and Type 3 child can be as much as eight and nine grade levels. This finding is true without exception for all Type 1, 2, and 3 children. In sum, all Type 1 children have been superior academic achievers without exception, Type 2 children are on or within one grade level of the grade norm, and Type 3 children fail to achieve grade level norms in all areas of standardized testing (Letteri, 1981).

Since the profile allows accurate descriptions and predications of cognitive processes in relation to academic achievement, we decided to attempt remediation of Type 2 and Type 3 children to determine the effect on their levels of academic achievement.

COGNITIVE PROFILE: REMEDIATION

Following and modeling after examples in the literature (Debus, 1970; Kagan, Pearson, and Welch, 1966; Siegelman, 1969), materials and strategies were developed for each of the seven dimensions of the Cognitive Profile. The purpose of these strategies was to train the individual in those areas of the Cognitive Profile shown to be deficient and to assist the individual to transfer these new strategies to all areas of academic achievement. In a controlled study (n=30) the experimental group (n=10) met with a trained remediator for one-hour sessions twice a week for 15 weeks. These training and transfer sessions were carried out in the child's school. The control group (n=20) identified as having the same cognitive profiles followed their normal daily routine. The experimental group was assisted in transferring their new strategies to the area of math. All children were retested at the end of the 15 weeks in the seven dimensions of the profile.

As expected, the experimental group showed significant gains and all displayed Type 1 profiles. The control group showed no change in Cognitive Profile types. Following a six month hiatus, all children in the study were administered standardized tests by the local schools (MAT). The experimental group showed an average gain in math of 3.65 grade levels while the control group had an average gain of only .75 grade levels. The study, although small, indicated that profiles could be changed, that transfer to academic areas could be achieved, and that the training and transfer strategies would be maintained for at least a six month period. Since that time, 15 case studies have been completed with the intent of improving the materials and strategies for both the training and the transfer procedures.

In a current study of six case studies ranging from third grade to seventh grade, following 10 weeks (20 hours) of training, an average improvement of two grade point levels has been demonstrated. Grade point averages have been determined by assigning the following grade weights: F-0; D-1; C-2; B-3; A-4. Measurement was by teacher-made tests.

COGNITIVE PROFILE: A LEARNED PROCESS

In a related study (Kuntz and Letteri, 1981), a significant correlation ($p <$ .05) was established between a mother's Cognitive Profile scores and those of her children under six years of age. No significant relationship was found between a mother's Cognitive Profile and children older than eight years. These results not only lend further support to the literature on early maternal influences on the child, but offer insight as to what the influences might be. Mothers may be transferring to a pre-school child the benefits and limitations of their own cognitive resources.

A further question posed by this research concerns verbal and non-verbal communications between mother and child. Using Chomsky's model of language acquisition, is it possible that the deep structure of language carries more than meanings of surface structure? Is it possible that this deep structure also carries messages on how to process data? On how to scan, focus, and compare data? The answer could have direct implications for child care in the home and in day care centers.

Conclusion

The Cognitive Profile of an individual resonates the central core of his learning capabilities. The profile determines how a child learns, has impact on what he learns, and ultimately, how he responds and adapts to all environmental influences.

If we are to address the question of optimal development for all children, perhaps we should start by assuring that all have appropriate Cognitive Profiles to give direction and force to their own development while providing the basis for skillful adaptation to, or modification of, their environments.

References

Bourne, L. E.; Ekstrand, B. R.; and Dominowski, R. L. *The Psychology of Thinking.* Englewood, N.J.: Prentice-Hall, 1971.

Debus, R. L. "Effects of Brief Observations of Model Behavior on Conceptual Tempo of Impulsive Children." *Developmental Psychology,* 1970, pp. 22–32.

Kagan, J.; Pearson, L.; and Welch, L. "The Modifiability of an Impulsive Tempo." *Journal of Educational Psychology* 57(1966): 359–65.

Kuntz, S., and Letteri, C. A. "Cognitive Profile of Mothers: Causal Factors in Determining Child's Profile." *Contemporary Education,* October 1981.

Letteri, C. A. "Cognitive Style; Implications for Curriculum." In *Curriculum Theory,* edited by A. Molnar and John Zahorik. Washington, D.C.: Association for Supervision and Curriculum Development, 1976.

————. "Cognitive Profile: Basic Determinant of Academic Achievement." *Journal of Educational Research,* March/April 1980, pp. 195–99.

————. "Cognitive Profile: Cross-Sectional Analysis." Technical Report #201, University of Vermont, Spring 1981.

Messick, Samuel. "The Criterion Problem in the Evaluation of Instruction: Assessing Possible, Not Just Intended Outcomes." In *The Evaluation of Instruction: Issues and Problems,* edited by M. Wittrock and E. E. Wiley. New York: Holt, Rinehart and Winston, 1970.

Santostefano, S. A. *A Bio-developmental Approach to Clinical Child Psychology: Cognitive Control, Cognitive Therapy.* Personality Series. New York: John Wiley & Sons, 1978.

Siegelman, E. "Reflective and Impulsive Observing Behavior." *Child Development* (40)1969: 1213–222.

Inventory of Learning Processes

Ronald R. Schmeck

From my theoretical perspective (Schmeck, in press), learning and memory are simply by-products of thinking: traces left behind by past information processing (Craik and Lockhart, 1972; Lockhart and Craik, 1978). Within this framework, a *learning strategy* is that pattern of information-processing activities that a person engages in when confronted by a learning task. If a person demonstrates a predisposition to favor a particular strategy, then he or she is manifesting a *learning style*. Thus, a style is simply a strategy that one uses with some cross-situational consistency.

I have spent six years developing a learning style measure consistent with these definitions. In developing my assessment instrument, I placed an emphasis on the information processes revealed by modern cognitive science. I have not included measures of attitudes, personality, preferences for time of day, physical environment, social climate, or cognitive style measures.

Since Messick (1976) defined cognitive styles as habitual modes of processing information, one could argue that a learning style is simply the cognitive style that one manifests when confronted by a learning task. According to Lewis (1976), I should be studying cognitive style rather than learning style since it is more "basic" than learning style. However, my experience with applying pre-existing cognitive style or personality measures in the educational context has been disappointing. Thus, I chose to develop my own measuring instrument directly within the educational context. I have labeled the instrument the *Inventory of Learning Processes*.

My colleagues and I (Schmeck, Ribich, and Ramanaiah, 1977) derived the inventory by factor analyzing the responses of 503 students to 121 self-report, inventory items. The items were developed by experts from various specializations within the general domain of human learning and memory with the objective of representing the research findings and processes of their specific areas of expertise. The processes were converted to behavioral descriptions phrased in terms of the environment and activities of a typical college student. The pool of items was administered to students at a large midwestern university and statistical procedures (factor analyses) were employed to develop scales for the inventory. Only factors containing five or more items were retained. The final Inventory of Learning Processes contained 62 of the original 121 items grouped into four scales which assess dimensions of learning behavior and conceptual activity characteristic of college students.

The first scale was called *Deep Processing*. It contains 18 items that assess the extent to which a student will critically evaluate, conceptually organize, and compare and contrast the information being studied.

The second scale revealed by the factor analysis contained 14 items which assessed the extent to which students will translate new information into their own terminology, apply it to their own lives, generate concrete examples from their own experience, and use visual imagery for the purpose of encoding new information. We call this scale *Elaborative Processing*. Elaborative Processing refers to the more concrete associations or examples that a person can generate from his or her own experience regardless of the level of Deep Processing employed. Elaborative Processing is an exercise in applying information to one's own life or personalizing it, while Deep Processing is a more "academic" exercise in verbal classification and categorical comparison.

Fact Retention is the third scale revealed by the factor analysis. The scale contains only seven items but it is a very useful predictor of academic performance. People who score high on the scale carefully process (and thus store) details and specific pieces of information regardless of what other processing strategies they might choose to employ.

The fourth scale is called *Methodical Study*. Those who earn high scores on the scale claim to study more often and more carefully than other students do and claim to employ methods similar to the systematic techniques recommended by the classic "How To Study" manuals (e.g., type your notes, outline the text, study every day, never cram for exams, etc.).

Schmeck, Ribich, and Ramanaiah (1977) report that the four scales of the Inventory of Learning Processes have acceptable reliabilities ranging from .79 to .88. They also report correlations among the scales ranging from .13 to .45. These intercorrelations were expected since the strategies being assessed are not necessarily independent of one another. I should point out, however, that subsequent research findings have revealed that the scales do have differential validity with regard to predicting academic performance. I would like to summarize some of these findings.

Predicting Academic Performance

My colleagues and I spent six years studying the learning styles (and strategies) revealed by the original factor analysis. Most of our research concerns the styles of college students, but the inventory also has been used with high school populations.* Perhaps the most definitive study for our present purposes is one conducted by Schmeck and Grove (1979) comparing the learning styles of 790 high and low college achievers. We used college grade point averages and scores on the American College Testing (ACT) entrance examination as our measures of academic achievement, and the Inventory of Learning Processes as our measure of learning style.

---

*Personal communications: E. McDaniel and J. Weinbaum, 1982.

We found that the most successful college students were significantly higher on Deep Processing, Elaborative Processing, and Fact Retention, and were slightly *lower* on Methodical Study. With this general profile in mind, I will describe the four constructs of the inventory by reviewing some of the other validity studies that have been conducted.

Deep Processing

First consider the *Deep Processing* scale. The student who earns a high score on this scale is very conceptual, spending time categorizing, critically evaluating the appropriateness of the categorizations, and comparing and contrasting categories. The strategy of Deep Processing seems to be the most powerful one revealed by the development of the inventory in that it is the scale that most frequently relates to performance in both classroom and laboratory.

It is interesting to construct a personality sketch for the Deep Processor. People who earn high scores on the Deep Processing scale are calm, confident, responsible, flexible, and have considerable self-insight with regard to their cognitive functioning.

- *Calmness* is suggested by the finding that the Deep Processing scale related negatively to neuroticism (Schmeck and Spofford, in press), manifest anxiety (Schmeck and Ribich, 1978), test anxiety (Schmeck and Ribich, 1978), and writing anxiety (Schmeck, McCarthy, and Meier, 1982).
- *Confidence* and *responsibility* are indicated by the positive relationships between Deep Processing and both self-efficacy, i.e., confidence and internality, i.e., personal responsibility on the locus of control dimension of personality (Schmeck, McCarthy, and Meier, 1982).
- *Flexibility* is indicated by the fact that Deep Processing relates positively to both independent and conforming achievement striving behaviors (Schmeck and Ribich, 1978), and to androgyny, i.e., absence of rigid sex roles (Tracy, Schmeck, and Spofford, 1980).
- *Self-insight* is indicated by the finding (Schmeck, McCarthy, and Meier, 1982) that subjects high on the Deep Processing scale are more accurate in estimating their ability to perform the various cognitive activities necessary to produce good written compositions.

What are the cognitive processes demonstrated by those who score high on the Deep Processing scale? Schmeck and Ribich (1978) found that those who earn high scores on the scale are considerably higher on critical thinking ability as indicated by scores on the Watson-Glaser Critical Thinking Appraisal.

In another study, Schmeck, Ribich, and Ramanaiah (1977) asked subjects to watch a videotaped introductory psychology lecture while supposedly trying to "judge its complexity." Afterward, subjects took an unannounced 30-item multiple-choice test composed of 15 test items demanding high level cognitive skill and 15 items requiring low level cognitive skill (Bloom, 1956). Subjects were not warned of the test because of our desire to determine whether style would have an effect even when situational demands were at a minimum.

Test results showed that performance on the test questions was related to the student's score on the Deep Processing scale, with Deep Processors scoring higher overall and earning especially high scores on higher level test questions which demanded greater thinking ability.

In other studies, subjects who earned high scores on the Deep Processing scale remembered more words when given cues that were semantic in nature (e.g., synonyms), while those who earned low scores remembered more words when given superficial, shallow cues (rhymes). Overall, it appears that those who score high on Deep Processing attend more to meanings and less to shallow, superficial aspects of the material being studied (Schmeck, in press). Ribich (1977) found that those who earned high scores on the Deep Processing scale were better at structuring information than those who were low on Deep Processing, and this success was independent of their intelligence as measured by the Otis-Lennon Mental Ability Test. Schmeck (1980) found that the inventory was clearly a better predictor of reading comprehension than was the Survey of Study Habits and Attitudes, and the Deep Processing Scale was clearly responsible for most of the predictive power of the inventory.

Biggs' (1979) SOLO scoring system is designed to evaluate the level of processing evidenced within a learning *outcome* (in the present context, the *answer* to an essay question). Schmeck and Phillips (in press) found that the Deep Processing scale was positively related to Biggs' measure of level of processing (Biggs, 1979) and both measures were positively related to scores on the Iowa Silent Reading Test. It is my view that the conceptual analyses that are routinely carried out by those who score high on the Deep Processing scale are responsible for their greater reading comprehension skills. I suspect that they attend more to ideas and the interrelationships among ideas and less to the precise wording of passages while they are reading.

Elaborative Processing

The second scale revealed by the factor analytic development of the Inventory of Learning Processes was labeled *Elaborative Processing*. Elaborative Processing is another way in which the student can form more intricate and enduring memory traces. When students process elaboratively they think of concrete associations or examples from their own experience and apply the information to their own lives, thereby personalizing it. Schmeck and Ribich (1978) found that students who score high on Elaborative Processing have greater mental imagery ability than those who score low. In addition, Ribich and Schmeck (1979) found that such students tend to reorganize information in very personal ways, using their own unique organizational systems. Schmeck, Ribich, and Ramanaiah (1977) found that individuals who score high on Elaborative Processing were significantly better at learning long lists of concrete words for a free-recall memory test.

Meier (1981) found that creative writing performance was significantly related to scores on the Elaborative Processing scale, but it was not related to scores on the Deep Processing scale. This suggests that the ability to personalize, concretize, and visualize information is more important in writing than is the more "academic" skill of abstracting, comparing, and contrasting abstractions. Similarly, McDaniel (1982) administered the Inventory of Learning Processes to 44 sophomore high school students enrolled in a special advanced placement English course. He reported that the Elaborative Processing scale was significantly related to teacher's ratings of students' verbal expression and ability to relate ideas from literature to real life.

Taken together, the Deep Processing and Elaborative Processing scales seem to assess a dimension of "thoughtfulness." There is a positive relationship between the *amount* of thought given to an idea and the *probability* that the idea will be recalled later. Also, there seems to be a relationship between the *type* of thought and the *quality* of recall. All thoughts are not created equal. Those that lead to categorization and comparison of chosen categories with other potential categories (Deep Processing) are more likely to improve recall. Likewise, those that translate ideas into personal terminology and operations and define it with personal experiences (Elaborative Processing) also contribute more to recall.

Fact Retention

The third inventory scale is one of *Fact Retention*. Schmeck and Ribich (1978) found that scores on the Fact Retention scale were related positively to achievement via conformity, suggesting that students with high scores on the scale follow instructions carefully. Also, Schmeck, Ribich, and Ramanaiah (1977) found that people who earn high scores on the scale tend to categorize information into narrow, precise categories and perform well on tests requiring memory for details and specific facts.

People who prefer to process details rather than broad ideas earn *high* scores on Fact Retention and *low* scores on Deep Processing. Those who prefer broad ideas to specific facts and details earn high scores on Deep Processing and low scores on Fact Retention. Either type of student is likely to perform well in the academic setting, since most academic exams require both conceptual understanding and retention of details. However, if the student is repeatedly faced with exams that test only for verbatim recall of details, he or she will probably develop the tendency to engage more in fact retention and less in deep processing. Also, it should be noted that the Deep Processing and Fact Retention scales are positively correlated, suggesting that the best fact retainers are also processing deeply. Some theorists (e.g., Morris, Bransford, and Franks, 1977) have argued that shallow processing is best when preparing for a low-level, fact retention type of test, but Schmeck and Spofford (1982) found that memory performance was superior following deep processing regardless of whether the subjects were given shallow or deep retrieval cues during the test. This suggested that even shallow (verbatim) tests are handled more easily by individuals who process deeply.

Methodical Study

Finally, there is the *Methodical Study* scale of the Inventory of Learning Processes. Schmeck and Ribich (1978) reported that scores on this scale were positively related to academic curiosity and to achievement via conformity, suggesting that students who score high on the scale are eager to succeed in academic work and follow instructions carefully. However, other studies have found that Methodical Study relates *negatively* to critical thinking ability (Schmeck and Ribich, 1978), verbal ability (Mueller and Fisher, 1980), and college entrance exam scores (Schmeck and Grove, 1979). The reason might be that some of the students who score high on Methodical Study are highly motivated but lack the ability necessary for Deep Processing. Their major strategy may be doing what they are told to do and rehearsing (i.e., repeating) information as often as they possibly can before the exam.

Needed Research

Future research should determine the extent to which learning style interacts with ability and developmental level. Students with less ability might be incapable of using certain learning strategies. This might also be true of individuals during the earlier stages of cognitive development. The relationships generally obtained between intelligence test scores and school achievement might precisely be due to intelligence placing limits on information processing activities; i.e., by limiting *thinking,* intelligence limits learning.

It is also likely that future research will reveal relationships between learning style and the stages of cognitive development described by both Jean Piaget (1963) and William Perry (1970). It is unlikely, for example, that one could process deeply before attaining the stage of formal operations described by Piaget and the relativistic and commitment phases described by Perry. Furthermore, there is evidence (Vu, 1977) that individuals may function at higher developmental levels in one academic content domain and at lower cognitive levels in other content domains. A student may engage in Deep Processing in social sciences while using Fact Retention and Methodical Study in the physical sciences (the reverse is equally possible). Similarly, aging might lead to changes in learning style. Labouvie-Vief (1977, in press) describes the elderly as deep processors who think in terms of global ideas and rules-of-thumb while retaining few details and specifics. Beyond the age of 50, I would expect scores on Deep Processing to increase and scores on Fact Retention to decrease.

Since I assume that a learning style is simply cross-situational consistency in the use of a particular learning strategy, and since research has shown that learning strategies are teachable, I also assume that learning styles can be modified. As I noted above, ability and developmental level place limits on learning styles, but I believe that many students can still significantly improve their academic performance by learning new strategies. I especially feel that students should learn to process information deeply and elaboratively, but an excessively persistent deep processor (a "globetrotter" according to Pask, 1976a, 1976b) might profit from some training in fact retention.

Dansereau and his colleagues (1979) and Holley et al. (1979) have shown that comprehension and retention of main ideas can be improved by teaching students a "networking strategy" that has students diagram text with node-link maps that illustrate the interrelationships among concepts. Such a networking strategy forces students to process information deeply. Similarly, Weinstein and her colleagues (Weinstein, 1975; Weinstein et al., 1979) have improved students' learning by teaching them to use elaboration strategies similar to those presumed to be assessed by the Elaborative Processing scale.

Reid (1981) used the items of the Deep Processing and Elaborative Processing scales of the Inventory of Learning Processes to derive exercises designed to teach students to process deeply and elaboratively. Pask (1976a, 1976b) has designed "learning to learn seminars" that teach students to develop what he calls a "versatile" style of learning. Versatile students employ analogies and general principles to structure information but also attend to the operational details that support the general argument.

I believe we need more research that would provide an opportunity to observe interactions between instructional treatments and learning styles. We need to determine which instructional treatments counteract the negative influences of certain styles and take advantage of the strengths of other styles. If, for example, classroom activities and homework exercises require deep and elaborative processing, they will counteract the bad effects of shallow-reiterative memorization and may, in the long run, actually *change* the student's style from shallow-reiterative to deep-elaborative.

References

Biggs, J. "Individual Differences in Study Processes and the Quality of Learning Outcomes." *Higher Education* 8(1979): 381–94.

Bloom, B. S. *Taxonomy of Educational Objectives: Cognitive Domain.* New York: David McKay Co., 1956.

Craik, F. I. M., and Lockhart, R. S. "Levels of Processing: A Framework for Memory Research." *Journal of Verbal Learning and Verbal Behavior* 11(1972): 671–84.

Dansereau, D. F.; Collins, K. W.; McDonald, B. A.; Holley, C. D.; Garland, J.; Diekhoff, G.; and Evans, S. H. "Development and Evaluation of a Learning Strategy Training Program." *Journal of Educational Psychology* 71(1979): 64–73.

Holley, C. D.; Dansereau, D. F.; McDonald, B. A.; Garland, J. C.; and Collins, K. W. "Evaluations of a Hierarchical Mapping Technique as an Aid to Prose Processing." *Contemporary Educational Psychology* 4(1979): 227–37.

Labouvie-Vief, G. "Adult Cognitive Development: In Search of Alternative Interpretations." *Merrill-Palmer Quarterly* 23(1977): 227–63.

———. "Individual Time, Social Time, and Intellectual Aging." In *Life Course Transition in Interdisciplinary and Cross-Cultural Perspectives,* edited by T. K. Hareven. New York: Guilford Press, in press.

Lewis, B. N. "Avoidance of Aptitude-Treatment Trivialities." In *Individuality in Learning,* edited by S. Messick. San Francisco: Jossey-Bass, 1976.

Lockhart, R. S., and Craik, F.I.M. "Levels of Processing: A Reply to Eysenck." *British Journal of Psychology* 69(1978): 171–75.

Meier, S. "Self-Efficacy Theory and Students' Writing Performance." Master's thesis, Southern Illinois University at Carbondale, 1981.

Messick, Samuel, ed. *Individuality in Learning.* San Francisco: Jossey-Bass, 1976.

Morris, C. D.; Bransford, J. D.; and Franks, J. J. "Levels of Processing Versus Transfer Appropriate Processing." *Journal of Verbal Learning and Verbal Behavior* 16(1977): 519–33.

Mueller, J. H., and Fisher, D. M. "Field Independence and Input Grouping in Free Recall." Unpublished manuscript, University of Missouri, 1980.

Pask, G. "Conversational Techniques in the Study and Practice of Education." *British Journal of Educational Psychology* 45(1976): 12–25. (A)

————. "Styles and Strategies of Learning." *British Journal of Educational Psychology* 46(1976): 128–48. (B)

Perry, W. G. *Forms of Intellectual and Ethical Development in the College Years: A Scheme.* New York: Holt, Rinehart & Winston, 1970.

Piaget, J. *The Origins of Intelligence in Children.* New York: Norton, 1963.

Reid, E. "Training Higher-Level Cognitive Skills." Doctoral dissertation, Southern Illinois University, 1981.

Ribich, F. D. "Memory for a Lecture: Effects of an Advance Organizer and Levels of Processing on Semantic and Episodic Memory." Doctoral dissertation, Southern Illinois University, 1977.

Ribich, F. D., and Schmeck, R. R. "Multivariate Relationships Between Measures of Learning Style and Memory." *Journal of Research in Personality* 13(1979): 515–29.

Schmeck, R. R. "Learning Styles of College Students." In *Individual Differences in Cognition,* edited by R. Schmeck and R. Dillon. New York: Academic Press, in press.

————. "Relationships Between Measures of Learning Style and Reading Comprehension." *Perceptual and Motor Skills* 50(1980): 461–62.

————. "Improving Learning by Improving Thinking." *Educational Leadership,* February 1981, pp. 384–85.

Schmeck, R. R., and Grove, E. "Academic Achievement and Individual Differences in Learning Processes." *Applied Psychological Measurement* 3(1979): 43–49.

Schmeck, R. R. and Lockhart, D. "Relationships Between Learning Styles and Three Measures of Achievement in a Research Methods Course." Unpublished manuscript, Southern Illinois University, 1982.

Schmeck, R. R., and Phillips, J. "Levels of Processing as a Dimension of Difference Between Individuals." *Human Learning* 1(1982): 95–103.

Schmeck, R. R., and Ribich, F. D. "Construct Validation of the Inventory of Learning Processes." *Applied Psychological Measurement* 2(1978): 551–62.

Schmeck, R. R., and Spofford, M. "Levels of Processing and Encoding Specificity: Does Processing Depth Make a Significant Independent Contribution to Recall Performance?" Paper presented at the Midwestern Psychological Association, Minneapolis, Minn., 1982.

————. "Attention to Semantic Versus Phonetic Verbal Attributes as a Function of Individual Differences in Arousal and Learning Strategy." *Contemporary Educational Psychology,* in press.

Schmeck, R. R.; McCarthy, P.; and Meier, S. "Self-Efficacy, Depth of Processing, Anxiety, and Locus of Control." Unpublished manuscript, Southern Illinois University, 1982.

Schmeck, R. R.; Ribich, F. D.; and Ramanaiah, N. "Development of a Self-Report Inventory for Assessing Individual Differences in Learning Processes." *Applied Psychological Measurement* 1(1977): 413–31.

Tracy, K.; Schmeck, R. R.; and Spofford, M. "Determiners of Vocational Interest: Sex, Spatial-Verbal Abilities, and Information Processing Style." Paper presented at the Midwestern Psychological Association Convention, St. Louis, 1980.

Vu, V. N. "Piaget's Formal Operations and the Acquisition of the Probability and Correlation Concepts of Graduate Students." Doctoral dissertation, Southern Illinois University, 1977.

Weinstein, C. E. "Learning of Elaboration Strategies." Doctoral dissertation, University of Texas at Austin, 1975.

Weinstein, C. E.; Underwood, V. L.; Wicker, F. W.; and Cubberly, W. E. "Cognitive Learning Strategies: Verbal and Imaginal Elaboration." In *Cognitive and Affective Learning Strategies,* edited by H. F. O'Neil and C. D. Speilberger. New York: Academic Press, 1979.

CHAPTER 7

The Grasha-Riechmann Student Learning Style Scales

Sheryl (Riechmann) Hruska
Anthony F. Grasha

The Grasha-Riechmann Student Learning Style Scales (GRSLSS) is one of the few instruments designed specifically to look at student differences in senior high school and college/university classrooms. The scales focus on how students interact with the teacher, other students, and learning. Because of this focus, the scales fall into the general learning style category of social-interaction models (Riechmann, 1980; Grasha, 1981), as opposed to other categories of learner differences such as cognitive styles or developmental-stage models.

Six styles are measured by the GRSLSS: Independent, Dependent, Participant, Avoidant, Collaborative, and Competitive. Each is described in Table 1, along with the classroom activities that students who are strong on each style tend to prefer.

Originally the six dimensions were thought to be three bipolar pairs or three sets of opposites. Research (Riechmann, 1972, 74; Andrews, 1981) has shown, however, that the Participant and Avoidant most consistently have this negative relationship (i.e., students who score highly on one scale are likely to score at the low end of the other scale). Results are mixed about the presence of a negative relationship between the Independent and Dependent scales. The Competitive and Collaborative scales appear to be independent.

Students prefer all six of the styles to some degree; no student prefers or adopts any one of the styles exclusively. Instead, they have learning style profiles which show varying strengths of preference for each of the six styles.

While learners generally prefer certain styles, this preference can and often does change depending on how the teacher structures the class. In other words, a student's style profile may change in response to the demands of a particular teacher's methods and assignments (Grasha, 1972).

Two versions of the GRSLSS are available. One of these—the *General Class Form*—asks students to rate statements based on all their classes. The other version—the *Specific Class Form*—asks students to indicate their style preferences relative to a particular course. These two versions of the instrument are used in somewhat different ways.

The General Class Form has been used by instructors at the beginning of a course to assess the learning styles of their students. This information helps instructors design instructional procedures to meet the style preferences of students. With these data, faculty can also be more sensitive to possible student discomfort with less familiar classroom roles (e.g., moving to a more independent learning situation, participating in experiential activities rather than lectures).

The Specific Class Form has been used as an outcome measure. Instructors trying innovative procedures or purposely trying to encourage one of the styles have used this version as a check on student style shifts in response to their efforts.

Both forms of the GRSLSS contain 90 items, with 15 items related to each of the six scales. Students are asked to judge themselves on a five-point scale in terms of how much they agree or disagree with each statement. A sample of items from each of the scales from the general version is given in Table 2.

Development of the instruments was based on the six styles identified by Grasha (1972). A "rational approach" was used to develop the items (Riechmann and Grasha, 1974). One set of students generated possible items on the basis of the style descriptions. Another set of students sorted a refined pool of these items into the category for which they thought the item was most appropriate. Items sorted into a given category with at least 70 percent consistency were used in the original version of the instrument. This initial form was shortened into the present form using inter-item correlations and reliability data. Factor analysis data have since confirmed the quality of the scales (Andrews, 1981).

Reliability data on the instrument have been collected. Test-retest reliability coefficients, with a seven day interval between testings, range from .76 for the dependent scale to .83 for the independent scale (N = 269).

Research Findings from Applications of the GRSLSS

Discipline differences. The General Class Form of the instrument was used to assess the presence of particular learning styles across disciplines (Grasha, 1976). The profiles of students in areas including psychology, education, physics, mathematics, chemistry, history, English, engineering, philosophy, and political science are not significantly different.

Graduate and undergraduate styles. At the University of Cincinnati, norms for differences between graduate and undergraduate courses are quite similar (Grasha, 1979). This finding has additional support in research by Mary Anne Dillon (1980) at Texas Woman's University. These data, taken in conjunction with the lack of strong discipline differences, suggest that the classroom styles students are encouraged to adopt are quite similar in most college learning situations.

Two and four-year institutions. Grasha (1979) also found notable differences between two and four-year college students. Two-year college students tend to adopt more dependent, more competitive, and more participant students roles than do students in four-year institutions.

Sex differences. Studies conducted with students of mixed majors have shown little or no sex differences in styles (Riechmann, 1972, 1974). Kraft (1976), however, finds that among physical education majors, males adopt competitive, avoidant, and independent roles to a higher degree than females. Women are much more participatory and slightly more dependent in their styles. This latter finding is similar to slightly higher dependent and participatory scores found in a sample of small-college nursing students (Swartz, 1976).

Age. In the GRSLSS norm study by Grasha (1979), students over 25 years of age were much more independent and participatory in their learning styles. Those under 25 showed higher levels of avoidance and competitiveness and lower levels of participation in the classroom. Similar findings among two-year college students have been reported by Eison and Moore (1979).

Relationship to grades. For the most part, scores on the GRSLSS are not related significantly to grades, excepting a weak but significant negative relationship between the Avoidant scale and grade point average, and a similar but positive correlation between the Participant scale and grades (Riechmann, 1972, 1974; Andrews, 1981). Review of the definitions of these two scales makes this finding easy to understand.

Teaching method and student style interactions. A variety of studies support the idea that student profiles formulated at the end of courses using interactive formats are quite different than student profiles from classes using a lecture format. Grasha (1972) found that interactive classroom procedures tend to encourage Collaborative, Participant, and Independent styles, while the latter foster Competitive, Dependent, and Avoidant styles. It appears that for these shifts in style to occur, teachers must make extensive use of a particular procedure. Occasional use does not seem to alter the styles students report using.

In addition to the shift in styles often associated with regular exposure to particular methods in a given class, a study by Andrews (1981) suggests that students may actually benefit more from classroom methods that closely fit their styles. Andrews found, for example, that students high on the Collaborative scale reported a strong benefit from participating in a peer-centered chemistry discussion section. In contrast, students with a strong preference for the Competitive style reported benefits from instructor-centered classes and not from participation in a peer-centered section.

More generally, students with strong Dependent and Participant styles reported being helped by both types of sections, while Independent and Avoidant students reported being helped by neither. Andrews found style differences about which aspects of the sections were particularly helpful. Students with "impersonal" styles (Independent, Avoidant, Competitive) found the text, handouts, and lectures to be most helpful. Those with strong "personal" styles (Collaborative, Participant, Dependent) found review sessions, study questions, and learning from other students most beneficial.

Findings from this study suggest that students with different learning styles find different methods and different aspects of courses helpful in their learning.

Uses of the GRSLSS

GRSLSS utilization has had positive outcomes for faculty and students. Information from the GRSLSS can be helpful for designing courses, developing sensitivity to learner needs, and facilitating students' learning.

Data from the instrument increase awareness of student differences in learning arising from various course components, and in preferences for particular teaching methods. With this awareness, faculty members are better able to respond to these differences, to appreciate the changes in style that go with changes in methods, and to make finer distinctions about which classroom activities or components are most useful to which students. In remaining with one method or adopting new methods, faculty members are often not aware of the consequences of these decisions for overall student learning and satisfaction. The GRSLSS underscores the importance of these decisions.

Students benefit from knowledge of their learning styles. Awareness of one's style helps explain why some courses are more comfortable or easier than others. Generally, the GRSLSS provides a framework against which students can assess the breadth of their readiness and ability to respond, with confidence and effectiveness, to a variety of learning formats.

If we are to help students be confident and effective learners, attention to learner differences and their interaction with classroom preferences, evaluations, and learning need to be taken into account. Because of its direct focus on classroom behaviors and preferences, the GRSLSS is a particularly straightforward instrument to use for these purposes. It has been used effectively by high school and higher education instructors to explore their teaching and to develop teaching approaches which increase student satisfaction and learning.

The complete instrument appears in the *Handbook of Faculty Development* (Bergquist and Philips, 1975), or is available from the authors.

Table 1
Student Learning Styles as Identified by Anthony Grasha and Sheryl Riechmann

Student Learning Style	Classroom Activity Preferences Based on Research Data
Competitive. This response style is exhibited by students who learn material in order to perform better than others in the class. They feel they must compete with other students in the class for the rewards of the classroom, such as grades or teachers' attention. They	*Competitive.* To be a group leader in discussion or when working on projects . . . To ask questions in class . . . To be singled out for doing a particularly good job on a class-related activity. No real preference for any one classroom method over another (e.g.,

view the classroom as a win-lose situation, in which they must always win.

lectures, seminars, etc.) as long as the method has more of a teacher-centered focus than a student-centered focus.

Collaborative. This style is typical of students who feel they can learn the most by sharing ideas and talents. They cooperate with teachers and peers and like to work with others. They see the classroom as a place for social interaction as well as content learning.

Collaborative. Lectures with class discussion in small groups . . . Small seminars . . . Student-designed and taught courses and classes . . . Group rather than individual projects . . . Peer determined grades . . . Talking about course issues outside of class with other students . . . Instructor group interaction.

Avoidance. This response style is typical of students who are not interested in learning course content in the traditional classroom. They do not participate with students and teachers in the classroom. They are uninterested or overwhelmed by what goes on in classes.

Avoidance. Generally turned off by classroom activities . . . Preferences include no tests . . . Self-evaluation for grading . . . No required readings or assignments . . . Blanket grades where everyone gets a passing grade . . . Does not like enthusiastic teachers . . . Does not prefer well-organized lectures . . . Does not like instructor individual interactions.

Participant. This style is characteristic of students who want to learn course content and like to go to class. They take responsibility for getting the most out of class and participate with others when told to do so. They feel that they should take part in as much of the class-related activity as possible and little that is not part of the course outline.

Participant. Lectures with discussion . . . Opportunities to discuss material . . . Likes both objective and essay type tests . . . Class reading assignments . . . Likes enthusiastic presentations of material . . . Prefers teachers who can analyze and synthesize material well.

Dependent. This style is characteristic of students who show little intellectual curiosity and who learn only what is required. They see teacher and peers as sources of structure and support. They look to authority figures for guidelines and want to be told what to do.

Dependent. Teacher outlines or notes on the board . . . Clear deadlines for assignments . . . Teacher-centered classroom methods.

Independent. This response style is characteristic of students who like to think for themselves. They prefer to work on their own, but will listen to the ideas of others in the classroom. They learn the content they feel is important and are confident in their learning abilities.

Independent. Independent study . . . Self-paced instruction . . . Problems that give the student an opportunity to think for himself . . . Projects that the student can design . . . Prefers a student-centered classroom setting over a teacher-centered one.

Table 2
A Sample of Items from the Grasha-Riechmann Student Learning Style Scales

General Version

Competitive
- To get ahead in class, I think sometimes you have to step on the toes of the other students.
- I feel that I must compete with the other students to get a grade.

Collaborative
- I think an important part of classes is to learn to get along with other people.
- I find the ideas of other students relatively useful for helping me to understand the course material.

Dependent
- I accept the structure a teacher sets for a course.
- Before working on a class project, I try to get the approval of the instructor.

Independent
- I study what is important to me and not necessarily what the instructor says is important.
- I work on class-related projects (e.g., studying for exams, preparing term papers) by myself.

Participant
- I am eager to learn about areas covered in class.
- I do my assignments whether I think they are interesting or not.

Avoidant
- I seldom get excited about material covered in a course.
- I try to spend as little time as possible on a course outside of class.

References

Andrews, J. "Teaching Format and Student Style: Their Interactive Effects on Learning." *Research in Higher Education* 14 (1981): 161–78.

Dillon, Mary Ann. "An Investigation of Learning Styles of Occupational Therapy Students." Master's thesis, Texas Woman's University, 1980.

Eison, J., and Moore, J. "Learning Styles and Attitudes of Traditional Age and Adult Students." Paper presented at Professional and Organizational Development Network, Berkeley, Calif., Conference, October 1979.

Grasha, A. F. "Observations on Relating Teaching Goals to Student Response Styles and Classroom Methods." *American Psychologist* 27(1972): 144–47.

———. Unpublished narrative data on the Grasha-Reichmann Student Learning Style Scales, 1979.

———. "Learning Styles: The Journey from Greenwich Observatory (1796) to Dalhousie University (1981): An Analysis and Synthesis." Paper presented at a conference at Dalhousie University, June 1981.

Kraft, R. E. "An Analysis of Student Learning Styles." *Physical Education,* October 1976.

Riechmann, S. "The Refinement and Construct Validation of the Grasha-Riechmann Student Learning Style Scales." Master's thesis, University of Cincinnati, 1972.

———. "The Relationship Between Student Classroom-Related Variables and Students' Evaluations of Faculty." Doctoral dissertation, University of Cincinnati, 1974.

———. "Learning Styles: Their Role in Teaching Evaluation and Course Design." *Resources in Education,* February 1980.

Riechmann, S., and Grasha, A. F. "A Rational Approach to Developing and Assessing the Construct Validity of a Student Learning Scale Instrument." *The Journal of Psychology* 87(1974): 213–23.

Swartz, P. "Learning Styles of Nursing Students in a Small College." Unpublished study, Gwynedd-Mercy College, 1976.

CHAPTER 8

The Practical Value
Of Learning Style Ideas

David E. Hunt

Why is the idea of learning style important? How can you find your way among the many different learning styles to select those that will be most useful?

Learning style is nothing more than a formal attempt to capture what goes on in effective communication. Learning style ideas attempt to make part of the teaching-learning and counseling transactions explicit—an explication practitioners themselves are much too busy to bring to consciousness, let alone describe in detail.

Our first step, therefore, is to get a feeling for this intuitive, implicit process which makes interpersonal communication possible, yet usually passes without notice. To get a first-hand understanding of this process, I ask you to reflect on what goes through your mind when you are communicating with another person.

Stop for a moment and imagine yourself in the following situation: As you are leaving work, you are stopped outside by a foreign visitor who inquires, in barely understandable English, how to find the nearest railroad station. What goes through your mind? Do you ask any questions before you reply to the request? What is your initial impression of the visitor?

Suppose further that the visitor does not understand your initial attempt at directions. What do you do next? Focus on your train of thought throughout all of this interchange. Notwithstanding the limitations of hypothetical situations, I hope that your reflection led you to a sharper awareness of certain identifiable processes in your experience.

How does the following two-step sequence fit with your analysis? An initial attempt is made to form an impression of the visitor (perhaps accompanied by a question or two to verify your impression) which in turn forms the basis for adapting your response to his request. Does it make sense to think of this interchange as two steps involving "reading" and "flexing" (Hunt, 1976) in which you form an impression and then act on this impression?

We cannot be this reflective, of course, in the moment when the split-second demands of the situation collapse this reading and flexing into the indistinguishable flow of conversational give-and-take. Reading and flexing are like perception and action, one leading to, or occurring simultaneously with, the other.

These two steps may also be viewed as "if . . . then" matching statements. We form a hunch about the other person in terms of "If this person is thus-and-so," which leads to an action statement, "then I should approach the person this way." You might have formed the impression, for instance, that a visitor would be familiar with maps, and therefore decided to draw instructions for him to find a place. It is very unlikely that in this case you would have gone through "if . . . then" formally by specifying that "*If* he knows about maps, *then* I will respond to his request with instructions on a map." What is more likely is that you formed an implicit hunch about the visitor which affected your way of responding.

I want you to become aware of this intuitive matching process because it is what learning style ideas help us to understand. Assuming that our response of drawing a map for the visitor is based on implicit matching, it is very similar to a formal matching prescription such as "If a person experiences events spatially, then I will use maps, globes, and atlases to communicate." Formal matching statements like this, in which the learning style description of spatial orientation serves to guide actions, are valuable because they make the matching process explicit, and therefore communicable. Indeed, the idea of learning style is important because it forms matching statements of the "if . . . then" variety and thereby clarifies what happens in reading and flexing.

Stop a moment to get a feeling for these two steps in whatever way is comfortable for you. If (hold out your left hand) then (hold out your right hand). See them in sequence: Reading → Flexing. Listen to them: Perception leads to action. In whatever way you wish, get the sense of reading and flexing, perception and action, if . . . then. This relationship is the theme for many variations: diagnosis to prescription, assessment to recommendation, and so forth.

What about matching in the classroom and counseling office? An experienced teacher makes a split-second judgment about a student's need for reassurance and provides it without ever formulating the matching principle "If a student has a high need for reassurance, then provide reward." In a similar way, a skilled counselor, on hearing his client report that his life is "muddy and grey," replies, "You want to get a clearer picture and add some color to your life," without ever thinking of matching to the visual representational systems or Neuro Linguistic Programing.

It is true that these instances of "matching in the moment" differ in duration from formal matching prescriptions, but they are similar in form and purpose. To acknowledge their similarity still leaves many unanswered questions: How can we distinguish between effective and ineffective "matching in the moment"? Will practitioners become more effective at matching in the moment by becoming more reflective and attempting to incorporate more formal matching principles? These and other questions must be considered at some point, but for now, I think that accepting the similarity between formal matching principles and the practitioners' matching in the moment gives us the beginning, necessary foundation for establishing communication between practitioners and researchers.

Evaluating and Selecting Appropriate Styles

Now I turn to the second question of how to evaluate the various learning style ideas in order to select the most useful. I propose three criteria, and use the Conceptual Level (CL) matching model (Hunt, 1979) to exemplify how to use them. Before elaborating on these criteria, I remind you that we are evaluating matching ideas or "If . . . then" statements, not simply a learning style description such as visual orientation. Reformulated in "If . . . then" terms, the Conceptual Level matching principle (Hunt, 1979)[1] states that "*If* a person is low in CL, *then* that person will learn better in a highly structured environment; *if* a person is high in CL, *then* the person will learn best in a low structure environment, or learn equally well in a variety of environments."

Such "If . . . then" matching statements can be evaluated by their (1) theoretical logic, i.e., can the statement be supported logically? (2) experimental evidence, i.e., can the statement be supported empirically by controlled experiments? and (3) intuitive agreement, i.e., does the statement agree with the implicit theories that practitioners use in practice? Note that this third criterion is mindful of the earlier discussion about the correspondence between intuitive "matching in the moment" and formal matching models.

Logical argument as criterion

If a person is characterized by a specific learning style, how can we logically derive a matched approach? One way is to consider the environmental approach as compensating for whatever the person lacks in the learning style. In the Conceptual Level matching model, for example, a person characterized as low CL is not capable of processing information in a complex manner, and therefore needs a highly structured environment that will compensate for this limitation. Many matching principles are implicitly based on this "deficit model" in which the underlying assumption is that the matched approach should compensate for what is missing in the specific learning style.

A contrast to this way of thinking is a view of a person's learning style as a source of strength to be utilized or enhanced. In this preferential model, an appropriate matching prescription is derived through a rationale of "playing to strength." For example, if a person is primarily visual in receiving information and representing thoughts, then the recommended approach is through that modality. In both compensatory and preferential matching (Snow, 1970) it is important to note that the "theoretical logic" involves implicit assumptions about the nature of personal learning, development, and change.

In the Conceptual Level matching model, the matching principles differ depending on whether one is taking a *contemporaneous* view of the person, i.e., attempting to facilitate present learning, or a *developmental* perspective, attempting to facilitate the growth and development of the learning style

---

1. This is only a very sketchy summary of the CL Matching Model since more thorough descriptions are available elsewhere, e.g., for the practitioner (Hunt, 1979) and researcher (Hunt, 1978; Miller, 1981).

itself. More specifically, when working with a person characterized as low in CL, the matching recommendation varies: For immediate purposes, "provide high structure," for long-term purposes, "provide high structure initially while gradually decreasing structure so that self-initiative can develop."

You will understand this criterion more clearly if you take a moment now to consider the logic of matching in several other learning style descriptions in this book, and also give some thought to the assumptions underlying the matching suggestion, e.g., "filling in deficits," "playing to strength," etc.

Experimental evidence as criterion

To some educational researchers, experimental evidence from controlled studies is the only criterion of matching principles. Some readers may be surprised, therefore, that I regard it as only one of several criteria. Because this criterion has been the most emphasized, it is probably easiest to describe. Continuing with the Conceptual Level matching principle, for example, experimental evidence comes from a study by Tomlinson and Hunt (1971) as follows: If eleventh grade students characterized as low CL were provided with a matched environment (the high structure of a rule-example order), their learning was optimal; if eleventh grade students characterized as high CL were provided matched environments (low structure of examples only), their *concept learning* was optimized.

Construct validity of the CL matching principle from about 30 experiments has recently been summarized by Miller (1981). It is important to note when considering such experimental evidence for a specific learning style matching principle, that the evidence always applies both to the specific "If . . . then" statement *and* to the measuring instrument used to characterize the learning style. In the Conceptual Level model, the evidence includes *both* the CL matching idea and the Paragraph Completion Method (Hunt et al., 1978) used to measure CL. The necessary coupling of concept and method is obvious to researchers but it may not always be so obvious to practitioners trying to evaluate the ideas as distinct from specific methods.

Intuitive experience as criterion

The best illustration of how this criterion operates for the CL matching idea is the reaction of a teacher who, after hearing me describe CL matching in terms of its theoretical logic and empirical evidence, commented, "I've been doing that for years but I didn't know there was a theory about it." The reader who wants to use this criterion might look at my paper, "How To Be Your Own Best Theorist" (Hunt, 1980), and use it to identify intuitive ideas from personal experience. Following are a few examples of intuitive "If . . . then" matching ideas that practitioners have identified using this procedure:

- "If a student has academic difficulty, then work with him or her on a one-to-one basis to try to overcome difficulties."
- "If a student has a social problem, then try to support the relationships

that 'work' for him or her now in order to build on these in wider context."

- "If a patient has little self-confidence, then help to facilitate the person's gleaning positive feedback from environment."

I do not maintain that these general matching ideas from practitioners are superior to, or more valid than, those that come from theory and research. Indeed, they must be put to test as well; but they cannot be tested until they are recognized.

Conclusion

In my brief comments I have emphasized the value of practitioners' implicit (and usually unexpressed) knowledge. Emphasis is required because this source of understanding has not always been acknowledged in the past since the source of knowledge has been only theories and experiments.

My emphasis on what teachers and counselors know does not mean that there is no value in psychological theory and research. I am simply trying to redress the imbalance and indicate that both parties can learn from each other. Not only can researchers gain better understandings of transactions by becoming aware of what practitioners know; but the practitioners, once they have identified their own knowledge, will be better able to learn more and gain new ideas from the researchers. Learning style can provide a basis for such communication to develop and thrive.

References

Hunt, D. E. "Teachers' Adaptation: Reading and Flexing to Students." *Journal of Teacher Education* 27 (1976): 268–75.

———. "Conceptual Level Theory and Research as Guides to Educational Practice." *Interchange,* 1977–78, pp. 78–90.

———. "Learning Style and Student Needs: An Introduction to Conceptual Level." In *Student Learning Styles.* Reston, Va.: National Association of Secondary School Principles, 1979, pp. 27–38.

———. "How To Be Your Own Best Theorist." *Theory into Practice* 19(1980): 287–93.

Hunt, D. E.; Butler, L. F.; Noy, J. E.; and Rosser, M. E. *Assessing Conceptual Level by the Paragraph Completion Method.* Toronto: Ontario Institute for Studies in Education, 1978.

Miller, Alan. "Conceptual Matching Models and Interactional Research in Education." *Review of Educational Research,* Spring 1981, pp. 33–84.

Snow, R. E. "Research on Media and Aptitudes." *Bulletin of the School of Education, Indiana University* 46(1970): 63–89.

Tomlinson, P. D., and Hunt, D. E. "Differential Effects of Rule-Example Order as a Function of Conceptual Level." *Canadian Journal of Behavioral Science* 3 (1971): 237–45.

CHAPTER 9

Personality Structure And Learning Style: Uses of the Myers-Briggs Type Indicator

Gordon Lawrence

Those who study teacher effectiveness seem to agree that the better teachers are able to see more of the complexities of a classroom and of the minds of their students. Yet, these teachers also have the capacity to tune out thousands of irrelevant and low-priority stimuli and attend to the essentials. In the hurly-burly of teaching, they somehow know what needs active response, what must be kept in the forefront, and what should be left on the periphery of attention.

As various constructs of learning style are proposed and subjected to experimentation, their developers want to help the teacher attend to the important variables of the classroom. The proof of a construct is in its usefulness. All conceptions of learning style must pass the ultimate test of practicality: Does this construct help teachers and students attend to the complex factors that affect learning without swamping them with too many variations and complexities?

In his view of personality types, the Swiss psychologist Carl Jung provided the best means I have found for drawing the diverse research on learning style into one conceptual scheme. His is a theory that calls attention to subtle variations in people yet keeps one focused on simple concepts of personality.

Jung's theory, presented in his book *Psychological Types* (1923), has been given scant attention by American educators. The task of making the theory visible and practical remained for Isabel Myers, who with her mother Katherine Briggs, developed the Myers-Briggs Type Indicator (MBTI) as a means of identifying Jungian personality types. With the 1980 publication of Myers' book, *Gifts Differing*, educators now have a resource that should extend the uses of Jung's ideas dramatically in the next few years.

The Myers-Briggs Type Indicator is a self-administering questionnaire concerned with Jung's theory of psychological types. It was first published in 1962 by Educational Testing Service as a research instrument, after 20 years of development by its authors. In 1975, Consulting Psychologists Press took over publication, and it became available for general professional use. The MBTI was developed with great care and has been used extensively in research since its publication. The research bibliography has over 600 entries examining personality type differences in academic aptitude and achievement, teaching and learning, career choice and satisfaction, marital relationships, organizational behavior and management styles, and counseling. As evidenced by this list of research topics, learning style is but one reflection of personality type.

Jung's Concepts Represented in the MBTI

Where other observers saw peoples' behavior as random and idiosyncratic, Jung saw patterns. "Psychological types" are patterns in the way people prefer to perceive and to make judgments. In Jung's theory, all conscious mental activity can be classified into four mental processes—two perception processes: sensing and intuition; and two judgment processes; thinking and feeling. What comes into consciousness, moment by moment, comes either through the senses or through intuition. Perceptions must be used to remain in consciousness. They are used—sorted, weighed, analyzed, evaluated, assigned into action, etc.—by the two judgment processes: thinking and feeling.

The Dominant Process

Everyone regularly uses all four processes, but we do not use them equally well. From childhood, each of us has come to rely on one process more than the others. It seems more trustworthy, so it is used more and becomes more mature and reliable. That one mental process becomes the centerpost, the core of the personality. People in whom *sensing perception* is the centerpost are above all else, practical people. Their close attention to data provided by the senses make them well attuned to immediate experiences, the literal facts at hand, the concrete realities.

People who have *intuitive perception* as the dominant process are naturally less tuned to sensory experience. Their consciousness is mainly filled with the meanings, associations, abstractions, theories, and imagined possibilities that do not depend directly on senses. Above all else, they believe in intuitive insights and imagination to set life's directions.

People in whom *thinking judgment* is the strongest mental process are logical and have orderly, analytical minds. All experience must fit into logical mental systems or the systems must be reworked to accommodate perceptions that don't fit. Children of this pattern may not seem logical by adult standards, but internally the drive is to test and organize all experience by logical criteria even if the logic is idiosyncratic! They naturally treat people and things (and themselves) objectively.

Finally, people with *feeling judgment* as the dominant mental process direct their lives toward human values and harmony, above all else. They weigh all experience as being harmonious or dissonant with the values and priorities of their own lives and others they care about. They are naturally more attuned to the subjective world of feelings and values and are more alert to the humane issues in any situation.

Polarity and Balance

If people had only one mental process they trusted and developed, their lives would be essentially one-dimensional. Unfortunately, we all know such people whose perceptions are not focused or tempered by good judgment. And we know others whose judgments are locked so tightly that they remained unrenewed by fresh perceptions.

In Jung's theory, the two kinds of perception—sensing and intuition—are polar opposites of each other. Similarly, thinking judgment and feeling judgment are polar opposites. In a sensing dominant person, intuition is necessarily the least developed and least trusted (and trustworthy) of the four mental processes. That is not an arbitrary feature of the theory, but rather a logical condition in human experience. In the instant that conscious attention is focused on sensing, it cannot also be focused on intuitions, and vice versa. I may shift quickly from one to the other, but cannot attend to both at once. Thus I attend to my intuitive perceptions and develop my intuitive capacities at the expense of my sensing perceptions.

The MBTI questions are constructed so that sensing choices are pitted only against intuitive ones, and thinking are pitted against feeling, making a perception scale that is independent from the judgment scale. The instrument reports a position for the respondent on each scale. The sensing-intuitive continuum runs from strongly sensing, to a slight preference for sensing, to a slight preference for intuition, to a strong preference for intuition. The thinking-feeling continuum is constructed in the same way. Thus the instrument has separate scales to correspond to these two different dimensions of personality type.

The Auxiliary Process

To avoid a one-dimensional personality, a person must develop a helping or auxiliary process to balance the dominant process. Because of the polarity concept just described, the auxiliary is always formed in the dimension other than the dominant one. A person having sensing or intuition as the dominant process, for example, will develop either thinking or feeling as the auxiliary process. Similarly, a person with thinking or feeling dominant will have sensing or intuition as the auxiliary process. Thus, combining dominant and auxiliary processes, eight sets are formed:

Dominant		Auxiliary		Dominant		Auxiliary
Sensing	with	Thinking		Intuition	with	Thinking
Sensing	with	Feeling		Intuition	with	Feeling
Thinking	with	Sensing		Thinking	with	Intuition
Feeling	with	Sensing		Feeling	with	Intuition

The meaning of the eight sets can be illustrated by the varied emphases in the left-hand column above. The sensing-with-thinking people focus their practical outlook on the aspects of the world that are readily subject to logical analysis—the objects, machinery, and the more impersonal transactions of life. In contrast, the sensing-with-feeling people attend primarily to the practical side of human needs. Still different in emphasis, the thinking-with-sensing people are those who wish to put their system of logical order on the practical matters of the world. And the feeling-with-sensing people are concerned primarily with harmonious relationships and seek to attain them through practical helpfulness.

The differences suggested here are subtle but not superficial. The intuition-with-thinking people, for example, may often test their intuitive inspirations with logical analysis, and the analysis may fault the inspiration. If the inspiration is compelling enough, however, no amount of illogicality in the idea will be enough to abort it. In a showdown, intuition will always prevail because it is the dominant process in those people. In contrast, the thinking-with-intuition person would always sacrifice the intuition in such a showdown.

Extraversion-Introversion

Jung identified a third dimension of personality structure that expands the 8 sets to 16. This third dimension is extraversion-introversion. Jung invented these terms, creating them from the Latin roots and assigning to them quite specific meanings which have been distorted, if not corrupted, in American common usage. Staying close to the Latin, extraversion means outward-turning and introversion means inward-turning. We all do both regularly, every day. We turn outside ourselves to act in the world, and we turn into ourselves to reflect. Action, of course, is blind and may be fruitless without reflection; and reflection that does not lead to action is futile. But each person is not equally "at home" in action and reflection. Extraverts will say, "When in doubt, act." Introverts will say, "When in doubt, reflect on the matter more deeply."

How does extraversion-introversion fit into the eight patterns already described? People who use their dominant process primarily to drive their actions in the world are extraverted. People who reserve the dominant process primarily for the personal inner world of thoughts and reflections are introverted.

The dominant process is the best introduction to a person; it tells the most about that person's personality. Extraverts, by definition, reveal their best first. What you see is what you get. Introverts, reserving their best for the inner world, their favored world, reveal mainly their auxiliary process to others. Only close associates will be allowed to see the most valued process in operation. We come to know introverts more slowly.

Consider, for example, how the extraversion-introversion dimension expands the thinking-with-intuition pattern. The extraverted version reflects those people who want to act in the world to organize and manage as much of it as they can, to extend their personal logical systems into the world around them—their favored arena for personal expression.

In contrast, introverted thinkers want to exercise their dominant process (thinking) mainly in the inner realm of private mental activity. They strive above all else to have orderly, logical minds. They use their auxiliary process, intuition mainly, to run their outer lives, and give the *appearance* of being intuitive dominants.

Simple symbols can show these ideas. Capital letters are used to represent the dominant process and small letters the auxiliary process. A circle is used to represent the dividing line between the inner and outer worlds that people live in.

F
s feeling judgment is dominant and extraverted, with sensing perception as auxiliary.

s
F feeling judgment is dominant and introverted, with sensing perception as auxiliary.

The people represented by the first symbol make their feelings public naturally and frequently. Their antennae are out to pick up feeling signals and they are the practical harmonizers and weavers of compromises.

The people represented by the second symbol have no less wealth of feeling, but it is reserved as a private process, to be revealed only to family and close friends. They take a receptive and quiet-helper role in contrast to the activist and often warmly-aggressive stance of those who have feeling dominant and extraverted.

The Fourth Dimension

Briggs and Myers elaborated Jung's ideas of psychological type and explicated a fourth dimension that is present but not highlighted in the descriptions already given. The fourth dimension is the attitude taken toward the outer world. When a *judgment* process is used to run one's outer life, as in $\overset{F}{\text{ⓢ}}$ and $\overset{t}{\text{ⓢ}}$, the natural drive is to have things decided, judged, settled, planned, organized, and managed according to plan. This is a judging attitude toward the outer world. In this personality pattern, the drive is always toward closure, toward having a settled system in place.

When a *perception* process is used to run one's life, as in $\overset{s}{\text{ⓕ}}$ and $\overset{S}{\text{ⓕ}}$, the natural drive is one of openness to new perceptions; staying flexible so as to adapt to changing circumstances and to experience as widely as possible. This is a perceiving attitude toward the world. In this personality pattern, the drive is toward keeping plans and organization to a necessary minimum so one can respond to new perceptions and adapt flexibly to new circumstances.

To summarize briefly, in Jung's theory of psychological types, all conscious mental activity occurs in two perception processes (sensing and intuition), and in two judgment processes (thinking and feeling). Everyone uses all four processes, but we differ in how much and how well we use them. In every person, one of the processes is dominant and indicates the basic way the person addresses life. If a person uses the dominant process mainly in the world of people and things, his or her orientation is called extraverted. If a person uses the dominant process mainly in the inner, private world of ideas and thoughts, he or she is called introverted. Balance in the personality is achieved by the development of a complementary mental process, so that both a perception and a judgment process can be used reliably.

The MBTI Profiles

The MBTI has four scales corresponding to the four dimensions of type theory, as shown in Table 1.

Table 1
Myers-Briggs Type Indicator

Four Preferences Are Scored To Arrive at a Person's Type

 Does the person's interest flow mainly to

The outer world of actions, objects, and persons?

EXTRAVERSION

The inner world of concepts and ideas?

INTROVERSION

 Does the person prefer to Perceive

The immediate, real, practical facts of experience and life?

SENSING

The possibilities, relationships, and meanings of experiences?

INTUITION

 Does the person prefer to make Judgments or decisions

Objectively, impersonally, considering causes of events and where decisions may lead?

THINKING

Subjectively and personally, weighing values of choices and how they matter to others?

FEELING

 Does the person prefer mostly to live

In a decisive, planned, and orderly way, aiming to regulate and control events?

JUDGMENT

In a spontaneous, flexible way, aiming to understand life and adapt to it?

PERCEPTION

© Center for Applications of Psychological Type, Inc., 1976.

The MBTI uses a shorthand designation for the eight characteristics: E for extraversion, I for introversion, etc. Note that N is used for intuition because the I is used for introversion.

The MBTI reports four scores, one for each scale, e.g., E_7, N_{21}, T_{45}, J_{17}. In this example, the person's type is <u>ENTJ</u>. The scores show a slight preference for extraversion, moderate preferences for intuition and judging, and a strong preference for thinking.

While type is reported and explained in four dimensions, it is not merely a combination of parts. Nor is it static as the term "type" often connotes. MBTI is a dynamic system, and each type is an integrated pattern. The brief descriptions of the 16 types highlight the strengths, the similarities, and differences of the types (Table 2).

Myers wrote extensive descriptions of each type, and at least a one-page description is given to people when their type is reported from the MBTI. Condensing the type descriptions into one table involves some oversimplification and distortion, so they should be used cautiously.

In the four-letter formula, two letters are underlined (e.g., ENTJ). "E" designates this type as an extraverted thinking type, with intuition as auxiliary. The two middle letters are the preferred mental processes. The underlined process, "T" in this case, is the dominant process.

In the table, the types are displayed with opposites across from each other, that is, types with all four dimensions different. For example, ENTJ and ISFP differ in all four letters. The areas of strength of the one are the weaknesses of the other. Opposites have the most difficulty communicating with each other. To find common ground they must make use of the less preferred and less trustworthy mental processes. Ironically, opposites stand to gain the most from each other because each represents to the other the direction in which the greatest opportunity for growth lies. Maturity in terms of type is the capability to use the appropriate process when it is needed.

The 16 types are arranged in the table so that the 4 with the same dominant process are together in quadrants: The 4 with thinking dominant are in the upper left quadrant; the 4 with feeling dominant in the upper right; the sensing dominant in the lower left; and the intuitive dominant in the lower right. This arrangement in quadrants provides a way of examining the relationships between personality type and learning style.

Learning Style and Type

Personality type is more fundamental than learning style. Learning style constructs are much more intelligible and useful against a backdrop of type. I hope to make that case convincingly in the paragraphs that follow.

In my judgment, the most essential relationship between type and learning style can be seen in the nature of the dominant mental process in each personality. Refer again to the brief descriptions of the 16 types and consider the differences represented by the quadrants, beginning with the thinking-dominant types. The young thinkers in school are energized by logically organized material. They thrive on things that can be analyzed, and resent what must be "learned" if it doesn't fit logically into their mental systems. They respond best to the teacher who is well organized and resist and resent the teacher whose organization is not logical. If they do not find logical orderliness in either the material or the teacher, they cannot bring their best energies and effort to the learning tasks.

The feeling-dominant types are in the upper right quadrant of the table. As the young feeling types start a new school year, they test the situation with two overriding criteria: Does the teacher care about me? And, is the subject matter something I can give my heart to? A caring relationship with the teacher can carry the young feeling types through many school tasks that do not interest them. When attachments both to the teacher *and* to the school subjects are effected, these children produce the best. With both conditions absent, they lose their primary motivation, and adjustments in instructional procedures and physical conditions are unlikely to make any difference.

Young sensing types, represented in the lower-left quadrant, may appreciate logical order and harmonious working relationships, but their learning motivation does not depend primarily on either. Above all else, they respond to what they see as practical and functional. Their criteria are: Can this teacher and this material show me something useful, skills that my senses can master and put to good use? These students are most likely to become lost when the teacher skips steps in explanations and directions, leaves large gaps for students' imagination to close, teaches abstractions without checking to see whether they connect with concrete realities in the students' lives, and teaches "facts" and "skills" that can only be put to real use at some indeterminate time in the future. Sensing types do their best mental work when their senses are most fully engaged ("I think best with my hands . . .").

The final group, the intuitive dominants, crave inspiration above all else. They are fully engaged only when their imaginations are fired with intriguing ideas and plans. For them, routine quickly becomes dull. Unless the teacher or the material inspires them, boredom drives them to seek out something else—anything to re-establish the inspirational charge. Often they resort to daydreaming, reading off-task material, or undermining the teacher. Their energy flows to wherever the inspiration is. When inspired, they are the most innovative of all types.

If teachers could learn just one thing about psychological types, it should be the power of the dominant process: that thinkers must pursue logical order; feeling types, follow their hearts; sensing types, strive to engage their senses in practical skills; and intuitives, follow whatever inspires.

Curriculum Biases

The typical curriculum of American schools was not designed to address differences in the learning styles of the various personality types. Educators today have inherited a mind set of what schooling is and should be, and that mind set favors some types and handicaps others. Two such biases are evident. The first is organizational. Schools expect students to work quietly, sitting quietly in their own seats most of the time. School learning is regarded essentially as a private, interior mental effort. That expectation fits introverted types well, but neglects the extraverts who learn best when they can test ideas in talk and action. For extraverts, action is a prelude to reflection. They are not well served by typical classroom expectations and practices. That bias might be tolerable if extraverts were a small minority of the population; however, research reported in the *MBTI Manual* clearly shows that the typical school has 70 to 75 percent extraverts.

The other major bias puts sensing students at a disadvantage. The curriculum materials are predominantly printed materials. The verbal and mathematical symbols on the printed page are the center of attention for most of the school day. Abstract symbols are the intuitive's preferred way of perceiving. In the sensing student's mind, however, abstract symbols are secondary to direct sensory experience. The more sensing types are engaged in new experiences, the more "sense" abstract symbols will make as representations of experience. Vicarious experience in books, valued by intuitives because it feeds imagination, is a pale substitute for young sensing students who believe that the concrete real world, as perceived by the senses, is far more important than symbols on a page.

In the United States, sensing types outnumber intuitives three to one, yet the schools' reliance on printed symbols as the main means of instruction serves the intuitive minority and handicaps the sensing majority.

When these two dimensions of type are combined, the distribution imbalance is even more dramatic; people with the extravert-sensing combination substantially outnumber the extraverts who prefer intuition, as well as the introverts.

ES types in school are likely to outnumber IN types as much as nine to one. Yet the typical patterns of schooling favor IN students. IS students can respond positively to the introversion bias of schools, and ENs are at home with the intuition bias, but the ES students—half the school population—have to work against their type disposition in most learning tasks. Little wonder that of the 500 people Isabel Myers identified from her base population as persons who dropped out of school before finishing eighth grade, more than 99 percent were type S.

IS	IN	I = 25%
19%	6%	
ES	EN	E = 75%
56%	19%	

S = 75%   N = 25%

Table 2
Brief Descriptions of the Sixteen Types

ENTJ	ISFP
Intuitive, Innovative ORGANIZER; aggressive, analytic, systematic; more tuned to new ideas and possibilities than to people's feelings.	Observant, loyal HELPER; reflective, realistic, empathic; patient with details, gentle and retiring; shuns disagreements; enjoys the moment.
ESTJ	**INFP**
Fact-minded, practical ORGANIZER; aggressive, analytic, systematic; more interested in getting the job done than in people's feelings.	Imaginative, independent HELPER; reflective, inquisitive, empathic, loyal to ideals; more interested in possibilities than practicalities.

I N T P

Inquisitive ANALYZER; reflective, independent, curious; more interested in organizing ideas than situations or people.

I S T P

Practical ANALYZER; values exactness; more interested in organizing data than situations or people; reflective, a cool and curious observer of life.

E S T P

REALISTIC ADAPTER in the world of material things; good-natured, tolerant, easygoing; oriented to practical, firsthand experience; highly observant of details of things.

E S F P

REALISTIC ADAPTER in human relationships; friendly and easy with people, highly observant of their feelings and needs; oriented to practical, firsthand experience.

I S T J

Analytical MANAGER OF FACTS AND DETAILS: dependable, decisive, painstaking, and systematic; concerned with systems and organization; stable and conservative.

I S F J

Sympathetic MANAGER OF FACTS AND DETAILS; concerned with peoples' welfare; dependable, painstaking, and systematic; stable and conservative.

E S F J

Practical HARMONIZER and worker-with-people; sociable, orderly, opinionated; conscientious, realistic, and well tuned to the here and now.

E N F J

Imaginative HARMONIZER and worker-with-people; sociable, expressive, orderly, opinionated, conscientious; curious about new ideas and possibilities.

I N F J

People-oriented INNOVATOR of ideas; serious, quietly forceful and persevering; concerned with the common good, with helping others find possibilities in themselves.

I N T J

Logical, critical, decisive INNOVATOR of ideas; serious, intent, highly independent, concerned with organization, determined, and often stubborn.

E N F P

Warmly enthusiastic PLANNER OF CHANGE, imaginative, individualistic; pursues inspiration with impulsive energy; seeks to understand and inspire others.

E N T P

Inventive, analytical PLANNER OF CHANGE; enthusiastic and independent; pursues inspiration with impulsive energy; seeks to understand and inspire others.

As a backdrop for making learning styles more understandable, type theory provides many insights. Only a few implications can be highlighted here. The accompanying table shows the typical work setting preferences of IS, IN, ES, and EN people, as identified by Myers. I have chosen to speak of "work settings" and to avoid asking people about their preferred "learning settings" because the latter term usually prompts them to visualize only the features of the typical classroom—which is biased and limited in its options. If a school faculty is skeptical about the importance of attending to learning styles, I ask them to check the items in Table 3 (a version of the table in which the four sets have no headings) and to examine the pattern of their check marks. Typically, a teacher will check either the right or left side of the table, and will leave one of the quadrants nearly void of checks. The empty quadrant is almost always the one opposite one's own pattern, as IS is opposite EN. Teachers usually teach true to type, and the empty set identifies the types of students they may have trouble reaching. The pattern of check marks graphically shows how much everyone, adult or child, values settings that support preferred ways of working. It also conveys the stress one is likely to feel in a learning setting that does not honor one's type.

Becoming an adult means, among other things, learning to function adequately in a variety of work settings. Adults put more checkmarks in the table than do children and distribute the checkmarks more widely. Children's apparently narrower range of work settings suggests that they may have fewer ways to learn effectively than do adults. Yet the argument could be made that schools typically offer fewer choices of work (learning) settings than the world offers to adults.

No doubt there are many variations in learning styles among extra-verted-sensing students. Every teacher I have worked with has been able to recall a variety of active and concrete learning experiences they have planned and provided for their students: constructing things, interviewing, writing and performing plays, developing science projects, collecting and cataloging, coaching or drilling other students, conducting field projects, producing a newspaper, etc. Teachers' main reason for not having more of these con-crete-active lessons is their sense that they must "cover the curriculum" more quickly than these activities allow. That pressure represents an attitude and priority of the school system much in need of re-examination.

The teaching of reading can illustrate the kinds of changes needed to remove the bias against extraverted-sensing students. The process of reading silently is, of course, an introverted one. Because reading consists of process-ing abstract symbols, teachers generally have assumed that reading should be presented to children as an introverted-intuitive task. They further assume that nearly all students should be able to experience reading as a natural process worth doing for its own sake.

The assumptions are false for many children. Teachers report that many of their students, particularly ES children, do not approach reading as an inherently interesting exercise, but rather get interested in it only as a tool, a means for gaining something important. For them, reading is not a preferred way of experiencing the world; direct action with tangible things is the much preferred way.

Table 3
I am likely to do my best work . . .

Directions: Put a check beside those items that are true for you, on all four lists. When you have finished that, go back over the four lists and draw a circle around the checkmark of items that are strongly true for you.

A Pattern	**C Pattern**
I am likely to do my best work in situations that:	*I am likely to do my best work in situations that:*
— will produce practical results, useful prod-ucts	— put me on my own initiative
— involve other people, group effort	— let me plan and carry out new projects
— have goals set in advance and let me work toward them in an orderly way	— involve other people in solving problems, such as group projects
— are real and not just dealing with theory	— let me create new ways of doing things
	— let me try out my ideas to see if they work, to see how other people react to them

— give me a clear picture of what other people are doing and what they regard as important
— have realistic schedules that don't expect too much too soon
— let me learn from first-hand experience, on the job
— let me use the practical skills and facts I possess
— give me a regular work schedule, but give me some variety and time to socialize, too
— let me work with concrete things, hands-on materials
— let me "think out loud" with other people

— don't require a detailed accounting of how I use my time
— pose problems needing more attention to the broad picture than to details
— provide variety and minimize routine
— let me figure out how to put theory into practice
— let me make mistakes without penalties and learn from the mistakes
— challenge my imagination

B Pattern

I am likely to do my best work in situations that:
— make practical sense to me
— have a clear organization in them
— are practical and realistic
— let me know just what is expected of me
— let me work at a steady speed, step-by-step
— require accuracy and careful attention to details
— require patience
— don't have many surprises in them
— let me use my practical experience
— let me use my memory for facts
— let me think through a problem by myself before I have to act on it

D Pattern

I am likely to do my best work in situations that:
— let me work in my head with my own ideas
— let me work toward solutions in my own way
— give me a chance to be creative
— let me set my own standards of quality
— let me work hard when I feel like it, and go easy when I need to
— don't burden me with too many routines
— have important ideas behind them
— give me ample time to think out my ideas before I have to act
— let me use my hunches and inspirations
— let me follow my curiosity
— let me work in depth on things of importance to me

While adult reading is mostly a silent, individual activity, type theory suggests that reading should be taught to many children as a social process: writing together and reading aloud; sharing stories; writing scripts to be acted; quizzing a partner on vocabulary and spelling; teaming in writing and critiquing letters, reports, and newspapers to be read by people whose opinions matter to the writers; reading aloud to younger people or to anyone else who will listen; and any other activities that present reading as a social transaction.

Type Theory as a Framework for Understanding Learning Style Research

Jung's theory of types has been supported with remarkable consistency by the research reported in the *MBTI Manual* and the CAPT bibliography (1981). Because of its comprehensiveness in characterizing the structure of conscious mental activity, I have found type theory to be by far the best means of organizing the diverse research on learning style. Keefe's useful chapter in *Student Learning Styles* (1979) clearly shows that the field of learning style consists of a wealth of diverse research and theorizing, but it is a wealth with few unifying threads. In my view, much can be gained by re-examining the field in light of type theory.

Here are a few considerations on learning style elements and their relationships to type.

Field dependent/independent: Type theory suggests that we consider what is in the "field" that people are sensitive to or independent of. If the field is rich with social cues and personal nuances, extraverts and feeling types can be expected to be more sensitive to these and less interested in disembedding impersonal meanings from the context. If abstract patterns are to be disembedded from a sensory-rich field, intuitive students are likely to give more attention to that task than are sensing students.

Reflectivity-impulsivity: Outcomes on this scale should correspond closely with introversion-extraversion, but two cautions are in order. Reflective is often interpreted to mean thoughtful—giving due consideration to things— and impulsive is often identified as its opposite. This interpretation tends to see the positive, mature side of introversion and the immature aspects of extraversion. Reflecting unduly means neglecting the need for timely action. The second caution is to emphasize the need for diagnostic data. Knowing which students are impulsive is not so valuable to the teacher as knowing what specific things stimulate the most reflection in the less mature extraverts; those things are important clues to what can help them develop. The corresponding question for introverts is, what do they value enough to encourage them into timely effective extraversion?

Reception styles: Most measures of reception style can be seen as varied ways of identifying the preference for sensing or intuition. Those who are familiar with type concepts may well agree with my classification, but the hypothesis remains to be tested. Modality preference, I believe, combines extraversion and introversion with sensing and intuition. Thus, ES-kinesthetic/motor, IS-visual/spatial, EN-spoken word, and IN-written word. Other reception styles can be sorted by pairs as favoring sensing or intuition.

Sensing	Intuition
focusing	scanning
preference for convention	tolerance for unrealistic experience
automatization	restructuring
perceptual/motor	conceptual

Attention styles: Measures of attention seem particularly susceptible to influence by personality type. The student who attends to high complexity in the working of an automobile may attend to much lower levels of complexity in social phenomena or in abstract schoolbook lessons. Persistence, anxiety level, and frustration tolerance are likely to depend very much on the interests of students, many of which are type-related. NTs, for example, are likely to persist, be less anxious, and more tolerant when working with abstract tasks that respond to logic. SFs are likely to persist and be less anxious about polishing social skills.

Expectancy styles: Measures of expectancy are likely to yield more useful data when type is taken into account. I will illustrate with three constructs. 1. Achievement motivation: What is the achievement goal—control (J) or understanding (P)? Practical utility (S) or conceptual clarity (N)? 2. Imitation: Who or what is regarded as a model to be imitated can be predicted to vary from type to type. 3. Risk taking vs. cautiousness: While extraverts are regarded more often as risk takers, and an ISTJ type would be regarded as definitely more cautious than an ENFP type, the main concern posed by type theory is that of identifying the arenas of risk taking and cautiousness each type would choose.

Finally, all of my experience and research confirm Dewey's adage that effort goes where interest is. The natural patterns of interests associated with the personality types are a rich resource that teachers need to know about. Teachers can't attend to all the idiosyncracies of all the students, but they can understand type concepts and anticipate the patterns of students. Teachers who know and use type theory report that it helps them keep learning styles in mind and see their students as individuals.

References

Center for Applications of Psychological Type. *Bibliography: The Myers-Briggs Type Indicator,* 1981. CAPT, 414 SW Seventh Terrace, Gainesville, Fla. 32601.

Jung, Carl. *Psychological Types.* New York: Harcourt Brace, 1923.

Keefe, James W. "Learning Style: An Overview." In *Student Learning Styles.* Reston, Va.: National Association of Secondary School Principals, 1979.

Lawrence, Gordon. *People Types and Tiger Stripes: A Practical Guide to Learning Styles.* 2d ed. Gainesville, Fla.: Center for Applications of Psychological Type, 1982.

Myers, Isabel Briggs. *MBTI Manual.* Palo Alto, Calif.: Consulting Psychologists Press, 1963, 1975.

———. *Gifts Differing.* Palo Alto, Calif.: Consulting Psychologists Press, 1980.

CHAPTER 10

Educational Cognitive Style Mapping

Seldon D. Strother

Each person is unique. Even identical twins have distinguishing characteristics. We come from different genetic, ethnic, and social backgrounds and the combination of these and other factors makes each of us individual. We need a precise method of describing the way that each individual searches for meaning.

No concept has had as great an impact on the educational process during the last decade as has individualized instruction. While no single learning variable can yet be said to outweigh all others in importance, learner characteristics, instructional strategies, and media forms, all seem worthy of exploration when searching for processes that may eventually effectuate individual learning.

Reviewers of educational research have suggested that there is a need for a unifying conceptual framework within which decisions can be made about the interrelationships of student characteristics, mode of presentation, learning objectives, type of learning, and subject content. The educational science of cognitive styles developed by Joseph Hill and his associates at Oakland Community College, Bloomfield Hills, Michigan, provides a vehicle within which we can analyze these interrelationships.

The Educational Sciences

The educational sciences were created to provide a conceptual framework and scientific language for the applied field of education that approaches the level of precision found in such fields as medicine, pharmacy, engineering, and law.

The following assumptions are essential to the concept of the educational sciences:

- Education is a process of searching for meaning.
- Human beings are social creatures with the capacity for deriving meaning from environment and personal experiences through the creation and use of symbols.
- Not content with biological satisfactions alone, human beings continually search for meaning.
- Cognitive style changes with a person's education and maturity.

The seven "sciences" are:

- Symbols and their meanings
- Cultural determinants of the meanings of symbols
- Modalities of inference
- Memory: Function—Concern—Condition
- Cognitive styles of individuals
- Teaching styles, administrative styles, and counseling styles
- Systemic analysis and decision making.

Educational cognitive style, the fifth science, includes: symbols and their meanings, cultural determinants of the meanings of symbols, modalities of inference, and memory.

Educational Cognitive Style

According to Hill* et al., "Cognitive Style is a unique means for describing an individual's mode of behavior in searching for meaning. It is reflected in an individual's disposition to use certain types of symbolic forms; in his derivation of symbol meanings from roles he has found most satisfying; and in the manner in which he reasons." A map of cognitive style provides a picture of the way a person derives meaning from his or her symbolic orientations, personal experiences, and ways of reasoning. Cognitive style reflects age, experience, and level of education. There are no good or bad cognitive styles; cognitive style is thought of as effective or ineffective only when it is considered in terms of a specific task to be accomplished.

Cognitive style is expressed as what mathematicians call a "cartesian product of sets," a non-arithmetic display of elements contained in two or more sets, showing possible combinations of the elements without actually breaking each down in graphic form.

The cartesian product representing cognitive style (G) is composed of the following sets: symbols and their meaning (S); cultural determinants of the meaning of symbols (E); modalities of inference (H). Hill defines cognitive style as the cartesian product of these three sets represented as:

$$G = \underline{(S)} \times \underline{(E)} \times \underline{(H)}$$

Set S—Symbols and Their Meanings

Two types of symbols, *theoretical* (e.g., words and numbers) and *qualitative* (e.g., sensory and code data), are basic to the acquisition of knowledge and meaning. Theoretical symbols differ from qualitative symbols in that the former present to the nervous system, and then represent to it, something different from sensory or coded data. The spoken word "cup," for example, is an auditory sensation that represents to the individual the physical object of a cup. In contrast, the visual image resulting from observing an actual cup

---

*Joseph E. Hill, Derek N. Nunney and Associates, Oakland Community College, Bloomfield Hills, Michigan

would be a qualitative symbol because it presents data directly to the senses. Both types of symbols are essential to the educational process, i.e., the process of searching for meaning.

There are two main types of *theoretical* symbols—*auditory* and *visual*—each of which can be divided into linguistic and quantitative elements. The classification of theoretical symbols is influenced by both an individual's educational level and the symbolic requirements of the educational task with which he or she is confronted. The theoretical symbols are:

- Theoretical Auditory Linguistic T(AL) is the ability to derive meaning from spoken words or graphic symbols.
- Theoretical Auditory Quantitative T(AQ) is the ability to derive meaning from the sound of numbers, mathematical symbols, and measurements.
- Theoretical Visual Linguistic T(VL) is the ability to derive meaning from printed words or graphic symbols; e.g., someone who reads with a high degree of comprehension.
- Theoretical Visual Quantitative T(VQ) is the ability to derive meaning from written numbers, mathematical symbols, and measurements.

Qualitative symbols are used to derive a variety of meanings from the environment and such personal experiences as feelings, values, and insight into self. In this context, qualitative symbols influence, and are influenced by, subcultural individualism. There are 18 qualitative symbols. Five of them are associated with sensory stimuli:

- Qualitative Auditory Q(A) is the ability to perceive meaning from nonverbal sounds.
- Qualitative Olfactory Q(O) is the ability to obtain meaning through the sense of smell—odors, aromas, etc.
- Qualitative Savory Q(S) is the ability to perceive meaning through the sense of taste—sour, sweet, bitter, etc.
- Qualitative Tactile Q(T) is the ability to perceive meaning through the sense of touch.
- Qualitative Visual Q(V) is the ability to perceive meaning from visuals that are not words or numbers.

Three qualitative symbols are programmatic in nature:

- Qualitative Proprioceptive Q(P) is the ability to combine or coordinate inputs from muscular functions into a specific response or operation which is monitored by sensory input, e.g., running to and catching a baseball, typing from written material, playing a musical instrument.
- Qualitative Proprioceptive Kinematics Q(PK) is the ability to synthesize a number of symbolic mediations into a performance of a complex physical activity involving motion, e.g., riding a bicycle, driving a car, flying a plane, bouncing on a pogo stick.
- Qualitative Proprioceptive Temporal Q(PTM) is the ability to synthesize a number of symbolic mediations into a performance of complex

physical activity involving timing, e.g., hitting a baseball, applying auto brakes in order to stop at a specific point, stepping on an escalator, and adjusting the tappets on an automobile.

The remaining 10 qualitative symbols are associated with cultural codes:

- Qualitative Code Empathetic Q(CEM) is the ability to put oneself in another's place, e.g., to know how it feels when someone hits his thumb with a hammer or is given a hypodermic injection (intramuscular).
- Qualitative Code Esthetic Q(CES) is the ability to enjoy the beauty of an object or an idea.
- Qualitative Code Ethic Q(CET) is commitment to specific values or duties. This commitment may not imply morality. A priest and a criminal are committed to a set of "values" which are different.
- Qualitative Code Histrionic Q(CH) is the ability to deliberately stage behavior to produce a desired effect. Playing a role which is designed to produce some particular effect on other persons; i.e., deliberate display of emotion for effect, fulfilling role expectations.
- Qualitative Code Kinesics Q(CK) is the ability to interpret bodily movements or nonverbal reactions, e.g., smiles and gestures.
- Qualitative Code Kinesthetics Q(CKH) willingness and interest in acquiring the ability to perform motor skills or effect muscular coordination according to recommended, or acceptable, form, e.g., bowling, golfing, diving, eating, typing, and writing.
- Qualitative Code Proxemics Q(CP) is the ability to judge the appropriate physical and social distance between oneself and another as defined by the other person, e.g., being able to recognize if you may put your arm around that girl or call the boss by his first name.
- Qualitative Code Synnoetics Q(CS) is personal knowledge of oneself, e.g., being able to set realistic goals and attaining them.
- Qualitative Code Transactional Q(CT) is the ability to recognize or establish with others a positive communication system which influences their actions or goals, e.g., to convince someone that your way is best, salesmanship, mediator, arbitrator.
- Qualitative Code Temporal Q(CTM) is the ability to respond or behave according to time expectations imposed on an activity by members in the role group associated with the activity.

Set E—Cultural Determinants of the Meanings of Symbols

The interpretations of sensations (i.e., the meanings that we assign to symbols) shape and are shaped by our culture. Culturally created rules of expression derived from social relationships are primary factors in the development of precepts and concepts in the educational science of cognitive style.** The main cultural influences, or "cultural determinants," of the

---

**In the educational science of cognitive style, a percept is defined as an individual's interpretation of a sensation, and a concept is defined as a shared, and agreed upon, interpretation of a sensation.

meanings of symbols, are family, associates, and individuality. Since the meaning ascribed to symbols plays an important part in an individual's mediation of both theoretical and qualitative symbols, these determinants are important to the educational enterprise.

We bring meaning to symbols not only as totally unique individuals but also as people who are influenced by friends and peer groups, and by those we consider to be our family. In most cases, one of these determinants plays a major and another a minor influence. The cultural determinants are listed below:

- Associates or Peers (A) are represented by the various groups with whom the person has the greatest contact. These contacts change throughout life.
- Family (F) is either an individual's immediate, extended, or surrogate family.
- Individuality (I) indicates the person who directs his or her own behavior and makes decisions.

Cultural determinants of the meaning of symbols can be expressed either singularly (F, A, and/or I) or in combinations.

Set H—Modalities of Inference

In the process of deriving meanings, we employ two basic types of reasoning: *induction* (from particular to general), and *deduction* (from general to specific). Inductive processes yield probability conclusions, and deductive processes produce conclusions that are necessary consequences of the premises and the chain of reasoning. Since the inductive processes are employed continually throughout life, greater emphasis is placed on them in the educational sciences than on the deductive processes that are required only in certain pursuits such as the study of mathematics.

The reasoning processes include:

- Magnitude (M) is categorical thinking; i.e., using rules, definitions, and/or classifications.
- Differences (D) is the emphasis on one-to-one contrasts of selected characteristics or traits.
- Relationships (R) is the comparison of two or more selected characteristics of traits through similarities.
- Appraisal (L) is the process of weighing magnitudes, differences, and relationships in reaching a probability conclusion.
- Deductive Inferential (Circle K) (K) is utilized most frequently in logical proofs, e.g., in mathematics and in symbolic logic.

Diagnostic Techniques

Individual cognitive style may be diagnosed by Empirical Mapping, Interest Inventory, Consultation/Interview, or by Administering a Battery of Tests (eclectic mapping).

Empirical Mapping is accomplished by recording behavior on the cognitive style elements over a period of time (observing repeated occurrences). The complexity of the observable behavior descriptions varies with chronological age, maturity level, and educational development.

Empirical Mapping is recommended for the kindergarten through fourth grade age group, but is appropriate at any level providing the overt behavior descriptions are realistic for the age group.

Interest Inventory is a self-evaluation tool that consists of statements that are characteristic of educational cognitive style elements. The statements are developed from the experiences of practitioners. The Cognitive Style Map resulting from an inventory represents one's preferred way of obtaining meaning from the environment.

Consultation/Interview requires a thorough understanding and acceptance of cognitive style mapping as a viable tool. This technique involves the use of inventory-type questions during dialog with the client, the ability to listen, and the observation of mannerisms that are characteristic of *observable* cognitive style behavior. Proficiency in using the method is gained only through practice.

Administering a Battery of Tests (Eclectic Approach) makes it necessary for the practitioner to administer instruments designed to measure verbal reasoning, listening comprehension, visual numerical comprehension, reading comprehension, oral numerical comprehension, grammatical usage, qualitative codes, qualitative-live choice, cultural effects, and inferential patterns.

Using selected items from existing standardized tests, it is possible to diagnose and profile an individual on the various cognitive style traits. Such a test battery is on file at the Oakland Community College Testing Center.* Items included in these tests either have been developed at the college or are taken from a variety of instruments, including the Iowa Tests of Educational Development, the Gates Reading Tests, the Vineland Social Maturity Scale, the Differential Aptitude Test, the Raven Matrices Survey, the Mueller Auditory Test, the Nottus Pattern Test, and the Science Research Associates batteries. The theoretical elements (listening comprehension T(AL), reading comprehension T(VL), numerical comprehension T(VQ), etc.,) are measured by using items from existing standardized tests.

Map Interpretation and Prescription Writing

Two forms of symbols are used in mapping cognitive style elements, one for *major* orientations and one for *minor* orientations. Methods of recording and classifying the data obtained from mapping instruments are optional, e.g., percentiles, raw score. Consider the use of percentiles:

1. A *major* means that a student scored above the 50th percentile on an element. Thus, a major T(VQ) would mean that on this test the

---

*Testing Center, Oakland Community College, Bloomfield Hills, Michigan

student demonstrated average or better ability to use numbers that he or she sees, and that he or she would probably be capable of succeeding in a regular math course.

2. A *minor* means that the student is probably adequate on a given style element. Thus a minor T′(VL) would mean that the student scored between the 25th and 49th percentile and would probably be satisfactory in an academic discipline that requires use of written words. He might need extra help, however, if the course has lengthy reading assignments.

3. *Negligible*—If the student scored lower than the 25th percentile, he or she might need review courses or perhaps assistance at the learning laboratory in order to succeed in a course like college algebra.

4. A *profile* is far more useful than any single element in interpreting or predicting behavior. A profile consists of all theoretical elements, qualitative elements, cultural determinants, and modality of inference elements.

A research base supports cognitive style mapping (not all inclusive). Shuert (1970) in an investigation of the cognitive style of successful mathematics students, found that the following elements of cognitive style were unique to the successful group:

- Major theoretical visual quantitative T(VQ)
- Major theoretical auditory quantitative T(AQ)
- Minor theoretical auditory linguistic T′(AL)
- Minor associates determinant A′
- Appraisal inference L
- Deductive inference K.

A study by Dehnke (1966) indicated that there seems to be a common cognitive style pattern among successful English teachers, as judged by their supervisors.

Fragale (1969) explored the individual and collective cognitive styles of those students enrolled in specific courses offered by the department of industrial technology and of those faculty members teaching the courses. He found that "collective styles" could be identified for both the teachers and the students studied.

The work of Wasser (1960), Schroeder (n.d.), and McAdam (1971) indicates a high probability of matching the cognitive style of the students with that of the teacher. Blanzy (1970) revealed that when programed instruction was used as the stimulus material, subjects whose cognitive styles included theoretical visual linguistic T(VL) and individuality (I) showed greater achievement gain than the subjects whose styles did not possess either of these elements.

These and other investigations support the feasibility of identifying a collective set of cognitive style elements for both teachers and students.

There are many trends in education today, including competency-based education, instructional development, and systematic planning to mention a few. Each of these has as its focus concern for the individual learner. Educational cognitive style appears to be a key in coming to know those characteristics.

References

Berry, J. J.; Sutton, T. J.; and McBeth, L. S. *Bibliography of the Educational Sciences with Commentary.* rev. ed. Bloomfield Hills, Mich.: Oakland Community College, 1975.

Blanzy, James John. "Cognitive Style as an Input to a Mathematics Curriculum System: An Exploratory Study in the Educational Sciences." Doctoral dissertation, Wayne State University, 1970.

Champlin, Nathaniel L. "Controls in Qualitative Thought." Doctoral dissertation, Columbia University, 1952.

Dehnke, Ronald E. "An Exploration of the Possible Isomorphism of Cognitive Style and Successful Teaching of Secondary School English." Doctoral dissertation, Wayne State University, 1966.

DeLoach, J. F. "An Analysis of Cognitive Style Disparity as an Antecedent of Cognitive Dissonance in Instructional Evaluation: An Exploratory Study in the Educational Sciences." Doctoral dissertation, Wayne State University, 1969.

DeNike, Lee. "An Exploratory Study of Cognitive Style as a Predictor of Learning from Simulation Games." Doctoral dissertation, Kent State University, 1973.

DeNike, Lee, and Strother, Seldon D. "A Learner Characteristic Vital to Instructional Development: Educational Cognitive Style." *Educational Technology,* September 1975, pp. 58–59.

———. *Media Prescription and Utilization as Determined by Educational Cognitive Style.* Athens, Ohio: Prescriptive Teaching.

Fragale, Marvin Joseph. "A Pilot Study of Cognitive Styles of Selected Faculty Members and Students in a Community College Setting." Doctoral dissertation, Wayne State University, 1969.

Fragale, Marvin J.; Svagr, Virginia; and Zussman, Steven. "Personalizing Human Interactions Utilizing Cognitive Style Mapping." Unpublished manuscript, Oakland Community College, 1971.

Guilford, J. P. "Dimensions of Intellect," International Colloquium on Factor Analysis, Paris, 1955: "The Structure of Intellect." Paper presented to National Academy of Sciences, Pasadena, California, November 1955.

Hand, James D. "Matching Programmed Instruction Packages and an Instructional Setting to Students in Terms of Cognitive Style: An Exploratory Study." Doctoral dissertation, Michigan State University, 1972.

Heffernan, Helen. "The Diverse Needs of the Learners to Be Served." Speech delivered at the National Conference on Rural Education at Oklahoma City, October 2, 1967.

Hill, Joseph E. "Cognitive Style as an Educational Science." Unpublished manuscript, Oakland Community College.

——— . "The Educational Sciences." Unpublished manuscript, Oakland Community College.

——— . "Symbols and Their Meanings." Unpublished manuscript, Oakland Community College, 1969.

——— . "A Synopsis of the Educational Sciences." Unpublished paper, Wayne State University, Detroit, 1967.

Hill, Joseph E., and Kerber, August. *Models, Methods, and Analytical Procedures in Educational Research.* Detroit, Mich.: Wayne State University Press, 1967.

Hill, Joseph E., and Setz., Betty D. "Educational Sciences at Oakland Community College." Unpublished paper, Oakland Community College, 1970.

Hill Educational Sciences Foundation. *The Educational Sciences: A Conceptual Framework.* West Bloomfield, Mich.: Hill Educational Sciences Foundation.

Hoogasian, Vaughn. "An Examination of Cognitive Style Profiles as Indicators of Performance Associated with a Selected Discipline." Doctoral dissertation, Wayne State University, 1970.

McAdam, Glenn F. "Personalizing Instruction Through the Educational Science of Cognitive Style and Teaching Style." Doctoral dissertation, Wayne State University, 1971.

Morshead, Richard W. "Toward an Educational Conception of Mental." Doctoral dissertation, Wayne State University, 1964.

Nunney, Derek N. *Educational Sciences Dissertation Abstracts* (67). Bloomfield, Hills, Mich.: Oakland Community College, December 1978.

Nunney, Derek, N., and Hill, Joseph E. "Personalized Educational Programs." *Audiovisual Instruction,* February 1972, pp. 10–15.

Rankin, Stuart C. "A Theory of an Isomorphism-Model-Hypothesis Method of Thought." Doctoral dissertation, Wayne State University, 1964.

Saunders, Thomas Frank. "A Philosophic Analysis into Emotion as a Category of Education and Psychology." Doctoral dissertation, Wayne State University, 1963.

Schroeder, Alran. "A Study of the Relationship Between Student's and Teacher's Cognitive Style and Student Derived Teacher Evaluations." Doctoral dissertation, Wayne State University, 1969.

Shuert, Keith L. "A Study to Determine Whether a Selected Type of Cognitive Style Predisposes One to Do Well in Mathematics." Doctoral dissertation, Wayne State University, 1970.

Strother, Seldon D. "An Analysis of Selected Cognitive Style Elements as Predictors of Achievement from a Didactic Film." Doctoral dissertation, Kent State University, 1973.

———. *The Way We Learn: Educational Cognitive Style.* Athens, Ohio: Prescriptive Teaching, 1975.

———. "The Classroom Learning Center with a Cognitive Style Mapping Interface." *T.H.E. JOURNAL: Technological Horizons in Education,* May 1980, pp. 42–44; 49.

Villemain, Francis I. "The Qualitative Character of Intelligence." Doctoral dissertation, Columbia University, 1952.

Wasser, Lawrence. "An Investigation into Cognitive Style as a Facet of Teachers' Systems of Student Appraisal." Doctoral dissertation, University of Michigan, 1960.

Wyett, Jerry L. "A Pilot Study to Analyze Cognitive Style and Teaching Style with Reference to Selected Strata of the Defined Educational Sciences." Doctoral dissertation, Wayne State University, 1967.

CHAPTER 11

Learning Style Inventory Development and Continuing Research

Gary E. Price

The Learning Style Inventory (Dunn, Dunn, and Price, 1975, 1978) is an instrument designed to assess how individuals in grades 3 through 12 prefer to learn. The variables, which encompass 24 areas derived from a content and factor analysis, are: (a) immediate environment—sound, light, temperature, and design; (b) emotionality—motivation, persistence, responsibility, and the need for structure or flexibility; (c) sociological needs—self, peers, adults, and/or varied; and (d) physical needs—perceptual preferences, time of day, food intake, and mobility (Figure 1).

Development of Learning Style Inventory

In the early 1970s, Rita Dunn extensively reviewed the literature, identifying the variables that affected student learning. Areas were identified and questions developed in each area. The initial instrument was called a learning style questionnaire, and included 223 items. This instrument was administered to several hundred individuals and reliability analyses were performed to show which items exhibited the highest internal consistency with each of the areas. Based on this analysis, the items that were found to be most consistent and reliable were used to develop the 1975 version of the Learning Style Inventory (LSI). This version was administered to 1,200 individuals in five states.

The items then were factor analyzed to establish a statistical and mathematical model for identifying independent and discrete areas. The factor analysis did not differentiate between individuals preferring to learn with one or two others and those individuals preferring to learn with several other people. Consequently, a combined factor was identified which is now called "a peer-oriented learner," one who prefers to learn not alone, but with either one, two, or several other people.

Questions designed to differentiate between tactile and kinesthetic preferences did not provide independence in those areas and were combined. The literature was reviewed to determine what "kinesthetic" and "tactile" might mean and how the terms were different. We defined tactile as the desire to

Diagnosing Learning Styles

STIMULI		ELEMENTS			
ENVIRONMENTAL	Sound	Light	Temperature	Design	
EMOTIONAL	Motivation	Persistence	Responsibility	Structure	
SOCIOLOGICAL	Peers	Self	Pair	Team	Adult	Varied
PHYSICAL	Perceptual	Intake	Time	Mobility	
PSYCHOLOGICAL	Analytic / Global	Cerebral Dominance	Impulsive / Reflective		

Designed by: Rita Dunn
Kenneth Dunn

learn by touching, and kinesthetic as the desire to learn by totally experiencing, being active, moving, feeling and/or being involved physically in one's learning.

A new set of items was developed for tactile and kinesthetic preferences and administered to 300 individuals. A subsequent factor analysis found that the LSI did differentiate between tactile and kinesthetic preferences. This information and other reliability analyses lead to the 1978 revision of the LSI.

We continued to use the factor analytic model to research the Learning Style Inventory and to improve its internal consistency and its ability to differentiate various areas that affect how people prefer to learn.

The factor analytic model was similarly used to develop an adult instrument, the Productivity Environmental Preference Survey (PEPS), (Dunn, Dunn, and Price, 1979). It was found that adults preferring to learn in the early morning and in late morning formed a continuum with people who prefer to learn in the afternoon and in the evening. (These areas on the LSI are not on a continuum; i.e., high scores in the morning do not necessarily result in low scores for the afternoon.) In addition, the factor analysis for adults indicated that supervisor-motivated and adult-motivated preferences were the same and should be combined on the adult version.

As a result of these differences, there are 21 areas on the PEPS and 24 areas on the LSI.

Research Applications of Learning Style

To date, there have been many research applications of learning style. These are reported elsewhere in this volume (Rita Dunn, p. 142). Several issues clearly suggest questions for future research. One such question involves matching teaching and learning style—encompassing both the way the student prefers to learn and the way the teacher prefers to teach. How the teacher prefers to teach may relate to the way he or she analyzes and synthesizes information. This teacher style in turn may interact with how students prefer to learn and how they analyze and synthesize information.

A similar question focuses on learning when there is a match or when there is dissonance between a teacher's and student's learning style.

Much research is developing in the area of brain functioning and in the interaction of brain functioning and learning style. At this point, there is little definitive data relating hemispheric dominance to actual learning. Available studies seem to indicate a great deal of variation among individuals in terms of information processing and brain organization (Levy, 1981).

A number of questions in ongoing research deal with maturation and adaptation. Maturation studies suggest that learning styles may change because of development. We do not know, however, whether preferences in learning style change primarily because of the changes in the individual, the person's ability to adapt to different types of instruction, or an interaction of the two. It is possible that individuals who are bright and flexible may more readily persist with inappropriate existing methods of instruction; whereas individuals who are not so flexible may not adapt so easily and may eventually drop out of school. It would be helpful to determine how changes in instruction influence a student's learning style and his or her ability to understand and process information.

Summary

Overall, the study of learning styles indicates that there are many differences among individuals and how they prefer to learn. Student learning styles change across grade levels, although it is not certain as to whether the changes are a function of development or maturation. Further research and analysis of how instruction relates to learning style should provide new insight into methodology so that teachers can respond more effectively in the classroom.

References

Dunn, R.; Dunn, K.; and Price, G. E. "Learning Style Inventory." Lawrence, Kans.: Price Systems, Inc., 1975, 1978.

———. "Productivity Environmental Preference Survey." Lawrence, Kans.: Price Systems, Inc., 1979.

———. "Learning Style Inventory Manual." Lawrence, Kans.: Price Systems, Inc., 1981.

Griggs, S., and Price, G. E. "Self-Concept Relates to Learning Style in the Junior High." *Phi Delta Kappan,* April 1981, p. 604.

Krimsky, J. S. "A Comparative Study of the Effects of Matching and Mismatching Fourth Grade Students with Their Learning Style Preferences for the Environmental Element of Light and Their Subsequent Reading Speed and Accuracy Scores." Doctoral dissertation, St. John's University, Jamaica, N.Y., 1982.

Levy, J. Presentation made at National Conference on Learning Style and Brain Research, New Orleans, La., November 14, 1981; see p. 173

Lynch, P. K. "An Analysis of the Relationships Among Academic Achievement, Attendance, and the Individual Learning Style Time Preferences of Eleventh and Twelfth Grade Students Identified as Initial or Chronic Truants in a Suburban New York School District." Doctoral dissertation, St. John's University, Jamaica, N.Y., 1981.

Pizzo, J. "An Investigation of the Relationship Between Selected Acoustic Environments and Sound, an Element of Learning Style, as They Affect Sixth-Grade Students' Reading Achievement and Attitudes." Doctoral dissertation, St. John's University, Jamaica, N.Y., 1981.

Price, G.; Dunn, R.; and Dunn, K. "Learning Style Research Report." Lawrence, Kans.: Price Systems, Inc., 1976, 1977.

CHAPTER 12

The Identification of Learning Styles Among Young Children

Janet Perrin

Every early childhood teacher is aware that some youngsters encounter frustration in school as early as kindergarten; they "tune out" and many never "tune in" again. I became interested in the identification of learning style characteristics of young children (K–2) because it was apparent that certain instructional experiences actually inhibited some young children's ability to learn.

The *Learning Style Inventory: Primary* (LSI:P) was designed to reveal the ways young children prefer to learn (learning style), and is based on the learning style model of Rita and Kenneth Dunn. The youngster, kindergarten through second grade, responds to pictures and questions that determine his or her learning style preferences in four broad areas.

The Environment

Sound: Does the child work well in absolute silence, or does he or she need some background sound to concentrate?

Light: Is the child comfortable in a brightly lighted room, or is he or she light sensitive and better able to concentrate with softer illumination?

Temperature: Does the child become distracted when he or she feels too warm or too cool?

Design: Does the child work better seated at a table or desk (formal design), or sprawled on the floor or in a soft chair (informal design)?

Emotional Tendencies

Motivation: Is the child eager to learn? Does he or she strive to please the teacher, family, or self?

Persistence and Responsibility: Does the child complete tasks? Does he or she accept and follow through on assignments?

Structure: Does the child follow directions? Is he or she able to make choices?

Sociological Needs

Peers

Adults   With whom does the child work best?

Alone

Physical Requirements

Perception: Does the child remember better when he or she uses visual, auditory, tactual, or kinesthetic materials—or a combination of these?

Intake: Is the child better able to concentrate if he or she nibbles or drinks something while working?

Time: Is the child's energy level higher in the morning, afternoon, or evening?

Mobility: Does the child lose interest if not permitted freedom to move around?

The LSI:P consists of 12 charts, each concerned with a distinct learning style element, an individual student profile form, and directions for administering and scoring. Teachers may test for one or several learning style elements at each session, depending on the ages and attention spans of the students.

Since young children often respond in ways they think will please their teachers, it is wise to acquaint the students with the format of a questionnaire before administering the Inventory. Assure them that there can be no wrong or right answers. Discuss the concept of learning styles and why it is important to know how each child learns best.

Administration is on an individual basis and students respond verbally. The entire Inventory takes approximately 20 minutes to administer. Teachers report that the value gained from personally interviewing each student justifies the time spent in administration. Figures 1 and 2 illustrate the "structure" element of the Inventory.

Figure 1.

Recent use of the LSI:P has yielded the following interesting data describing the learning style preferences of 75 randomly selected, first grade students.

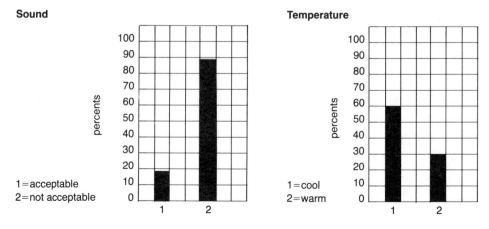

Light

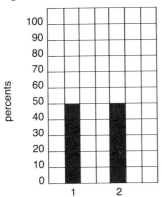

1=low
2=bright

Design

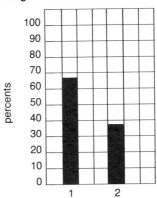

1=formal
2=informal

Structure

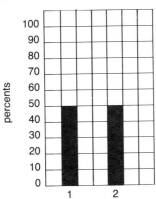

1=needs
2=needs little

Mobility

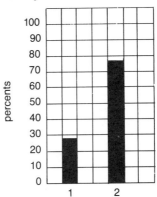

1=requires
2=does not require

Intake

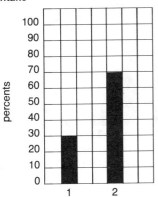

1=requires
2=does not require

Responsibility, Persistence

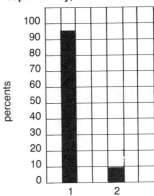

1=is
2=is not

Time

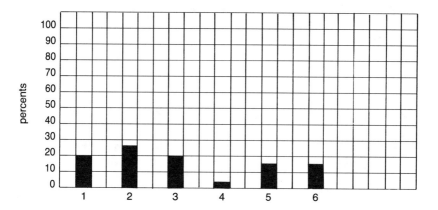

1=morning
2=afternoon
3=evening
4=morning
   and evening
5=morning
   and afternoon
6=afternoon
   and evening

Sociological

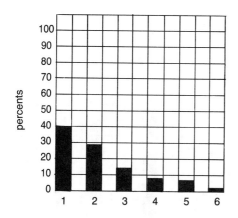

1=alone
2=adult
3=peers
4=alone, peers
5=adult, peers
6=alone, adult

Motivation

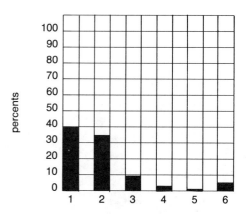

1=adult, teacher, and self
2=teacher, adult, and self
3=adult, self, and teacher
4=teacher, self, and adult
5=self
6=unmotivated

Perception

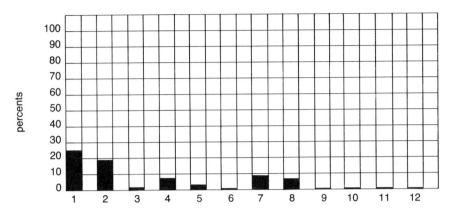

1=kinesthetic, visual	4=tactual, visual	7=visual, kinesthetic
2=kinesthetic, tactual	5=tactual, auditory	8=visual, tactual
3=kinesthetic, auditory	6=tactual, kinesthetic	9=visual, auditory
	10=auditory, kinesthetic	
	11=auditory, tactual	
	12=auditory, visual	

The LSI:P includes a grid system for the hand scoring of each learning style element. The completed grid shown in Figure 3 provides a composite learning style profile of the student.

Fraction scores closest to unity (one) are considered elements important to the youngster's learning style. Instructional environments and strategies for individual students may be developed directly from the student profile form (Figure 4).

This developing instrument was used by teachers in more than 400 school districts throughout the United States, between 1977 and 1981. In response to input on its administration, scoring, and interpretation, the Inventory has been revised several times.[1] It is through such continuing experimentation with learning style instruments, and through an increased awareness and sharing among educators, that learning styles may become the central focus of instruction.

---

1. Copies of the experimental instrument may be obtained from the Center for the Study of Learning and Teaching Styles, St. John's University, Utopia Parkway, Jamaica, NY 11439.

Figure 2.

Element: *Structure*

Introduction

Display the picture.

(Point to picture 1) The little boy in this picture likes to have his teacher show him exactly what to do and when to do it.

(Point to picture 2) The little boy in this picture likes to decide for himself what to do and when to do it.

I am going to ask you a few questions about how you like to do your schoolwork.

Questions

1. When you do your schoolwork:
    1. Do you like your teacher to tell you what to do next?
   or
    2. Do you like to decide yourself what to do next?

2.   1. Do you like your teacher to tell you exactly how to do something?
   or
    2. Do you like to do things your own way?

3. In school do you like your teacher to:
    1. Check each part of your work as you are working?
   or
    2. Check all of your work at the end of the day?

4. In school do you like to get:
    1. One page of your work at a time?
   or
    2. Many pages of your work at one time?

5. Let's look at the picture again. Remember, in this picture (point to 1) the little boy likes his teacher to show him exactly what to do and when to do it. In this picture, (point to 2) the little boy likes to decide for himself what to do and when to do it. Which picture shows the way you like to do your schoolwork? (Have the child point to the picture or respond verbally.)

Figure 3.
STUDENT PROFILE

NAME __Joshua__

GRADE __/__ TEACHER __2__ DATE _____

Sound

						Score
not acceptable	1	1		1	1	1/5
acceptable			2			4/5
Response	2	2	1	2	2	

Light

						Score
low			1	1	1	2/5
bright	2				2	3/5
Response	1	2	2	2	1	

Temperature

						Score
cool	1	1	1	1	1	0/5
warm						5/5
Response	2	2	2	2	2	

Design

						Score
formal	1	1	1	1	1	0/5
informal						5/5
Response	2	2	2	2	2	

Sociological

							Score
alone	1	1			1	1	1	0/5
adult		2					2	3/5
peers			3					4/5
Response	3	2	3	2	2	3	3	

Structure

						Score
needs		1		1	1	2/5
needs little	2		2			3/5
Response	1	2	1	2	2	

Intake

						Score
does not require		1	1	1	1	1/5
requires	2					4/5
Response	1	2	2	2	2	

Time

						Score
morning	1		1	1	1	0/4
afternoon		2		2	2	1/4
evening						4/4
Response	2	3	3	3	3	

Responsibility & Persistence

						Score
is not	1	1	1	1	1	0/5
is						5/5
Response	2	2	2	2	2	

Mobility

						Score
does not require		1		1	1	2/5
requires	2		2			3/5
Response	1	2	1	2	2	

Motivation

							Score
teacher							3/3
adult						2	2/3
self						3	2/3
unmotivated	4	4	4	4	4	4	4	0/7
Response	3	1	2	2	1	3	1	

Perception

									Score
tactual					1	1	1		2/5
auditory	2		2	2	2		2		0/5
visual		3					3		3/5
kinesthetic			4				4		4/5
Response	3	1	3	3	1	4	4	4	4

Figure 4. Prescription based on Learning Style Inventory: Primary Profile

Joshua—Sound is acceptable 4/5; Warm temperature 5/5; Informal design 5/5; Works with peers and adult; Requires intake 4/5; Works in the evening 4/4; Motivated by teacher, adult, self; Kinesthetic, visual, tactual.

Prescription: Assign Joshua to work in a carpeted area with pillows on the floor in a warm section of the room. Nutritious snacks should be available. Provide opportunities for team and paired assignments and frequent teacher interaction. Assign projects and resources for use at home in the evening. Assign multi-sensory resources, particularly kinesthetic tasks and projects accompanied by visual stimuli.

CHAPTER 13

Reading Styles: Key to Preventing Reading Failure

Marie Carbo

The tragic mismatching of reading programs and individual learning styles hinders learning, causing many youngsters to struggle, become frustrated, and fail. As a result, thousands of students develop an aversion to reading, undergo years of extensive and costly remediation and, too often, drop out of school.

For the past seven years, I have conducted research on reading and learning styles, taught severely learning disabled youngsters to read through their individual learning styles, and developed and tested the *Reading Style Inventory*. Both the research and my personal experiences suggest that countless students with reading difficulties have been mistaught. Restak (1979) has documented the auditory superiority of girls over boys and boys' tendency to be kinesthetic longer than girls. Considering that phonics and teacher lecture predominate in many primary reading programs, it is not surprising that boys have lower reading achievement than girls in the primary grades and outnumber girls in special reading and learning disabilities classes about four to one (Johnson and Greenbaum, 1980).

Only recently have educators begun the important task of exploring and researching a diagnostic-prescriptive approach to improving reading instruction. This critical shift in focus from attempts to discover the best reading approaches for *all* students toward efforts to discover the best reading approaches for a *particular* youngster based on learning style diagnosis can have a far-reaching, positive effect on the quality of reading instruction in the future.

Learning Style Research

Research indicates that achievement increases when youngsters are taught according to their individual learning styles. Students, for example, read significantly better when taught with the amount of sound (Pizzo, 1981) and/or light preferred (Krimsky, 1981), and when they learn through their modality strengths (Bursuk, 1971; Carbo, 1978, 1980; Donovan, 1977; Urbschat, 1977; Wepman and Morency, 1975).[1]

---

1. It is important to note that much of the previous research matching reading method and modality preference has serious methodological shortcomings such as the use of unreliable or incorrect instrumentation and inadequate treatment controls.

Martin found that some youngsters learn best when provided with structure in the form of specific rules and limited choices, while others require little guidance. Scheduling high school truants at the time of day they prefer to learn results in significantly improved attendance (Lynch, 1981). Copenhaver (1979) and Cafferty (1980) report that matching learning and teaching styles results in significantly higher student achievement.

Conversely, in each of these studies, when students' learning styles were mismatched with instructional practices, achievement declined significantly.

Most of these studies were brief. When a student's educational program and learning style are mismatched for a prolonged period of time, the impact on that student's ability to learn may be profound indeed, causing failure, defeat, embarrassment, and anger.

Past research has demonstrated quite conclusively the negative effect of reading failure on a youngster's self-concept and subsequent school career. Clearly, prevention of reading failure through learning style diagnosis, evaluation, and prescription must become a major educational priority for the 1980s.

A position statement issued by the International Reading Association states, "Differences in the learning styles and abilities of children emphasize the need for a variety of approaches to meet those individual needs ("There's More to Reading," 1979). As a result of Public Law 94-142, every handicapped youngster must have a yearly Individualized Education Plan (IEP) that includes not only information about the child's performance levels but a "specific statement describing the child's learning style" (1977).

Matching Reading Methods and Learning Styles

Every reading method demands specific learning style preferences and learner strengths (Carbo, Spring 1980, September 1980). A preference describes the manner in which a youngster likes to learn, whereas a strength indicates an ability or skill possessed by the student. Matching an individual student's learning style preferences and strengths with complementary reading methods improves that youngster's chance for success. A reading method that is based on the most fundamentally incorrect assumptions about how a particular student learns will cause the most severe reading problems for that youngster.

Perceptual preferences and strengths usually are the most critical learning style elements for success with a reading method. A student might need the structure provided by the phonic method, but if he or she does not have the *auditory* abilities necessary to succeed with phonics, then that would be the wrong method to select.

The following is an abbreviated checklist of the learning style characteristics needed to succeed with three commonly used reading methods. A detailed listing may be found in the *Reading Style Inventory Manual* (Carbo, 1981b).[2]

---

2. The *Reading Style Inventory* (manual, sample test, and computer printout) is available for $11.50 from Marie Carbo, P.O. Box 41, Williston Park, N.Y. 11596.

LANGUAGE-EXPERIENCE METHOD

The student:
_____ learns best through his or her visual and tactual senses.
_____ enjoys working in an informal atmosphere.
_____ can work when people are talking.
_____ likes to work primarily with peers and alone.
_____ is motivated and persistent and needs little teacher direction.

PHONIC METHOD

The student:
_____ learns best through his or her auditory sense.
_____ enjoys working in a formal atmosphere.
_____ is adult-motivated.
_____ can learn in a group and can sit and attend for long periods.
_____ needs to work with structured materials and needs teacher direction.

INDIVIDUALIZED METHOD

The student:
_____ has good visual memory.
_____ is able to learn alone with minimal interaction with peers and teachers.
_____ can make choices from many possibilities.
_____ is not in need of a great deal of structure and teacher direction.
_____ does not need to work with structured reading materials and enjoys working in an informal atmosphere.

Diagnosing Individual Reading Styles

The current availability and extensive use of performance level tests has led to the common practice of grouping students for reading instruction according to their skill deficiencies and/or reading scores, with little or no regard for *how* an individual child learns best and should be taught. The Reading Style Inventory (RSI), based on the learning style model of Dunn and Dunn (1978), was developed to help educators select the best reading methods, materials, and teaching procedures for an individual student.

The RSI identifies 30 learning style elements that affect an individual's ability to learn to read and comprise that student's individual "reading style." It is a two-part, 52-item inventory that can be individually or group administered in approximately 30 minutes to students in grades 2 through 12. After a student's RSI is scored, the answers are grouped into patterns. Those reading methods and materials that most nearly match the youngster's reading style are recommended, with necessary modifications. Reading methods and materials that mismatch the student's learning style are also listed.

A research study conducted using the RSI with 293 second, fourth, sixth, and eighth graders yielded test-retest reliability coefficients ranging from .67

to .77 for the 13 RSI scales (Carbo, 1981b). Additional studies with larger and more representative populations of students are planned for the near future.

The following sample statements are excerpted from the perception section of the RSI.

a) When I look at words, I often mix up letters like "b" and "d."	b) When I look at words, I almost never mix up letters like "b" and "d."

a) I usually need to place my finger under the words I'm reading.	b) It doesn't help me to place my finger under the words I'm reading.

a) Many times it's hard for me to remember the sounds letters make.	b) I always remember the sounds letters make.

a) When I'm not sure how to spell a word, it helps me if I write it down.	b) When I'm not sure how to spell a word, it doesn't help me if I write it down.

Comparing Reading Styles Across Grade Levels

The 293 students tested in grades two, four, six, and eight using the Reading Style Inventory differed significantly on 10 elements of reading style. Second graders demonstrated significantly less visual and auditory strength, higher preferences for tactual and kinesthetic stimuli, and a greater need for intake and mobility than the other grades under study. Second graders were significantly more teacher-motivated and self-motivated, and preferred to read alone significantly less than fourth, sixth, and eighth graders.

Implications

These findings suggest that beginning programs need many tactual and kinesthetic resources with ample opportunity for movement and intake. It appears that as students progress in school they tend to enjoy reading less and are not encouraged to read as much by their teachers. High-interest reading programs that are responsive to individual reading styles are needed so that boys and girls continue to experience their initial enthusiasm for reading. Many young students need opportunities to interact with their teacher and peers during reading. Intermediate and junior high school students like materials that permit them to read alone. Individualized programs with a variety of books and programed/computerized materials appear to be good choices for older students.

Only 28 percent of the youngsters in this research preferred to read in the morning and many of these were second graders. It would seem that most students do *not* prefer to read in the morning—the very time of day many teachers schedule reading instruction. Older students demonstrated independent reading styles and seemed to need more choices with less teacher direction than second graders who preferred few choices and careful, exact directions from the teacher.

Comparing the Reading Styles of Good and Poor Readers

The 293 students in the RSI study were classified according to reading level and differed significantly on 10 reading style elements. On the elements of perception, intake, and mobility the reading styles of poor readers were quite similar to those of the second graders. The poor readers demonstrated significantly less visual and auditory strength, higher preferences for tactual-kinesthetic stimuli, and a greater need for intake and mobility. They were significantly more peer-motivated, less self-motivated and responsible, and preferred fewer choices than good readers. The poor readers did not prefer to read in the morning and liked their work checked significantly faster than good readers.

Implications

These findings corroborate the research of Price, Dunn, and Sanders (1980). Poor readers prefer tactual-kinesthetic experiences within an informal, highly structured environment that permits them to move about and that provides for intake. The rarity of such programs leads one to hypothesize that the reading styles of poor readers probably are not sufficiently matched in the lower grades, perhaps leading to the persistence of a need for tactual-kinesthetic stimulation, mobility, and intake in the upper grades. It would seem critical to design reading programs for the peer-motivated, tactual-kinesthetic youngsters with high mobility, quiet, and intake needs.

The overwhelming majority (86 percent) of students in the RSI study preferred to read, at least some of the time, in an informally designed area (rugs, soft chairs, and pillows). Reading environments that accommodate many reading styles are needed, especially those that provide quiet, warmth, informality, and intake—the reading style preferences of poorer readers.

Beginning Reading Programs Based on Learning Style Research

In a study of the learning styles of 3,972 subjects, Price (1980) found that young children learn most easily tactually and kinesthetically. Visual modality strength developed next, and not until grades five or six are most youngsters able to learn easily through their auditory sense. Price's findings are corroborated by the research listed in Figure 1. Keefe (1979) has reported that, "Perceptual preference seems to evolve for most students from psychomotor (tactual-kinesthetic) to visual and aural as the learner matures."

Young students tend to be global rather than analytic. They learn best when information is presented as a gestalt or whole. Many may not be ready for the step-by-step presentation of phonic rules until second or third grade. Burton (1980) found that kindergartners recalled significantly more dissimilar words (e.g., elephant, fun, circus) than similar words (e.g., cat, fat, mat). Most beginning phonics books contain similar words. It may be advisable to utilize phonics materials in the later grades if students need them and if they have the auditory and analytic abilities to recall this kind of information easily.

A particularly effective whole-word, global approach for young readers is tape-recorded storybooks followed by games about the books (Carbo, 1978, 1979). With this method, children see and hear words simultaneously within the context of high-interest stories and then practice the vocabulary presented in game form. This procedure has significantly increased the comprehension and word recognition of beginning readers and disabled readers.

Based on this research, beginning reading programs might well benefit from some redesign:

- Teach through the tactual-kinesthetic-visual senses with many "hands-on" activities.
- Use global reading methods, such as language-experience and tape-recorded storybooks.
- Provide sufficient structure and opportunities for movement and intake in an environment that includes some informal areas.

Teaching Reading Through Individual Reading Styles

To prevent reading failure and increase enjoyment and achievement, several beginning steps should prove useful.

1. Identify individual reading styles and use complementary reading methods, materials, and teaching procedures.

2. Try global reading methods, particularly with young readers and poor readers, reserving phonics for analytic youngsters with auditory strengths who can be successful with this approach.

3. Provide multisensory reading materials for youngsters who need tactual-kinesthetic reinforcement to learn. Use games, activity cards, multisensory instructional packages, beaded letters, etc.

4. Provide sufficient structure for those who need it, especially young readers and poor readers. Number and color-code materials, limit choices, give clear directions, and provide time limits for the completion of work. For the motivated, persistent, responsible youngster who is self-structured, allow more choices, give fewer directions, and provide more flexible time limits.

5. Allow youngsters to read with peers, a friend, teachers, alone, etc., depending upon the child's sociological preferences. Try computerized and programed materials for students who prefer reading alone, and games and small group techniques for those who learn best by interacting with peers.

6. Establish quiet reading sections a sufficient distance from noisier areas. The latter might be placed in hallways or alcoves.

7. Create at least two sections within a classroom by placing file cabinets or bookcases perpendicular to a wall. Design one area where youngsters may read with one peer or in small groups; provide one small, informal area containing rugs, pillows, and a soft chair.

8. Schedule reading at various times of the day, when feasible, to accommodate the preferred time of the day for your students. Be particularly sensitive to the energy highs of poor readers and use these times to teach reading. Tape record some lessons so that youngsters can listen to the recording at the time of day they learn best.

9. Provide snack periods throughout the day for students in need of intake.

Most young children come to school with the enthusiasm, interest, and the ability to learn to read. The beginning years of reading instruction are precious—not one minute should be wasted. We know that most five and six-year-olds are global, tactual, kinesthetic, visual learners. They need to touch and feel to learn. They are captivated easily by wondrous folk and fairy tales and the great children's literature. Yet beginning reading programs across the nation continue to demand that students sit quietly (most young students *need* mobility), in hard chairs (most young students *prefer* informality), and listen carefully (most young children are *not* auditory) to phonic rules (most young students are *not* analytic).

Unfortunately, too many students are not taught the way they learn best, so they fail. They undergo countless years of remediation—often being mistaught again and again. We must translate learning style research into practical classroom procedures. As reading programs are matched with individual reading styles, students will have a better chance to learn to read naturally, easily, and enthusiastically. Teaching through individual reading styles can help to prevent reading failure and its costly, debilitating effect on students.

Figure 1.
Summary of Selected Modalities/Methods Research

Investigator(s)	Subjects	Modalities* or Methods† Compared	Dominant Modality Reported
Waugh (1971)	Kindergartners	Visual, Auditory*	Visual
Burton (1980)	Kindergartners	Visual, Auditory†	Visual
Freer (1971)	First Graders	Visual, Auditory†	Visual
Pulliam (1945)	Second Graders	Visual, Kinesthetic†	Kinesthetic
Otto (1961)	Second Graders	Visual, Auditory, Kinesthetic*	Kinesthetic
Mills (1956)	Seven Year Olds	Visual, Auditory, Kinesthetic†	Visual
Waugh (1971)	Second Graders	Visual, Auditory*	Auditory
Bruininks (1970)	Third Graders	Visual, Auditory†	Visual
Mills (1956)	Eight Year Olds	Visual, Auditory, Kinesthetic†	Kinesthetic
Otto (1961)	Fourth Graders	Visual, Auditory, Kinesthetic*	Visual
Cooper & Gaeth (1967)	Fourth Graders	Visual, Auditory*	Visual
Russell (1938)	Fifth Graders	Visual, Auditory*	Auditory
Cooper & Gaeth (1967)	Twelfth Graders	Visual, Auditory*	Auditory

References

Bruininks, Robert H. "Teaching Word Recognition to Disadvantaged Boys." *Journal of Learning Disabilities,* January 1970, pp. 28–36.

Bursuk, L. "Sensory Mode and Lesson Presentation as a Factor in the Reading Comprehension Improvement of Adolescent Retarded Readers." Doctoral dissertation, City University of New York, 1971.

Burton, Elizabeth. "An Analysis of the Interaction of Field Dependent/Field Independent Learning Styles and Word Type as They Affect Word Recognition Among Kindergartners." Doctoral dissertation, St. John's University, 1980.

Cafferty, Elsie. "An Analysis of Student Performance Based upon the Degree of Match Between the Educational Cognitive Style of the Teachers and the Educational Cognitive Style of the Students." Doctoral dissertation, University of Nebraska, 1980.

Carbo, Marie. "Teaching Reading with Talking Books." *The Reading Teacher,* December 1978, pp. 267–73.

———. "How to Play with a Book." *Early Years,* February 1979, pp. 72–74.

———. "An Analysis of the Relationships Between the Modality Preferences of Kindergartners and Selected Reading Treatments as They Affect the Learning of a Basic Sight-Word Vocabulary." Doctoral dissertation, St. John's University, 1980.

———. "Matching Reading Method and Learning Style." *Learning Styles Network Newsletter,* Spring 1980, p. 5.

———. "Reading Style: Diagnosis, Evaluation, Prescription." *Academic Therapy,* September 1980, pp. 45–52.

———. *Reading Style Inventory.* E. Williston, N.Y., 1980, 1981a.

———. *Reading Style Inventory Manual.* E. Williston, N.Y., 1981b.

Chomsky, Carol. "After Decoding What?" *Language Arts* 53(1976): pp. 288–96.

Cooper, J. C., Jr., and Gaeth, J. H. "Interactions of Modality with Age and with Meaningfulness in Verbal Learning." *Journal of Educational Psychology* 58(1967): 41–44.

Copenhaver, Ronnie. "The Consistency of Student Learning Styles as Students Move from English to Mathematics." Doctoral dissertation, Indiana University, 1979.

Donovan, Margaret Ann. "The Relationship of Modality Preferences and Programs Used in Initial Reading Instruction." University of Hawaii, 1977, *Dissertation Abstracts International*, 39/01-A, 85.

Dunn, Rita, and Carbo, Marie. "The Reading Gamble: How to Improve the Odds for Every Youngster." *Learning* 8(1979): 34; 36; 40; 43.

————. "Modalities: An Open Letter to Walter Barbe, Michael Milone, and Raymond Swassing." *Educational Leadership,* February 1981, pp. 381–82.

Dunn, Rita, and Dunn, Kenneth. *Teaching Students Through Their Individual Learning Styles: A Practical Approach.* Reston, Va.: Reston Publishing Co., 1978.

Dunn, Rita; Carbo, Marie; and Burton, Elizabeth. "Breakthrough: How to Improve Reading Instruction." *Phi Delta Kappan,* May 1981, p. 675.

Freer, Frank J. "Visual and Auditory Perceptual Modality Differences as Related to Success in First Grade Reading Word Recognition." Doctoral dissertation, Rutgers University, 1971.

Johnson, C. S., and Greenbaum, G. R. "Are Boys Disabled Readers Due to Sex-Role Stereotyping?" *Educational Leadership,* March 1980, pp. 492–96.

Keefe, James W. "School Applications of the Learning Style Concept." In *Student Learning Styles: Diagnosing and Prescribing Programs.* Reston, Va.: National Association of Secondary School Principals, 1979.

Krimsky, Jeffrey. "A Comparative Study of the Effects of Matching and Mismatching Fourth Grade Students with Their Learning Style Preferences for the Environmental Element of Light and Their Subsequent Reading Speed and Accuracy Scores." Doctoral dissertation, St. John's University, 1982.

Lynch, Peter. "An Analysis of the Relationships Among Academic Achievement, Attendance, and the Individual Learning Style Time Preferences of Eleventh and Twelfth Grade Students Identified as Initial or Chronic Truants in a Suburban New York School District." Doctoral dissertation, St. John's University, 1981.

Martin, Michael Kenneth. "Effects of the Interaction Between Students' Learning Styles and High School Instructional Environment." Doctoral dissertation, University of Oregon, 1977.

Mills, Robert E. "An Evaluation of Techniques for Teaching Word Recognition." *The Elementary School Journal,* January 1956, pp. 221–25.

Otto, Wayne. "The Acquisition and Retention of Paired Associates by Good, Average and Poor Readers." *Journal of Educational Psychology* 52(1961): 241–48.

Pizzo, Jeanne. "An Investigation of the Relationships Between Selected Acoustic Environments and Sound, an Element of Learning Style, as They Affect Sixth Grade Students' Reading Achievement and Attitudes." Doctoral dissertation, St. John's University, 1981.

"Policies for the Development of Written Individualized Programs." Editorial, *Exceptional Children* 43(1977): 358–59.

Price, Gary E.; Dunn, Rita; and Sanders, William. "Reading Achievement and Learning Style Characteristics." *The Clearing House* 54(1980): 223–26.

Pulliam, R. A. "Indented Word Cards as a Sensory-Motor Aid in Vocabulary Development." *Peabody Journal of Education* 23 (1945): 38–42.

Restak, Richard M. "The Other Difference Between Boys and Girls." In *Student Learning Styles: Diagnosing and Prescribing Programs.* Reston, Va.: National Association of Secondary School Principals, 1979, pp. 75–80.

Russell, R. D. "A Comparison of Two Methods of Learning." *Journal of Educational Research* 18 (1938): 235–39.

"There's More to Reading Than Some Folks Say." A position statement from the Board of Directors of the International Reading Association, in a letter from the President, Roger Farr, November 3, 1979.

Urbschat, Karen Spagenberg. "A Study of Preferred Learning Modes and Their Relationship to the Amount of Recall of CVC Trigrams." Doctoral dissertation, Wayne State University, 1977.

Waugh, R. P. "The Relationship Between Individual Modality Preference and Performance Under Four Instructional Procedures." Doctoral dissertation, University of Oregon, 1971.

Wepman, Joseph, and Morency, Anne. *Perceptual Development and Learning: An Experimental Study on Modality Reading Instruction. Section II. Final Report.* U.S. Department of Health, Education and Welfare: ERIC Document Reproduction Service ED 125 164, 1975.

CHAPTER 14

Measuring the Productivity Preferences of Adults

Kenneth J. Dunn

The Productivity Environmental Preference Survey (PEPS) is the first comprehensive approach to an adult's individual productivity and learning style. The PEPS instrument can be an important and useful first step toward analyzing the conditions under which an adult is most likely to produce, achieve, create, problem-solve, or learn.

Careful analysis of each person's profile data will identify those elements that are critical to his or her productivity style. Further, the instrument aids in prescribing the type of environment, working conditions, activities, and motivating factors that would maximize individual output. Finally, those productivity elements that are characteristic of highly rated employees may be used to establish criteria for recruiting, screening, and selection decisions.

The Productivity Environmental Preference Survey analyzes individual adult's personal preferences for each of 18 different elements and was developed through content and factor analysis. It is a comprehensive approach to the identification of how adults prefer to function, learn, concentrate, and perform in their occupational or educational activities in the following areas:

- Immediate environment (sound, temperature, light, and design);
- Emotionality (motivation, responsibility, persistence, and the need for either structure or flexibility);
- Sociological needs (self oriented, colleague oriented, authority oriented, and/or combined ways); and
- Physical needs (perceptual preferences(s), time of day, intake, and mobility).

Questions concerning each area are presented; selected responses tend to reveal highly personalized characteristics that, when combined, represent the ways in which an individual prefers to work or concentrate. The 21 factors (based on 18 elements) include the following:

1. Sound
2. Light
3. Warmth
4. Formal Design
5. Motivated/Unmotivated
6. Persistent
7. Responsible
8. Structure
9. Learning Alone
10. Peer Oriented Learner

11. Authority Oriented Learner
12. Several Ways
13. Auditory Preferences
14. Visual Preferences
15. Tactile Preferences
16. Kinesthetic Preferences

17. Requires Intake
18. Morning/Evening
19. Late Morning
20. Afternoon
21. Needs Mobility.

Administration of the PEPS Instrument

The 100 questions are answered on the Likert Scale, i.e., Strongly Agree (5) to Strongly Disagree (1). Because many of the questions in the instrument are highly relative and subjective, individuals are encouraged to give immediate reactions to each question on an impulsive, "feeling" basis to avoid too much reflection and analysis.

Interviews often are valuable in administering the survey. The one-to-one relationship that develops as the supervisor questions an individual about his or her productivity preferences can provide new insights into a person's attitudes, motivational framework, and thinking that might not be possible through written checklists, scales, or other directed responses.

Selected Research Studies Using the Productivity Environmental Preference Survey

Initial correlational studies were conducted during the 1976–1980 period to determine whether differences existed among adults at various levels of academic involvement and employment. In a limited number of instances, specific productivity style characteristics were assessed to determine possible patterns with implications for improved performance. Although the data is too sparse for any generalizations to be offered, some conclusions were drawn based on observations and employer/supervisor reports which offer promise of increased productivity and other benefits if PEPS were used extensively as a diagnostic-prescriptive instrument.

1. *Executives in Training* (N=123)

Young, upwardly mobile executives in a large corporation varied widely in their response to the Productivity Environmental Preference Survey, yet all 123 were trained and worked in the same environment. Planning and careful change based on their responses increased productivity, motivation, and positive attitudes toward both themselves and the organization for which they worked.

A. *While concentrating on work-related assignments, a substantial number preferred:*

Music or Different Types of Sound in the Environment	25
Bright Light	37
Formal Design (straight chair, desk)	54
Structure and Direction from Supervisors	36
Working Alone	46

Learning by Listening	5
Learning by Seeing, Reading	26
Learning by Doing (involvement in real life experiences)	70
Working Early in the Morning	36
Beginning Work at 10 a.m.	36
Mobility, Ability To Move Around on the Job	23

B. *Another group preferred:*

Quiet	13
Low Light	6
Structuring Their Own Schedules and Work	25
Working with Peers	29
Not Learning by Listening	43
Not Learning by Viewing	25
Working in the Afternoon	41
Not Moving Around on the Job	15

2. Male-Female Graduate Students

Females in this sample tended to prefer a formal design, structured schedules and directions, a variety of learning situations (alone, with peers, with adults, in pairs, etc.), and less authority. Males preferred a less formal design and less structure, but were authority oriented.

3. Male-Female Undergraduate Students

In a relatively large sample (females 124 and males 98), the females preferred brighter light, a warm learning environment, structure, and kinesthetic learning (by firsthand involvement, "whole body" activity, or real-life experiences).

The males preferred dimmer light, a cooler learning environment, less structure, and non-kinesthetic learning.

4. Undergraduate Students

Living Off Campus (N=151)	Living on Campus (N=71)
Preferred:	
Dim light	Brighter light
Learning with peers	Learning alone
Learning in the morning	Learning in several ways
	Learning in the evening

5. Productivity Style and Grade Point Averages

A. Undergraduate Students (N=148) GPA 2.90.

Those students were responsible; preferred mobility, working in the early morning, learning by listening and through a variety of ways, but not kinesthetically.

Their sense of responsibility and ability to move about (mobility) contributed most to their grade point averages.

B. *Graduate Students* GPA 3.44.

Of greatest consequence was motivation, learning in an informal design, learning in the afternoon, learning by listening, and *not* being authority-oriented (nonconforming). Also important were learning in the late morning, kinesthetic and visual learning, structure, peer orientation, and a need for warmth. This group did *not* prefer mobility, intake (food and drink), and learning alone.

Another group of studies was conducted to determine whether adult learning/productivity style appeared to be related to either Global/Analytic, Field Dependent/Independent, or Right/Left Hemispheric inclinations. The population for this investigation was comprised of graduate students at a large urban university.

6. *Global Cognitive Style* (N=41) From Sigel's Cognitive Style Test (1967).

Those who scored as high globals were highly motivated and preferred the late morning and the afternoon, bright light, learning alone, and an informal design.

They did not require mobility, were not persistent, were not authority-oriented, and did not prefer to learn in several ways.

7. *Right and Left Handed* (N=41) From Zenhausern's Hemispheric Activation Test (1979).

Right	Left
Preferred sound	Preferred quiet
Motivated	Less motivated
Responsible	Less responsible
Peer oriented*	Learning in several ways
Visual*	Auditory and tactile
Early morning or evening	Late morning and afternoon*
Less persistent	More persistent

*Contributed most to the Discriminate Equation

8. *Field Dependent and Field Independent* (N=41) From Witkin's Embedded Figures Test (1971).

Field Independent	Field Dependent
Preferred mobility	Preferred structure
Preferred sound	Late morning
Preferred formal design	Learning alone
Learning in several ways	Learning kinesthetically
Learning visually	Were self-motivated
Were more responsible	
More persistent	

Implications

Data on learning/productivity preferences have implications for recruiting, selecting, evaluating, matching, promoting, planning, designing, special programing, working patterns, and time schedules.

Schools, corporations, and other organizations could identify the productivity style elements that are characteristic of consistently high performance employees. Those characteristics then could be used in screening and selecting the potentially best candidates for specific situations.

Another important use would be the identification of those elements that are critical to an individual employee's productivity style. Supervisors, with the aid of the employee, then could prescribe the type of environment, working conditions, and activities that would capitalize on those productivity style characteristics.

This hypothesis was substantiated by the Director of Instruction of the Antilles Consolidated School Systems, U.S. NAVSTA, in Ceiba, Puerto Rico (Peeples, 1981) who used the PEPS to identify the productivity styles of a group of media specialists who were involved in a participatory management approach.

Using the composite and individual information made available through the instrument, staff members began to share their knowledge of themselves with each other. Tasks requiring a cohesive small group were self selected by peer oriented learners; research and creative problem solving were tackled by those who indicated they preferred to work alone. The individuals who were authority oriented began to emerge as thoughtful, task oriented leaders in a leaderless group.

One year later the supervisor wrote that the PEPS not only served as a key to team building, but also to time management for the director who had increased time to focus energy on areas other than the conventional supervision tasks.

A simple application was employed by the author to test his administrative council on time preference. Eleven of 12 administrators and supervisors preferred working, thinking, solving, and creating early in the morning. All council meetings, previously held at 2:15 p.m., were changed to 8 a.m.

The improvements were astonishing. Afternoon meetings had always consumed two to three hours despite strong management efforts at control. Since the meeting time was changed, breakfast has been served from 8:00 to 8:20 and the meeting is over by 9:15 or 9:20. Problem solving ability and creative alternates have improved and, best of all, the meeting time has been reduced to one hour.

References

Dunn, Rita, and Dunn, Kenneth. "Learning Style as a Criterion for Placement in Alternative Programs." *Phi Delta Kappan,* December 1974, pp. 275–79.

Dunn, Rita, and Dunn, Kenneth. *Administrator's Guide to New Programs for Faculty Management and Evaluation.* West Nyack, N.Y.: Parker Publishing Co., 1977.

Dunn, Rita, and Dunn, Kenneth. *Teaching Students Through Their Individual Learning Styles: A Practical Approach.* Reston, Va.: Reston Publishing Co., 1978.

Dunn, Rita, and Dunn, Kenneth. "Learning Styles/Teaching Styles: Should They?—Can They?—Be Matched?" *Educational Leadership,* January 1979, pp. 238–44.

Dunn, Rita; Dunn, Kenneth; and Price, Gary E. "Learning as a Matter of Style." *The Journal,* School Administrators Association of New York State, Fall 1976, pp. 11–12.

———. "Diagnosing Learning Styles: A Prescription for Avoiding Malpractice Suits Against School Systems." *Phi Delta Kappan,* January 1977, pp. 418–20.

———. "Identifying Individual Learning Styles and the Instructional Methods and/or Resources to Which They Respond." Paper presented at the annual conference of the Association for Supervision and Curriculum Development, Houston, Texas, March 1977.

———. "Identifying Individual Learning Styles." In *Student Learning Styles: Diagnosing and Prescribing Programs.* Reston, Va.: National Association of Secondary School Principals, 1979, pp. 39–54.

Fiske, Edward B. "Teachers Adjust Schooling to Fit Students' Individuality." *The New York Times,* Tuesday, December 29, 1981.

Kaiser, H. F. "The Varimax Criterion for Analytic Rotation in Factor Analysis." *Psychometrika* 23(1958): 187–200.

Lemmon, Patricia. "Step by Step Leadership into Learning Styles." *Early Years,* January 1982.

Marcus, Lee. "A Comparison of Selected 9th Grade Male and Female Students' Learning Styles." *The Journal,* School Administrators Association of New York State, January 1977, pp. 27–28.

Maslow, Abraham. *Motivation and Personality.* New York: Harper & Row, 1954.

Moore, Leo B. "How to Manage Improvement." *How Successful Executives Handle People: 12 Studies on Communication and Management Skills.* Boston. *Harvard Business Review,* 1951–1960, pp. 111–112.

Peeples, Gay. "Diagnosing Adult Learning Styles to Promote Managerial Change." *Learning Styles Network Newsletter,* Winter 1981.

Price, Gary E. "Research Using the Productivity Environmental Preference Survey." Paper presented at the Second Annual Conference on Teaching Students Through Their Individual Learning Style, New York City, July, 1980.

Price, Gary E.; Dunn, Rita; and Dunn, Kenneth. "Identifying Individual Learning Styles and the Instructional Methods and/or Resources to Which Handicapped Youngsters Respond." *Early Childhood Education.* Wayne, N.J.: Avery Publishing Group, 1977, pp. 221–27.

Price, Gary E.; Dunn, Rita; and Dunn, Kenneth. *Productivity Environmental Preference Survey; PEPS Manual.* Lawrence, Kans.: Price Sytems, 1979, 1981.

Rummel, R. J. *Applied Factor Analysis.* Evanston, Ill.: Northwestern University Press, 1970.

Zenhausern, Robert; Dunn, Rita; Cavanaugh, David P.; and Everle, Betty M. "Do Left and Right 'Brained' Students Learn Differently?" *The Roeper Review,* September 1981, pp. 36–39.

Teaching Students Through Their Individual Learning Styles: A Research Report

Rita Dunn

T hose of us who became involved with learning styles during the 1960s were impressed with the increased achievement that resulted when students' unique characteristics were responded to in laboratory settings (Dunn, 1971; Dunn and Shockley, 1970, 1971). It took years of further experimentation to develop a practical system that teachers could use to address 30-36 different style elements in the same classroom (Dunn and Dunn, 1972, 1975, 1978); it was almost a decade before sufficient data verified that system's positive impact on instruction in many states (Cavanaugh, 1981; Fiske, 1981; Lemmon, 1982).

Researchers at St. John's University's Center for the Study of Learning and Teaching Styles have been experimenting with some 21 different elements of style (see Diagnosing Learning Styles model, p. 116). Well-designed and carefully-conducted research now documents that teaching students through their individual learning styles results in: (1) increased academic achievement; (2) improved attitudes toward school; and, (3) reduced discipline problems. It is important that teachers and administrators become aware of that research so that they understand the need for learning styles instructional programs in our schools.

The following questions are ones that practitioners should begin asking. Because a single investigation may reveal data that supports several answers, the questions have been coded so that readers easily can match each question with its research base. Thus, if you are interested in the studies that document answers to a specific question, find that question's symbol and then refer to the Research Chart on p. 146.

Question 1: Can students identify their own learning styles? (Code: A)

Responses from more than 150,000 learners reveal that most students can describe how they will learn best; some cannot, and others can only describe preferences for those learning style elements that are very important to them.

No one is affected by all the elements of learning style (as identified by the *Learning Style Inventory*, Dunn, Dunn and Price, 1978). Most people respond strongly to between 6 and 14; a few people are strongly influenced by 18. When an element is unimportant to students, they are unaware of specific reactions to it, and, therefore, when questioned about their behaviors often respond, "It depends. . . ." They cannot answer definitively because their responses to that element depend on their interest in the topic, the people with whom they are working, and/or other possibilities. That specific element itself does not influence their learning.

On the other hand, when an element *is* important to youngsters, most can verbalize their preferences and dislikes. An element that is *extremely important* to an individual (we call it a "strong preference,") can be identified easily by most people.

To illustrate, one need only examine the research conducted by Farr, 1971; Domino, 1970; Cafferty, 1980; Copenhaver, 1979; Krimsky, 1982; Lynch, 1981; Pizzo, 1981; and Shea, 1983. The students in those studies were administered a self-report instrument in which they were asked to identify the ways in which they would achieve best. Experimental investigations revealed that when taught as they had indicated, students did, indeed, achieve better than when they were taught in ways that differed from their preferences.

Question 2: Does teaching through learning styles increase academic achievement? (Code: B)

This publication does not provide enough space to permit a complete listing of studies corroborating that students learn more, more easily, and remember better when they are taught through their preferred learning styles, but the following documents will serve as indicators: Cafferty, 1980; Carbo, 1980; Domino, 1970; Douglass, 1979; Farr, 1971; Krimsky, 1982; Pizzo, 1981; Shea, 1983; Tannenbaum, 1982; Trautman, 1979; Urbschat, 1977; White, 1981.

Prior to the Carbo data, research was contradictory about the importance of using students' perceptual strengths to teach reading. Carbo's review of the literature, however, exposed poor designs, misinterpretations of data, and faulty conclusions of previous studies where few relationships were evidenced between modalities and treatments. Her investigation demonstrated that matching modality strengths and treatments is mandatory for many children to learn to read well.

White's (1981) study is instructive in that it found nonconforming students do not learn through conformity but must be given choices from among appropriate alternatives. White revealed that independent students learn better through methods that foster independence rather than conformity.

Note that these studies were conducted at all levels—*college* (Domino, 1970; Farr, 1971), *high school* (Cafferty, 1980; Douglass, 1979; Tannenbaum, 1982), *junior high school* (Trautman, 1979; White, 1981), *elementary school* (Krimsky, 1982; Pizzo, 1981), and *primary* (Carbo, 1980; Urbschat, 1977). Furthermore, regardless of grade level, Kaley (1977) showed that learning style can predict *reading* achievement better than I.Q.

Question 3: Does teaching through learning style improve students' attitudes toward school? (Code: C)

Perhaps because new concepts must demonstrate increases in achievement before educators will consider adopting them, fewer studies focus on improved attitudes than on grades and scores. Evidence shows, however, that youngsters' attitudes about their schools, their teachers, and learning improve when they are taught by methods, resources, or programs that respond to their unique characteristics (Domino, 1970; Copenhaver, 1979; Pizzo, 1981).

Other interesting investigations not listed in the chart related to attitude and contrast the self-concept of students who do well, with those who do poorly in reading and mathematics. Achieving youngsters invariably exhibit learning styles that differ from underachieving ones (Hudes, Saladino, and Meibach, 1977; Dunn, Price, Dunn, and Sanders, 1979; Dunn, Price, and Sanders, 1981; Griggs and Price, 1981).

Question 4: Does teaching through learning style reduce discipline problems? (Code: D)

One of the most important studies in this area (Lynch, 1981) verified the following at the secondary level:

- When matched for their time-of-day preference and permitted to change teachers, chronic truants attended school more frequently (an amazing 3.54 units per ten-week marking period).
- A significant interaction occurred between degree of truancy, time-of-day preference, and English teacher assignment.
- Initial truants attended school *less* frequently (.51 units) when assigned to the *same* English teacher for two consecutive years.

Another study (Carruthers and Young, 1980) of 50 eighth grade math students from rural and inner-city schools revealed that those students whose learning preferences matched the time assigned to their math classes were less of a discipline problem than those who were mismatched. In addition to reductions in truancy, fewer discipline problems, and the need for fewer motivational influences, one alternative junior high school in New York City reversed negative achievement, attitude and behavior trends of delinquent adolescents merely by teaching them through their learning styles (Dunn, 1981). In a relatively affluent high school, a learning styles-based program produced not only significant academic gains but a decline in truancy and discipline problems (Cavanaugh, 1981).

Question 5: Do students learn effectively when taught through their *preferred* learning styles? (Code: E)

The Cafferty, 1980; Domino, 1970; Farr, 1971; Krimsky, 1982; Lynch, 1981; Pizzo, 1981; and White, 1981, investigations all used self-report instruments that asked students either how they preferred to learn (when given a choice) or how they actually did/would learn most easily. Each of those studies revealed statistically significant gains when students were taught in ways they said they preferred to learn.

Question 6: Does learning style change, or is it consistent? (Code: F)

Price's (1980) studies revealed that selected style elements tend to be stable over time, whereas others appear to parallel the growth curve. A total of 3,972 subjects in grades 3 through 7 completed the Dunn, Dunn, and Price *Learning Style Inventory* (LSI) during the 1979-1980 school year. Some of the significant findings were:

- The higher the grade level, the less preference was indicated for formal design, structure, and teacher motivation.
- Self-motivation decreased during grades 7 and 8, but a gradual increase was evidenced in each of the grades thereafter.
- The higher the grade level, generally, the less motivated are students. The biggest shift occurs between grades 7 and 8, with grade 11 showing the highest percentage of unmotivated learners.
- The strongest need to learn with peers occurs in grades 6 through 8; the lowest need is in grade 12, followed by grade 9.
- The younger the child, the more tactual and kinesthetic he or she is, followed later by the development of visual strengths, and beginning with grades 5 and 6, the development of auditory strengths.

Corroborating Price's extensive study, Copenhaver (1979) evidenced that students' styles remain consistent *regardless of the subject being studied:* (1) students have significantly more positive attitudes toward a subject when their learning styles are similar to their teachers' teaching styles; (2) a wide range of learning styles exists among students in every class; and, (3) many different teaching styles are necessary if teachers are to respond to the diversity of learning styles among their students.

Thus, learning style seems to remain consistent during a given period— certainly during a single year. It can change over time. When an element affects an individual strongly, that element tends to be consistent for a longer time. When an element is unimportant to an individual, it tends to be less consistent, depending on interest, motivation, peer orientations, and the effects of those elements that *do* affect him or her strongly. In this entire report, the only statement that is based more on *observation* than on "tightly designed" research is the last. We currently are accumulating data on the consistency of elements that are "unimportant" to an individual at given stages of school life.

Question 7: How reliable are learning style identification instruments?

Because of the increasing popularity of this movement, new instruments purporting to measure learning styles are appearing with regularity. It can take years to develop a reliable and valid instrument. Many psychological instruments have low reliabilities, and some are normed on highly specific populations, making them inappropriate for other groups. It is important to use the "right" instrument for the "right" population. Unreliable instruments lead to unreliable data.

When choosing a test to identify students' learning styles, be certain that it is accompanied by a printed manual that provides: (1) reliability and validity data; (2) studies that *employed* the instrument; (3) the grade levels and types of youngsters for whom the test is appropriate; and, (4) the author(s)' credentials. Write the authors and request the titles of published articles that describe research studies that used the instrument. Read the journals in which those studies were published; check the grade levels and populations that comprised the sample; obtain the names and addresses of administrators or teachers who actually used the test; write and ask for reactions. In those ways you can check the instrument's appropriateness with the populations for whom the author suggests it can be used. If such data is available, and you are satisfied with the responses, certainly use the instrument. If not, consider another instrument.

Question 8: Have we broken the learning style code?

We know a great deal about learning style, but there is a great deal more to learn. At St. John's University's Center for the Study of Learning and Teaching Styles, each research project reveals new information that both triggers new insights and requires additional investigations of related questions. The next decade perhaps will provide a learning breakthrough for every child, but focused activity and quality professional research will be critical to the effort. We hope that the best minds and talents will share in that task.

Research Chart

Researcher, Title of Research, Date	Population	Findings
Elsie Cafferty, "An Analysis of Student Performance Based upon the Degree of Match Between the Educational Cognitive Style of the Teachers and the Educational Cognitive Style of the Students," Doctoral dissertation, University of Nebraska, 1980.	1,689 Teacher/ High School Student Pairs	1. The greater the match between the student's and the teacher's style, the higher the student's grade point average. 2. The greater the mismatch between the student's and the teacher's style, the lower the student's grade point average.
(Codes A, B, E)		
Marie Antonetti Carbo, "An Analysis of the Relationships Between the Modality Preferences of Kindergartners and Selected Reading Treatments as They Affect the Learning of a Basic Sight-Word Vocabulary," Doctoral dissertation, St. John's University, 1980.	Kindergarten Children	1. When reading treatments were matched to perceptual preferences, significantly higher reading scores resulted at the .01 level.

(Code B)

Ronnie W. Copenhaver, "The Consistency of Learning Style as Students Move from English to Mathematics," Doctoral dissertation, Indiana University, 1979.	76 High School Students	1. Students' learning styles remain consistent regardless of the subject being studied. 2. Significantly more positive attitudes resulted when students' styles were similar to their teachers'. 3. A wide range of learning styles exists in each class.

(Codes A, C, F)

George Domino, "Interactive Effects of Achievement Orientation and Teaching Style on Academic Achievement," ACT Research Report 39 (1970) : 1–9.	100 College Students	1. Students taught in ways they believed they learned scored higher on tests, fact knowledge, and efficiency than those taught in a manner dissonant from their orientation.

(Codes A, B, C, E)

Claudia B. Douglass, "Making Biology Easier to Understand," *The American Biology Teacher,* May 1979, pp. 277–99.	High School Students	1. When inductive students used inductive materials and when deductive students used deductive materials, achievement increased; when the students and the resources were mismatched, less academic achievement was realized.

(Code B)

Beatrice J. Farr, "Individual Differences In Learning: Predicting One's More Effective Learning Modality," Doctoral dissertation, Catholic University, 1971.	72 College Students	1. Individuals accurately predicted the modality in which they would achieve superior academic performance. 2. It was advantageous to learn and to be tested in the preferred modality. 3. The above advantage was reduced when learning and testing were both in the nonpreferred modality.

(Codes A, B, E)

Jeffrey S. Krimsky, "A Comparative Study of the Effects of Matching and Mismatching Fourth Grade Students with Their Learning Style Preferences for the Environmental Element of Light and Their Subsequent Reading Speed and Accuracy Scores," Doctoral dissertation, St. John's University, 1982.	32 Elementary Students	1. When matched with their light preferences, students showed significantly higher reading speed and accuracy scores, at the .001 level. 2. Students who were mismatched achieved significantly *below* the matched group.

(Codes A, B, E)

Peter K. Lynch, "An Analysis of the Relationships Among Academic Achievement, Attendance, and the Individual Learning Style Time Preferences of Eleventh and Twelfth Grade Students Identified as Initial or Chronic Truants in a Suburban New York School District," Doctoral dissertation, St. John's University, 1981.	136 High School Students	1. When matched with their time-of-day preference and mismatched for teacher assignment, chronic truants attended school more frequently (3.5 units per ten-week marking period). 2. A significant interaction (at the .01 level) occurred among degree of truancy, learning style preference, and English teacher assignment, suggesting that time preference was a factor in the reversal of truancy patterns.

(Codes A, D, E)

Jeanne Pizzo, "An Investigation of the Relationships Between Selected Acoustic Environments and Sound, an Element of Learning Style, as They Affect Sixth Grade Students' Reading Achievement and Attitudes," Doctoral dissertation, St. John's University, 1981	64 Elementary Students	1. When students were matched with their need for either sound or quiet preferences, significantly higher reading and attitude scores resulted, at the .01 level. 2. Students who were mismatched, achieved significantly *below* the matched students.

Thomas C. Shea, "An Investigation of the Relationship(s) Among Preferences for the Learning Style Element of Design, Selected Instructional Environments, and Reading Test Achievement of Ninth Grade Students To Improve Administrative Determinations Concerning Effective Educational Facilities," Doctoral dissertation, St. John's University, 1983.	32 Ninth Graders	1. When students were matched with their learning style preference for design, statistically significantly higher reading scores resulted at the .01 level. 2. Students who were mismatched for informal design achieved significantly lower than when matched.

(Codes A, B, C, E)

Rhoada K. Tannenbaum, "An Investigation of the Relationship(s) Between Selected Instructional Techniques and Identified Field Dependent and Field Independent Cognitive Style as Evidenced Among High School Students Enrolled in Studies of Nutrition," Doctoral dissertation, St. John's University, 1982.	100 High School Students	1. When students were matched with complementary resources, statistically significant higher scores resulted, at the .045 level. 2. Students who were mismatched achieved significantly *below* the matched students.

(Code B)

Paul Trautman, "An Investigation of the Relationship Between Selected Instructional Techniques and Identified Cognitive Style," Doctoral dissertation, St. John's University, 1979.	Junior High School Students	1. There is no difference between the relative achievement of analytic and global students when they are taught through materials that match their styles.

2. When students were matched with complementary resources, significantly higher scores resulted at the .01 level.
3. Students who were mismatched achieved significantly *below* the matched students.

(Code B)

Karen S. Urbschat, "A Study of Preferred Learning Modes and Their Relationship to the Amount of Recall of CVC Trigrams," Doctoral dissertation, Wayne State University, 1977.	135 Primary Children	1. Perceptual strengths can be identified among first graders. 2. Superior and significant results occurred when the treatment was matched to the appropriate modality. 3. Most of the first graders in the study found it easier to learn through either a *visual* or a combined *auditory/visual* approach. 4. *Regardless of the child's perceptual strength,* a treatment that included a visual approach achieved significance at .05 level with auditory, visual, and auditory/visual children. (This study **did not include tactual** or **kinesthetic** treatments).

(Code B)

Regina T. White, "An Investigation of the Relationship Between Selected Instructional Methods and Selected Elements of Emotional Learning Style upon Student Achievement in Seventh and Eighth Grade Social Studies," Doctoral dissertation, St. John's University, 1981.	80 Junior High School Students	1. Highly persistent and highly responsible students achieved significantly higher than those with low persistent and responsibility scores. 2. A positive relationship was revealed between the *Learning Style Inventory* subscales of persistence and responsibility and the *California Psychological Inventory* subscale of achievement via conformity (Ac). Students identified as being persistence and responsible were identified as *manifesting conforming behavior.* 3. Comparatively, less persistent and less responsible students do not learn through conformity; it is likely that they would learn more easily through acceptable choices.

(Codes B, E)

References

Cafferty, Elsie. "An Analysis of Student Performance Based upon the Degree of Match Between the Educational Cognitive Style of the Teachers and the Educational Cognitive Style of the Students." Doctoral dissertation, University of Nebraska, 1980.

Carbo, Marie Antonetti. "An Analysis of the Relationships Between the Modality Preferences of Kindergartners and Selected Reading Treatments as They Affect the Learning of a Basic Sight-Word Vocabulary." Doctoral dissertation, St. John's University, 1980.

Carruthers, Stephen A., and Young, L. Andrew. "Preference of Condition Concerning Time in Learning Environments of Rural Versus City Eighth Grade Students." *Learning Styles Network Newsletter,* Spring 1980, p. 1.

Cavanaugh, David P. "Student Learning Styles: A Diagnostic/Prescriptive Approach to Instruction." *Phi Delta Kappan,* November 1981, pp.202–03.

Copenhaver, Ronnie W. "The Consistency of Student Learning Styles as Students Move from English to Mathematics." Doctoral dissertation, Indiana University, 1979.

Domino, George. "Interactive Effects of Achievement Orientation and Teaching Style on Academic Achievement." ACT Research Report 39 (1970) : 1–9.

Douglass, Claudia B. "Making Biology Easier to Understand." *The American Biology Teacher,* May 1979, pp. 277–99.

Dunn, Kenneth. "Madison Prep: Alternative to Teenage Disaster." *Educational Leadership,* February 1981, pp. 386–87.

Dunn, Rita. "Individualizing Instruction Through Contracts—Does It Work with Very Young Children?" *Audiovisual Instruction,* March 1971, pp. 78–80.

Dunn, Rita, and Dunn, Kenneth. *Practical Approaches to Individualizing Instruction: Contracts and Other Effective Teaching Strategies.* Nyack, N.Y.: Parker Publishing Co., 1972.

——. *Educator's Self-Teaching Guide to Individualizing Instructional Programs.* Nyack, N.Y.: Parker Publishing Co., 1975.

——. *Teaching Students Through Their Individual Learning Styles: A Practical Approach.* Reston, Va.: Reston Publishing Co., 1978.

Dunn, Rita, and Shockley, Alonzo H. *Better Education Through Community Involvement.* New York: Freeport Public Schools, Pursuant to a U. S. Office of Health, Education and Welfare grant, under the supervision of the New York State Education Department (1970).

——. *That a Child May Reach: Expanded Education in Freeport.* New York: Freeport Public Schools, Pursuant to a U. S. Office of Health, Education and Welfare grant, under the supervision of the New York State Education Department (1971).

Dunn, Rita; Price, Gary E.; and Sanders, William. "Reading Achievement and Learning Styles." *The Clearing House,* January 1981, pp. 223–26.

Dunn, Rita; Price, Gary E.; Dunn, Kenneth; and Sanders, Willian. "Relationship of Learning Style to Self-Concept." *The Clearing House,* November 1979, pp. 155–58.

Farr, Beatrice J. "Individual Differences in Learning: Predicting One's More Effective Learning Modality." Doctoral dissertation, Catholic University, 1971.

Fiske, Edward B. "Teachers Adjust Schooling to Fit Students' Individuality." *The New York Times,* Tuesday, December 29, 1981.

Griggs, Shirley A., and Price, Gary E. "Self Concept Relates to Learning Style in the Junior High." *Phi Delta Kappan,* May 1981, p. 604.

Hudes, Sonia; Saladino, Antoinette; and Meibech, Donna Siegler. "Learning Style Subscales and Self-Concept Among High Achievement Third Graders." *The Journal,* School Administrators Association of New York, Fall 1977, pp. 7–10.

Kaley, Stephanie Beth. "Field Dependence/Independence and Learning Styles in Sixth Graders." Doctoral dissertation, Hofstra University, 1977.

Krimsky, Jeffrey S. "A Comparative Study of the Effects of Matching and Mismatching Fourth Grade Students with Their Learning Style Preferences for the Environmental Element of Light and Their Subsequent Reading Speed and Accuracy Scores." Doctoral dissertation, St. John's University, 1982.

Lemmon, Patricia. "Step By Step Leadership into Learning Styles." *Early Years,* January 1982.

Lynch, Peter. "An Analysis of the Relationships Among Academic Achievement, Attendance, and the Individual Learning Style Time Preferences of Eleventh and Twelfth Grade Students Identified as Initial or Chronic Truants in a Suburban New York School District." Doctoral dissertation, St. John's University, 1981.

Pizzo, Jeanne. "An Investigation of the Relationships Between Selected Acoustic Environments and Sound, an Element of Learning Style, as They Affect Sixth Grade Students' Reading Achievement and Attitudes." Doctoral dissertation, St. John's University, 1981.

Price, Gary E. "Which Learning Styles Elements Are Stable and Which Tend to Change?" *Learning Styles Network Newsletter,* Autumn 1980, p. 1.

Shea, Thomas C. "An Investigation of the Relationship(s) Among Preferences for the Learning Style Element of Design, Selected Instructional Environments, and Reading Test Achievement of Ninth Grade Students To Improve Administrative Determinations Concerning Effective Educational Facilities." Doctoral dissertation, St. John's University, 1983.

Tannenbaum, Rhoada. "An Investigation of the Relationship(s) Between Selected Instructional Techniques and Identified Field Dependent and Field Independent Cognitive Styles as Evidenced Among High School Students Enrolled in Studies of Nutrition." Doctoral dissertation, St. John's University, 1982.

Trautman, Paul. "An Investigation of the Relationship Between Selected Instructional Techniques and Identified Cognitive Style." Doctoral dissertation, St. John's University, 1979.

Urbschat, Karen S. "A Study of Preferred Learning Modes and Their Relationship to the Amount of Recall of CVC Trigrams." Doctoral dissertation, Wayne State University, 1977.

White, Regina T. "An Investigation of the Relationship Between Selected Instructional Methods and Selected Elements of Emotional Learning Style upon Student Achievement in Seventh and Eighth Grade Social Studies." Doctoral dissertation, St. John's University, 1981.

CHAPTER 16

Developing a Framework for the Study of Learning Style in High-Level Learning

Bruce M. Shore

Recognized learning styles cover a wide range of variables from cognitive processes to social preferences, from subject matter to gender differences. There are three particularly evident gaps, however. First, notwithstanding several efforts to put some conceptual order in the array of available measures (Keefe, 1981), there is still little order among them, considerable redundancy, and little guidance for the educator wishing to use a subset for predictive or explanatory purposes (the work reported by Letteri, 1981, is among the most obvious contributions to such guidance).

Second, apparently no attention is given in any of the available research to taxonomically related differences in the level of the content being learned (in terms of the work of Bloom and his colleagues, or others). This is of critical importance where high-level learning is of particular interest, such as in postsecondary education or in the education of the gifted at any level.

Third, the research makes little progress in closing the gap between the largely psychometric orientation of learning-styles measures and the more explicit process-orientation of cognitive psychology. This report outlines one attempt to glean some direction from existing research toward filling the first gap, in pursuit of research on the second. Less direct attention is given to the third. The overall focus of this paper is in the direction of academic performance.

In addition to learner and subject differences, research on learning styles must take account, among other contextual variables, of the taxonomic level of the learning. We may well have to stop relying so heavily on tests that define learning styles in terms of the present state of the learner, and perhaps become more oriented to some future state, however transitory. The trend is certainly recognized in the measurement of academic potential or intelligence (Horn, 1979): "There will be emphasis in measuring complex learned capacities of a kind that characterizes adult thinking, in contrast to tests designed for school children" (p. 229). Flavell (1976) similarly asks "What adult-like knowledge and behavior might constitute the development target here, toward which the child gradually progresses?" I wish Horn had written "learning" rather than "learned," but both he and Flavell express well how an interest in the gifted is consistent with the study of learning by university personnel engaged in research.

I have chosen to use doctoral research as an example of high-level learning and to search in this context for some limitation in the range of learning styles to be considered. Some of the studies considered are also of interest to Schmeck (1981), but his studies and others have dealt with more simply defined performance variables.

Learning Style, Ability Differences, and University-Level Learning

Pask (1975) studied differences in learning styles of students characterized as "holists" versus "serialists." Later (1976) he showed that when these styles were matched to different instructional strategies, learning was facilitated. Traditional task analyses in problem solving or learning are hierarchical, but Pask maintains that effective performance requires different entry points, skipping steps where necessary. Marton and Säljö (1976) studied text learning by university students and found that they also operated at two distinct levels of processing—surface-level and deep-level. The former learning was directed at what the author said, the latter at what he meant. Depending on which the instructor might want to test, this could affect performance success. Kirby and Das (1977) studied another conceptualization of processing (simultaneous versus successive) and found that the highest achievement was obtained by students high in both types of ability. A degree of adaptiveness as well as the specific ability is involved. Such flexibility is also a part of successful performance on traditional problem-solving tasks that involve overcoming "psychological set." The main difference between these processing strategies is their dependence (successive) or not (simultaneous) on the original temporal order of the input. Similarly, Getzels and Csikszentmihalyi (1976) described the performance of their successful artists as both stimulus-seeking and stimulus-reducing. The variables are different, but the idea of functioning in more than one mode remains. Two decades ago, Barron (1958) suggested that the abilities to cope with ambiguity and to hold many divergent ideas in consciousness at once were among the notable characteristics of creative architects and artists.

Several discussions arising from Piaget's contributions, especially regarding differences in learning strategies associated with development, led Flavell (1976) to wonder about students who have the appropriate procedures to solve certain problems yet still fail to do so. He postulates the idea of metacognition (p. 232) or awareness of one's own cognitive processes. Metacognition suggests the interesting hypothesis about successful graduate students and researchers not only having certain abilities but being flexible and adaptable, and aware of them and how they work.

Domino (1968) showed in a naturalistic study that independent, as opposed to conforming achievement motivation, measured by the California Personality Inventory (CPI), is related to college performance requiring independent or conforming behavior, respectively. Research is possibly an example of performance requiring independence. In a following experimental study, Domino (1971) confirmed this aptitude-treatment interaction (Cronbach and Snow, 1977). Not only did students matched in achievement and instructional style perform better, they more positively evaluated their instruction. Peterson (1977), adding ability and manifest anxiety (common in gifted students) to the measures used in a model aptitude-treatment-interaction study with grade nine students, found significant interaction effects on success. The instruction had been varied in structure and student participation.

These studies suggest that there is merit in seeking particular combinations of both student characteristics and instructional conditions which might enhance student learning.

A Learning Style Framework

This short overview suggests an imperfect hierarchy of learning style or cognitive style operation.

1). The first of the dimensions refers to the existence or not of operative learning styles, and in effect, denotes the richness of strategies available to the learner. Lowest, and clearly related to very poor academic performance, is the absence of any useful learning strategy observable in cases of extreme learning disability, emotional upset, or limited ability. Every new type of learning is an insurmountable challenge. Even with 20 correct replies to "type x" questions on "page y," a return to page "w" leads to failure. Only speculation supports this level since some learning styles have been reported for less extreme examples of disability (Carbo, 1981). Enough anecdotal evidence could probably be collected, however, to at least hypothesize the level.

A higher level of this learning style operation is simply the existence of one or more operative learning styles, even exclusively at the extreme of a bipolar concept. When appropriate to some learning situation, success will occur.

2). A second dimension involves a degree of flexibility, adaptability perhaps in the Piagetian sense. On one hand learners may redefine the problem in terms of their own cognitive strengths. A verbally proficient person scoring highly on a field-independence test (such as the Portable Rod and Frame or Embedded Figures Test) might verbalize all the cues and treat the task as verbal (Shore, Hymovitch, and Lajoie, 1981) or perhaps switch to a spatial mode and complete the test as it was planned to operate. Similarly, some examination takers reshape questions so they can tell us what they do know.

The second dimension comes from cognitively oriented studies and comprises degrees of metacognitive awareness. Not enough has been written about metacognition yet to suggest ways of scaling it, but the concept is very attractive, inherently and in its origins. A single effective learning style could lead to the avoidance of sure-to-lose learning situations and the careful choice of courses or careers. With varied, flexible, adaptive learning styles come the possibilities for predicting successful learning in situations where the content is fluid, where the demands on the learner differ (e.g., course-work versus thesis). Knowing how one thinks could be a major factor in learning efficiency. In this case, the onus for matching could rest with the learner. If Landa (1974) is correct, even metacognition may be a learnable heuristic.

Research Implications

Two questions ensue, one conceptual and one empirical. Conceptually, we must ask whether existing learning style measures fit on the grid created by these two variables—metacognition (adaptiveness) and style. For example field-independence-dependence might fit as a line diagonally, from low/low (dependent) to high/high (independent) perhaps equidistant from the two axes, since it may be absent, dominant in one direction, or adaptable, and may be accompanied by varying degrees of metacognition. The Schmeck, Ribich, and Ramanaiah (1977) scale may be represented as a line slightly more parallel to the adaptiveness axis, since it offers variance across style availability yet seems to demand a modicum of metacognition to be reliable. Zenhausern's (1979) scale may be more parallel to the metacognitive axis since it seems to provide an index of a single bipolar style, but to vary more according to the testee's reports of preferred tasks. Hunt et al.'s (1978) "conceptual level" might be represented as a line perpendicular to and halfway along the styles axis since the tester makes the inference about need for structure. Any level of metacognition might be operative, but it is not apparently revealed by the measure.

All these are intended as very imprecise representations. The purpose is not to supplant existing notions of learning style, but to help select subsets which conceptually allow all levels of combinations of metacognition and style to be sampled by an appropriate selection of learning style measures.

The second hypothesis is that it should, at a particular time, be possible to represent individuals as dots on this grid, and that the location will be positively correlated with successful high level learning. Perhaps lower level tasks (e.g., at Bloom's "knowledge of specifics" level, preponderant in the content of schooling) are not sufficiently intellectually demanding to require variety in learning style approach or metacognition.

Our plan, just underway, is to map many important learning style concepts on our grid to validate the grid conceptually. Then we propose to collect data on style and success from high-level learners and empirically test the framework in a cross-section of university disciplines.

References

Barron, T. "The Psychology of Imagination." *Scientific American* 25(1958): 789–93.

Carbo, M. "Learning Style: Key to Understanding the Learning Disabled." *Learning Styles Network Newsletter* 2(1981): 5.

Cronbach, L. J., and Snow, R. E. *Aptitudes and Instructional Methods.* New York: Irvington (Wiley-Halstead), 1977.

Domino, G. "Differential Predictions of Academic Achievement in Conforming and Independent Settings." *Journal of Educational Psychology* 59(1968): 256–60.

———. "Interactive Effects of Achievement Orientation and Teaching Style on Academic Achievement." *Journal of Educational Psychology* 62(1971): 427–31.

Flavell, J. H. "Metacognitive Aspects of Problem Solving." In *The Nature of Intelligence,* edited by L. B. Resnick. Hillsdale, N.J.: Earlbaum (Wiley), 1976, pp. 231–35.

———. "Metacognition." Paper presented at the annual meeting of the American Psychological Association, Montreal, August 1980.

Getzels, J. W., and Csikszentmihalyi, M. *The Creative Vision: a Longitudinal Study of Problem Finding in Art.* New York: John Wiley & Sons, 1976.

Green, B. F. "Current Trends in Problem Solving." In *Problem Solving: Research, Method and Theory,* edited by B. Kleinmuntz. New York: John Wiley & Sons, 1966, pp. 3–18.

Horn, J. L. "Trends in the Measurement of Intelligence." *Intelligence* 3(1979); 229–40.

Hunt, D. E.; Butler, L. F.; Noy, J. E.; and Rosser, M. E. *Assessing Conceptual Level by the Paragraph Completion Method.* Toronto: OISE, 1978.

Keefe, J. W. "Assessing Student Learning Styles: An Overview." Paper presented at the Major Conference on Student Learning Styles and Brain Behavior, New Orleans, November 1981; see page 43.

Kirby, J. R., and Das, J. P. "Reading Achievement, IQ, and Simultaneous-Successive Processing." *Journal of Educational Psychology* 69(1977): 564–70.

Landa, L. N. *Algorithmization in Learning and Instruction.* Englewood Cliffs, N. J.: Educational Technology, 1974.

Letteri, C. A. "Cognitive Profiles." Paper presented at the Major Conference on Student Learning Styles and Brain Behavior, New Orleans, November 1981; see page 68.

Marton, F., and Säljö, R. "On Quantitative Differences in Learning: 1—Outcome and Process." *British Journal of Educational Psychology* 46(1976): 4–11.

Newell, A., and Simon, H. A. "GPS, a Program That Stimulates Human Thought." In *Computers and Thought,* edited by E. A. Feigenbaum and J. Feldman. New York: McGraw-Hill, 1963.

Olson, D. "Notes on a Cognitive Theory of Instruction." In *Cognition and Instruction,* edited by D. Klahr. Hillsdale, N.J.: Earlbaum, 1976.

Pask, G. *The Cybernetics of Human Learning and Performance.* London: Hutchison, 1975.

———. "Styles and Strategies of Learning." *British Journal of Educational Psychology* 46(1976): 128–48.

Peterson, P. "Interactive Effects of Student Anxiety, Achievement Orientation, and Teacher Behavior on Student Achievement and Attitude." *Journal of Educational Psychology* 69(1977): 779–92.

Polya, G. *How To Solve It: A New Aspect of Mathematical Method,* 2d ed. New York: Doubleday (Anchor), 1957.

Resnick, L. B., and Glaser, R. "Problem Solving and Intelligence." In *The Nature of Intelligence,* edited by L. B. Resnick. Hillsdale, N.J.: Earlbaum (Wiley), 1976, pp. 205–30.

Schmeck, R. R. "Inventory of Learning Processes." Paper presented at the Major Conference on Student Learning Styles and Behavior, New Orleans, November 1981; see page 73.

Schmeck, R. R.; Ribich, F.; and Ramanaiah, N. "Development of a Self Report Inventory for Assessing Individual Differences in Learning Processes." *Applied Psychological Measurement* 1(1977): 413–41.

Shore, B. M.; Hymovitch, J.; and Lajoie, S. P. "Processing Differences in the Relation Between Abilities and Field-Independence." *Psychological Reports,* 1981.

Zenhausern, R. *Differential Hemispheric Activation Instrument.* New York: St. John's University, 1979.

Part Three

Brain Behavior
Research
and
Application

CHAPTER 1

The Brain*

by Richard M. Restak

To Aristotle, the brain was merely a cooling system for the blood as it left the heart. Assyrians favored the liver as the seat of the "soul." The Egyptians who embalmed the pharaohs carefully preserved most major organs in special jars—but not the brain, thinking it inconsequential.

Natural philosophers and physicians in ancient Greece eventually ascertained the true state of affairs—some centuries before the birth of Christ—but enlightenment gave rise to mysteries of a subtler sort. Granted that the brain is, after all, the center of conscious experience. Granted that it governs the way we perceive, think about, and react to the world; holds our memories in trust; sows, germinates, tends, reaps, harvests, and husbands our emotions; sustains our very sense of self. Given all that, how does the organ *work*?

The functioning of the brain has been variously likened to the workings of a telephone switchboard, a railway system, a computer. None of these models has proved entirely adequate. So far as we know, the brain is unlike any other structure in the universe, and perhaps only the vast universe itself presents conceptual problems of equal complexity.

In terms of "hardware" alone, we are dealing with an organ composed of 10 to 15 billion highly differentiated yet profoundly interlocked brain cells. Beyond issues of structure lurk questions that transcend biology. "Know thyself," Socrates advised. But can one, really?

The issues posed by "the brain" are as broad as life itself. What happens inside our heads when we write poetry, solve a puzzle, conduct business, fall in love? What made Rembrandt Rembrandt? Why are we sad or happy? How do we learn? Why do we forget? How do we remember? What is mental illness? What causes it? How "real" is "perception"? Driven by curiosity, altruism, or professional ambition (and what, incidentally, is the source of *these* drives?), hundreds of researchers in America and Europe are engrossed in such questions. Here and there, they are closing in on something that may approximate the truth. Here and there, they have run into a fog bank.

*Adapted from the *Wilson Quarterly*, Summer 1982. Copyright 1982 by the Woodrow Wilson International Center for Scholars.

Mapping the Hemispheres

The research conducted by Roger Sperry, Torsten Wiesel, and David Hubel that led to a Nobel Prize in 1981 involved the study of the two cerebral hemispheres. While their research was carried out during the past 25 years, the first investigations into the functioning of the hemispheres occurred nearly 25 centuries ago. The investigator was the Greek, Hippocrates (ca. 460–377 B.C.).

Hippocrates was the first to suggest that the brain was the organ of the mind. In his treatise *On the Sacred Disease* (epilepsy), he wrote: "Not only our pleasure, our joy, and our laughter, but also our sorrow, pain, grief, and tears arise from the brain, and the brain alone." A meticulous observer, Hippocrates also noticed that a sword wound to the right side of a soldier's head would affect only the left side of the body—and vice versa. From this, he concluded that "the brain of man is double." There matters rested for more than two millenniums.

While the Romans, Arabs, and medieval Christians often mused on the locus and nature of "mind" and "soul," it was not until the 19th century that brain research came into its own.

In 1861, a young French physician named Paul Broca published an account of a patient in the Salpetrière who had suffered a stroke years earlier. Rather than rendering him completely mute, however, the stroke had allowed the patient to speak in short, laborious, telegraphic sentences (e.g., "I went restaurant food"), a condition Broca called *aphasia*. Examination of the patient's brain after death revealed a precise area of destruction in the left cerebral hemisphere that, Broca postulated, was responsible for speech.

Examination of other patients later corroborated Broca's assertion and initiated a lively interest (which continues) in correlating behavior with discrete parts of the brain. Thus, we can now "map" the brain in a rough sort of way, pinpointing which portions are generally involved with vision, smell, movement, bodily sensation. One of the unintended consequences of the work of Broca and others was to lend impetus to the already popular "science" of phrenology, which, though misguided, did spur further interest in brain/behavior research.

Meanwhile, other researchers busied themselves with the larger implications of a human brain made up of two hemispheres. In 1844, an English physician, A.L. Wigen, published a little-noticed paper *(The Duality of the Mind)* describing the illness, death, and autopsy of a lifelong friend and patient. At the autopsy, Wigen discovered to his amazement that his friend, who had been neurologically normal in every respect, possessed only *one* cerebral hemisphere. "If only one cerebrum was required to have a mind," Wigen concluded, "the presence of two hemispheres [the normal state] makes possible and perhaps even inevitable the possession of two minds."

Wigen's speculations remained largely untested until the 1940s when brain researchers began cutting the *corpus callosum* (a tract of nerve fibers, also called the *cerebral commissure,* connecting the two hemispheres) to prevent seizure discharges from being relayed from one hemisphere to the other. The earliest researchers reported that the operation had no detectable effect on behavior. Clarification of the true situation awaited the Nobel Prize winning efforts of Sperry and his colleagues. They demonstrated in "split-brain" subjects that each hemisphere is specialized for carrying out certain functions. Thus, in general, the right hemisphere is specialized for functions that deal with nonverbal processes (e.g., drawing, spatial awareness) while the left hemisphere is dominant for language.

While work with split-brain subjects has contributed immensely to our understanding of the hemispheres, the implications of that work have often been oversimplified. Some have claimed that Western society may be overly dependent on logical, linear, "left hemisphere" processes while Eastern thought is more "holistic" in its orientation. Some American educators have jumped on the bandwagon by suggesting that classroom techniques be modified to encourage freer expression of the "silent, non-dominant" right hemisphere.

When the Blind Can See

We should remember, however, that commissurotomy has been performed on very few people, all of whom have suffered unusual, chronic brain disease or disabling seizure disorders. Moreover, most authorities believe that hemisphere specialization can be altered profoundly by events early in life (e.g., birth trauma, infection). Thus, it is risky to leap from pathological cases to speculation about how the two hemispheres operate in presumably "normal" people.

Cooperation rather than competition between the two hemispheres seems to be the situation prevailing under most conditions. Both hemispheres, relying on different modes of information processing, operate in tandem to construct a continuous model of reality. Contradictions are resolved via interhemispheric connections—principally but not exclusively the corpus callosum. There are other important connecting links located deep beneath the cerebral hemispheres, where subcortical nerve cells serve as relay points enabling the two hemispheres to "talk" with each other. A significant degree of "processing," it appears, is carried out here long before nerve signals ever reach the cerebral cortex.

Take the phenomenon of "blind sight."

Penetrating injuries to the back of the head sustained by soldiers during World War I first revealed to researchers that the posterior parts of the brain, the occipital lobes, are involved in vision. Soldiers lost their sight in proportion to the amount of damaged "visual cortex." In the most devastating wounds, vision was lost altogether, an often cited "proof" that vision was "located" in the occipital lobes. But it turns out that things aren't nearly that simple.

For example, if a flash of light or sudden movement occurs in front of a blind person and he is asked to point in the direction of the visual stimulus, he will respond correctly 85 percent of the time. This is possible because of the connections that still exist between the eyes and portions of the brain far below the cerebral hemispheres. In monkeys, these connections are so developed that, in the event of cerebral damage to the visual cortex, the animals may recover useful sight. The phenomenon of "blind sight" also shows that the brain's performance is not dependent on consciousness, for the blind person insists that he is unable to "see" any visual stimulus at all.

Synthesizing Perception

The visual cortex, it turns out, is the seat of *conscious* awareness. But often we perceive things *unconsciously*. Waking from a sound sleep to the noise of a ringing telephone is an example. The visual area of the brain, neurobiologists now think, is more concerned with the *interpretation* of visual stimuli rather than simply with "sight." Immediately adjacent to the area for visual reception in the cortex are the visual association areas, which correlate what we see with what we hear, taste, touch, and smell. The resulting "product" of this interlocking system is our perception of reality. I do not mean to imply that the "real world" is only a construction of our brain. That form of idealism died out with Bishop Berkeley. It does suggest, however, that we impose *meaning* upon our perceptions.

The cerebral cortex is responsible for the synthesis of sight and sound and touch into a coherent whole. Usually, this synthetic process occurs effortlessly, but, on occasion, the process breaks down. For example, a patient with *visual agnosia* may be incapable of recognizing an object or person by vision alone. Though not blind, he must touch the object or hear the person speak in order for recognition to occur.

It is sobering to think that the ability to "make sense" of our world is at the mercy of the slightest alteration in the amount of blood delivered to the brain. A person who has suffered a stroke may be incapable of understanding speech or written language. He may fail to recognize that his own arms and legs belong to him. Some of these lost functions may be recovered after a time, indicating that the brain has great recuperative powers and can "reassign" certain tasks (e.g., speech) to undamaged areas. But the degree of recovery is almost always incomplete.

Interestingly, if the injury occurs early enough, total "refit" is possible. A child of eight or nine can suffer brain damage or even the complete loss of a cerebral hemisphere and yet go on to develop normally—as apparently happened with Dr. Wigen's patient. But by age 10 or 12, the prognosis will be similar to that for an adult: a largely irreversible loss of function. Why? Neurobiologists cannot say for sure. The brain's recuperative powers are thought to depend on an early "plasticity." As times goes on, specialization takes over and specific functions establish "squatter's rights" in one hemisphere and not the other.

Brain researchers are now trying to discover precisely why this occurs and whether the brain's early plasticity can ever be regained. There are some hopeful signs. For example, as Michael Gazzaniga, director of the Division of Cognitive Neurosciences at Cornell University, has shown, the right hemisphere is capable of primitive speech (on the level of a six- or eight-year-old child). It is possible, then, that drawing, speaking, writing, and other abilities exist "holistically" within the brain, at least potentially, and are not limited to specialized "centers" within one hemisphere or the other.

"No, I Can Never Say 'No'!"

The notion of "holistic" brain functioning can be traced back 120 years. During the 1860s, a dour and solitary English neurologist, John Hughlings Jackson, developed the novel theory that the central nervous system has a complex "vertical" organization with many functions somehow represented at different levels, starting with the lowest (and, biologically, most ancient) spinal cord level and proceeding up to the rarified realm of the cerebral cortex. Jackson's theory was based on his observation that a circumscribed injury never leads to a *complete* loss of function—even Broca's "aphasic" patient was able to speak, albeit clumsily.

As proof of a multilevel organization, Jackson cited a patient of his who could not voluntarily speak the word "no," but one day blurted out in frustration: "No, Doctor, I can never say 'no'!" A similar anomaly has been observed in stroke victims who, under the power of a strong emotion, can move a paralyzed limb. Such performances are possible, according to Jackson, because the brain is able to utilize alternative pathways that, under ordinary circumstances, are either totally unused or merely complementary to the main pathway. The difference is perhaps analogous to parallel highways, one old and one new.

Jackson's theory of alternative brain pathways met with disbelief in his own time, but many modern brain researchers now find it fits both research findings and common sense observations. In their view, mental processes should be regarded as complex functions that are diffused throughout the brain and nervous system, not "localized" (à la Broca).

A creative tension persists today between the view that the brain can be understood by separating it into functional areas and the opposite orientation, which holds that mental life is a single, indivisible, "holistic" phenomenon, a function of the whole brain working in a unitary fashion. Some neuroscientists straddle the fence by postulating that the most basic brain functions (movement, sight) can be localized while symbolic activities (thought, the exercise of "will") cannot. Like the Missouri Compromise, this gallant effort does not quite do.

The exercise of "will," for instance, may be electrically distributed throughout the brain even when the resulting action is extremely localized in its final form. If a person in an experimental situation is instructed to move his finger at any time he wishes, the first recorded electrical event preceding the movement is a widespread "readiness potential" that can be recorded over a large area of both cerebral hemispheres. Only several milliseconds later can a distinct readiness potential be recorded specifically from the "hand area" of the motor cortex.

Widely separated parts of the brain are required for carrying out the simplest of actions. Voluntary movement of the hands, for instance, is virtually impossible without the cerebellum which designs movements that must be "preprogrammed" since they occur too fast and too "unthinkingly." Electrical recordings taken just before I put pen to paper might well register "readiness" in the sensory cortex, cerebellum, and motor control centers beneath the cortex, as well as in the limbic system, the "emotional area" of my brain.

The most convincing proof that the brain is organized along functional rather than strictly anatomical lines comes from stimulation studies of the exposed cerebral cortex. Because the brain does not contain pain fibers, a person undergoing a neurosurgical procedure can remain awake while parts of his cerebral cortex are stimulated with an electronic probe. From such "fishing expeditions," scientists have learned that the various parts of the body are represented on the cortex not according to *size* but in proportion to usefulness. The thumb and the tongue, for instance, occupy a huge area, while the small of the back and the chest wall have only tiny representations.

The Archaeology of the Self

During the 1950s, neurosurgeon Wilder Penfield and his colleagues at the Montreal Neurological Institute made a startling discovery. They learned that past events in a patient's life could be mentally "brought to life" by an electrode applied to the temporal lobe—the "interpretive cortex" as Penfield called it. Although bodily movements could also be induced, these movements never proceeded beyond crude clutching or grasping motions. Electrodes could not elicit responses requiring fine motor control or coordination, because the stimulation never involved part of a willed act or "program" such as we use when carrying out a complex movement. Penfield's work was, in fact, one of the earliest indications that *acts* rather than separate muscle movements are programmed within the brain.

Penfield's patients frequently reported that, upon stimulation, everything around them seemed to have occurred before. One patient heard his mother speaking on the telephone. Another patient experienced the vivid hallucination of riding in a car around Fordham Square in the Bronx with his father.

Throughout, the patients remained fully aware that their strange mental experiences did not correspond to any events actually taking place in the operating theater, but were somehow the direct result of the surgeon's electrical probe. It was obvious to Penfield that "there is, beneath the electrode, a recording mechanism for memories of events. But the mechanism seems to have recorded much more than the simple event. When activated, it may reproduce the emotions which attended the original experience. . . ."

The temporal lobe is the center for the integration of experience. Here sight and sound and touch are synthesized into three-dimensional reality bounded in space and time. Disturbances within the temporal lobe, such as temporal lobe epilepsy, result in emotional distortions. Time and space may seem elongated or foreshortened. Anxiety may alternate with feelings of cosmic unity. The individual may express a sense of oneness with all of creative matter. Or he may cringe in fear, gripped by a terrible existential *angst*.

Fyodor Dostoyevsky, a temporal lobe epileptic, described in *The Idiot* the ecstasy that accompanied the onset of an epileptic attack. "[T]here was always one instant," he wrote, "just before the epileptic fit—when suddenly in the midst of sadness, spiritual darkness, and oppression, his brain seemed momentarily to catch fire and in an extraordinary rush all his vital forces were at their highest tension."

THE HUMAN BRAIN

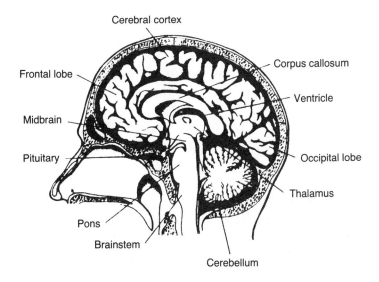

Adapted from The Conscious Brain, *by Steven Rose,* © 1973 by Steven Rose. By permission of Alfred A. Knopf, Inc.

Enclosed within a bony skull and three enveloping membranes, the human brain is nourished by the one and one-half pints of blood pumped through it each minute. Since the time of our hominid ancestors, the human brain has grown in size by 300 percent, more than any other part of the body.

Our own sense of certainty, personal cohesion, and familiarity with our surroundings are dependent on the smooth functioning of the temporal lobe. The temporal lobe is an extension of the ancient limbic system, which in lower animals is concerned with smell. In higher mammals and man, the smell function has decreased in importance to be replaced by vision and hearing. Indeed, in humans, the *rhinencephalon,* once concerned with smell, has become associated with emotion.

Studies of ancient brain structures have been carried out at the Laboratory of Brain Evolution and Behavior of the U.S. National Institute of Mental Health in Poolesville, Maryland. The director, Dr. Paul MacLean, who originated the term limbic system, compares the human brain to an archaeological site. The outermost portion, the cerebral cortex, which is highly developed in man, envelops deeper layers that contain structures shared with our reptilian and mammalian forebears.

MacLean believes that many of our mental processes are related to those that prevailed in ancient subhuman forms. For instance, human aggressiveness is a carry-over from a time when hominids often faced a simple choice: Kill or be killed. In modern society, by contrast, aggressiveness generally leads only to trouble. The tension between, say, talking peace and preparing for war can be understood, according to MacLean, as "schizo-physiology," a split between the thinking portions of our brain (the cerebral cortex) and the feeling portions (the limbic system). In epilepsy and certain forms of mental illness, especially schizophrenia, dysfunctions in the limbic system produce emotional reactions that are "irrational" —out of touch with reality. Brain researchers are now trying to develop drugs that will harmonize the limbic and cerebral structures.

The Question of Language

During the past few years researchers have abandoned many entrenched beliefs about brain function. Freed from conceptual straitjackets, they have undertaken imaginative "I wonder what would happen if . . ." kinds of excursions into unknown territory. Thus, Dr. Floyd Bloom, director of the Arthur Vining Davis Center for Behavioral Neurobiology at the Salk Institute in San Diego, has investigated memory by injecting small amounts of vasopressin (a neuropeptide) into the brain ventricles of rats previously trained to jump onto a pole in order to avoid a painful electric shock. Bloom found that these rats retained "memories" of their training for longer periods of time than did rats injected only with salt water. Bloom later performed experiments on people, with similar results. Neuropeptides, he believes, may signal "that the survival of the animal is challenged and that the animal had best be attentive to its surroundings" —thereby enhancing memory. It is not too far-fetched to think that various neuropeptides will, one day, be assumed into the repertoire of pharmacology for humans.

ELECTRONIC "WINDOWS"

The first tool that provided a "window" into brain functioning was the electroencephalogram (EEG), developed 57 years ago by a German psychiatrist, Hans Berger. A shy, reclusive man, greatly interested in psychic phenomena, he rarely spoke publicly of his belief that the human brain generated spontaneous electrical signals that could be measured and interpreted. Not until 1934 were Berger's findings confirmed.

Among the newest and most exciting instruments of exploration are CAT and PET scanners. The CAT (*computerized axial tomography*) scanner combines conventional X rays with computer techniques to provide, in essence, a cross section of the brain or any other part of the body. Since its introduction in 1972, the CAT scan has revolutionized medicine by allowing neuroscientists to envision the subtle structural changes within the brain that accompany tumors and strokes. The newer PET (*position emission tomography*) scanner reveals activity within the brain—what is going on metabolically or chemically. For instance, an injection of glucose tagged with a radioactive "tracer" can be tracked through the brain to the site where it is metabolized.

BEAM (*brain electrical activity mapping*) uses computers to produce a color contour map of the electrical activity at the brain's surface. The computers can also be used in "evoked potentials" studies to average out the background "noise" that is present even when the brain is "idling." This enables neuroscientists to trace elementary sounds and flashes of light through multiple "way stations" within the brain. A single clicking sound, for example, can be broken down into eight different components starting with the ear and extending up to the auditory cortex. Abnormalities point to the location and, often, the nature of a disease.

An interest in behavior is shared by brain scientists of diverse persuasions and interests. Why do animals—and people—act the way they do? What brain events correspond with conscious experience? For instance, what is going on in my brain when, in a restaurant, I order a chocolate soufflé? How does it differ from events that would accompany my choosing apple pie à la mode instead? Implicit in such questions is the assumption that there must exist correlations between my choices and the events going on in my brain. But what are they?

The answer immediately introduces two levels of discourse masquerading as only one. To choose a chocolate soufflé is an act of will. It requires the use of words in a language that will be meaningful to the waiter and involves innumerable variables that can never be reduced to an explanation at the level of a chemical slipping across a synapse. Why am I in the restaurant in the first place? What does my ordering of a highly caloric dessert imply about my attitude toward obesity?

To ask such questions is immediately to participate in a long-standing debate regarding the place of language in human motivation. To some researchers, human language is only a more sophisticated version of the kinds of communication seen in lower primates. Attempts to teach chimps to speak have, on occasion, been declared successful; yet, invariably, the "language" has been revealed as only a clever form of imitation or, in the words of Sir Edmund Leach, a series of "circus tricks."

Nothing But, Nothing More

The debate over the uniqueness (if such it is) of human language and culture has great implications for brain research. And, if Sir Edmund is correct, then the social sciences—sociology, psychology, anthropology, and the rest—can never be based on the kinds of rules that govern the natural sciences; human attitudes, voting behavior, choices can never be predicted, or even explained with any precision. In other words, a detailed study of the brain is not ever going to shed much light on why I choose a chocolate soufflé over pie à la mode. As Leach put it, the capacity to make choices, which is linked to language, "represents a major discontinuity with the rest of nature." Our biology may *constrain* our behavior, but it does not *dictate* it.

How, then, is the mind related to the brain? "Reductionism," the simplest and currently the most popular view among nonbiologists, assumes that the mind is nothing more than the brain. As Carl Sagan wrote in *The Dragons of Eden*, "My fundamental premise about the brain is that its workings—what we sometimes call 'mind'—are a consequence of its anatomy and physiology and nothing more." Sagan's "nothing more" is a first cousin of the "nothing but . . ." argument ridiculed a few years ago by Arthur Koestler: "Love is *nothing but* sublimated sexuality. The mind is *nothing but* the brain and so on." Such "nothing but" arguments reduce complex biological phenomena to principles everyone *thinks* he is familiar with. In neurobiology, the argument takes the form: "If we only knew enough about the brain, all of the mysteries concerning 'mind' would disappear."

Yet everything that we have learned about the brain over the years points away from any simplistic relationship between neurons and the expression of mind. Performance is not confined to any specific portion of the brain but is "spread out." The brain is thus highly localized yet exhibits confounding "nonspecificity." Brain researchers still have not resolved this conundrum, and perhaps never will.

What Is "Understanding"

Can the brain understand itself? There is no way for us to stand back and "objectively observe" the brain or even theorize about it, without encountering constraints that are inherent in our neuronal networks. To what extent can "reality" or "truth" be ascertained when the inquiring organ—the brain—itself exhibits significant perceptual biases that can never be altered?

In 1922, Werner Heisenberg, a student of Danish physicist Niels Bohr, asked his mentor: "If the structure of the atom is as closed to descriptive accounts as you say, if we really lack a language for dealing with it, how can we ever hope to understand atoms?" Bohr's response could be applied to our attempt to "understand" the human brain: "I think we may yet be able to do so. But in the process we may have to learn what the word 'understanding' really means."

In recent years, physicists have joined forces with brain researchers. From this marriage of "hard" and "soft" science have come some impressive advances in our capacity to observe the brain. The advent of CAT scans has laid bare the structure of the human brain in ways that formerly were impossible without wielding saw and scalpel and actually "taking a look." PET and BEAM scans let us see the brain "in action."

But the marriage has sometimes been stormy, for physics, ever since the development of quantum mechanics, has been an extraordinarily "counterintuitive" discipline. Its principles are not readily grasped. It does not "make sense" in the same way that Newtonian physics did. As Heisenberg put it, "All the words or concepts we use to describe ordinary physical objects such as position, velocity, color, size, and so on become indefinite and problematic if we try to [apply them to] elementary particles."

Quantum theory is essentially an improvisation that is taken to be "true" only because it works. Gary Zukav, who surveyed the world of modern physics in *The Dancing Wu Li Masters,* wrote of quantum theory: "It is not necessarily how nature 'really is,' it is only a mental construction which correctly predicts what nature probably is going to do next."

A similar uncertainty exists in our study of brain organization. It simply isn't possible to know what is taking place among all of the 10 to 15 billion neurons and their interconnections. Spontaneous nerve cell discharges cannot be predicted nor does a given neuron discharge in a predictable manner even when affected by the same stimulus twice in a row. Getting a "fix" on an individual neuron is very much like trying to predict the location of a specific subatomic particle at a given moment. It can't really be done. As a result, no neuroscientist can ever exert experimental control over the internal state of a human brain. In a sense, then, choice, whim, and free will are rooted in the very structure of the brain itself.

This is not to say, incidentally, that brain functioning is strictly "free form." On the contrary, randomness at the micromolecular level is offset by behavioral constraints. Within the human brain, certain biases exist from birth that structure experience along certain lines. The infant, for instance, is born with the capacity to differentiate color, discriminate background noise from pure tone, even recognize and prefer the human face over all competing visual stimuli. An infant only moments out of the womb will turn its head in the direction of a voice (it prefers a female pitch), inquisitively searching for the source of the sound. Where does such a newborn infant learn such responses? Obviously, infant behavior is not learned at all. Such findings are bringing about a reconsideration of the ideas of Immanuel Kant, who held that all experience is organized according to the categories of our thought. In other words, our ways of thinking about space, time, and matter are predetermined by the structure of our mind.

Our visual system, for example, is limited to only a small segment of the electromagnetic spectrum—namely the radiation of wavelength from about 380 to 760 millimicrons. (The total range of wavelengths in the electromagnetic spectrum is from 0.00005 millimicrons to several miles.) This narrow segment contains all the colors that can be seen by the human eye. Thus, the very concept "color" depends on the neurological mechanism operating between eye and brain. Even within the visible spectrum we are not totally "free." The eyes are more sensitive to yellow-green than to violet, blue, or red.

These predispositions to perceive and behave in certain ways form the basis for recent sociobiological theories regarding individual as well as cultural development.

Brain researchers have also discovered lately that some of our most cherished ideas about how we perceive "reality" are wrong. Vision, for instance, is not based on the brain working as a kind of slide projector that receives impressions "ready made" for the eyes. Instead, the cells that gather information from the light receptors in the retina respond best to a spot of light of a particular size and in a particular point of the visual field. This information is conveyed to receptor cells in the visual cortex that are arranged according to columns that respond to variation in the angle and orientation of the lines in the visual field. Reality is a two-way street: We impose "meaning" on the world even as the world holds up cue cards.

Of even greater importance was the discovery that these recognition patterns within the brain's visual cortex required outside stimulation in order to develop normally. In a child with strabismus (crossed eyes), one of the eyes is usually suppressed in favor of the "dominant" eye. If this imbalance is not corrected, vision is lost in the eye not in use. For this reason, strabismus and cataracts are now operated on early in life. The importance of environmental stimulation of brain function persists throughout life and tells us much about ways to prevent senility. Simply put, the brain (like a muscle) must be used in order to maintain its optimal functioning. Everything else being equal, it is the actively involved, mentally stimulated elderly person who is least likely to develop senility.

We have learned much that is useful and much that is provocative about the brain during the past few decades, but it is too early to say how far we have advanced in mapping the *terra incognita* inside our skulls. Sir Charles Sherrington, a Nobel Prize-winning neurophysiologist, once referred to the brain as an "enchanted loom" that "weaves a dissolving pattern, always a meaningful pattern, though never an enduring one; a shifting harmony of subpatterns." What is most obvious today is our inability to understand these subpatterns. How are they formed? What is the guiding principle by which billions of neurons can be "orchestrated" to produce a symphony or a sonnet, a poem or play, a PET scanner or paradigm, a Trianon or a trance? We do not, of course, know.

But our ignorance on this score may be beside the point. While brain researchers remain bedeviled by frustrated curiosity, their findings have greatly improved the quality of our lives. They have enabled us to detect and, increasingly, to cure a variety of brain disorders and offered new hope to the mentally ill. Brain science has revolutionized certain forms of therapy, particularly for victims of strokes, and vastly increased our understanding, still imperfect, of the psychology of learning, of affection, of aggression.

If the workings of the brain remain elusive, even that has its uses. It reminds us that human beings are a race apart, special in a way they continually try to define and explain, never succeeding, but still the only creatures on Earth to whom it has occurred to make the attempt.

References

When Lord Byron bemoaned "the petrifactions of a plodding brain," he was unaware that his own brain was about twice the average size. This discovery, made after the poet's death in 1824, delighted those who believed intelligence to be a function of brain size. The idea seemed to make sense.

Unfortunately, writes biologist Steven Rose in **The Conscious Brain** (Knopf, 1973, cloth; Vintage, 1976, paper), most of the "sensible" ideas about the human brain have turned out to be wrong. In this case, Rose notes, "when a correction is made for body size, then the brains of all humans are closely matched in weight and structure, Einstein's or Lenin's with that of . . . a 'simpleton.' "

Rose's book is one of the best overall introductions to the subject. He traces man's concepts of the brain from the "hydraulic system" envisioned by René Descartes in the 17th century to our own preoccupation with the innards of computers.

It is still impossible to explain, he writes, just how "two fistfuls of pink-gray tissue, wrinkled like a walnut, [can] store more information than all the libraries of the world."

Two fine supplements to Rose's book—each profusely illustrated—are Keith Oatley's **Brain Mechanism and Mind** (Dutton, 1972, cloth & paper) and Colin Blakemore's **The Mechanics of Mind** (Cambridge, 1977, cloth & paper).

More adventurous readers may wish to sample Gordon Rattray Taylor's **The Natural History of the Mind** (Dutton, 1979, cloth; Penguin, 1981, paper). Reading Taylor is like hearing one of the late John Coltrane's tenor saxophone solos: We are led up, down, around, and all over the place, but in the end one likes having made the effort.

One of the tragedies of brain research is that much of what we know is a consequence of injury or disease. As Howard Gardner observes in **The Shattered Mind** (Knopf, 1975, cloth; Vintage, 1976, paper), what no doctor may do out of curiosity—"selectively destroy brain tissue"—is done every day by fate. The results are revealing, sometimes baffling. What is one to make of a person who can interpret "DIX" as the Roman numerals for "509" but is unable to pronounce the letters as a word—as "Dicks"?

"Holism" in the neurosciences—a conviction that the brain must be studied as an integrated whole, rather than as merely the sum of its "mechanical parts"—is eloquently defended by Russian neurophysiologist Aleksandr Romanovich Luria in **The Working Brain** (Basic, 1973, cloth & paper). He deftly covers rather esoteric subject matter in straightforward prose, without ever a trace of condescension.

Luria's brilliant and prolific disciple was Karl Pribram, whose **Languages of the Brain** (Prentice-Hall, 1971, cloth; Wadsworth, 1977, paper) is recognized as a modern classic.

Pribram ponders neurological experiments that over the years have confounded brain researchers, developing along the way his notion of the brain as a hologram

What is the relationship between mind and brain? **Consciousness and the Brain** (Plenum, 1976), edited by Gordon Globus, Grover Maxwell, and Irvin Savodnik, offers no definitive answers, although the speculative essays in this collection are eminently readable. The most valuable philosophical investigation of mind and brain is still Gilbert Ryle's **The Concept of Mind** (Barnes & Noble, 1949, 1975).

Ryle's target was the old Cartesian notion of "duality" —a conception of mind and body as different in their very natures. Ryle so demolished this view that none dared again propose a dualistic theory of the brain until John C. Eccles came along.

Rarely does a Nobel laureate in medicine set out his ideas in a text intended for undergraduates, but Sir John did just that in **The Understanding of the Brain** (McGraw-Hill, 1973; 2nd ed., 1976, paper only). Eccles explains with precision and elegance how nerve cells communicate with one another, though his dualist convictions force him into some tricky intellectual acrobatics.

The recent enthusiasm for computer simulations of the human brain is effectively challenged in **Computer Power and Human Reason** (W. H. Freeman, 1976, cloth & paper). Author Joseph Weizenbaum concedes the apparent "plausibility" of viewing man as a "sophisticated machine" but adds that, scientifically, the notion is simplistic.

Morally, Weizenbaum contends, this notion constitutes a "slow-acting poison." "What," he asks, "could it mean to speak of risk, courage, trust, endurance, and overcoming when one speaks of machines?" And what would a "deterministic" concept of the brain do to our belief in "moral responsibility"?

The relevance of physics to the brain sciences may not be immediately apparent to the general reader. But physics has a great deal to tell us, and a good place to discover why is in Richard L. Gregory's **Mind in Science: A History of Explanations in Psychology and Physics** (Cambridge, 1981). In this lucid, colorful, and demanding book, Gregory, a neuro-psychologist, ranges widely, from Babylonian myth to relativity theory, from the nature of light to the nurture of intelligence.

We live in two worlds, Gregory explains, a world that we see and perceive, and an underworld that we do not see but can *also* (with ingenuity) perceive: the everyday world of color, hardness, "reality" versus the lately discovered world of atoms and quantum mechanics. Do these worlds know each other? How?

"Brains," writes Gregory, "construct predictive hypotheses of aspects of the world which are generally useful for survival. [Most brain hypotheses] are largely at variance with the realities of physics. Our perceptual and conceptual hypotheses float free, even from things that seem most immediately sensed and known, to create and journey into realms of fantasy, myth, poetry, and illusion. Sometimes the fantasy traveler returns to bring gifts back to our world."

Some of these gifts of knowledge are unwelcome, unfriendly, disturbing; others are joyous, benign, enlightening. What, one wonders, would our reaction be if one gift someday turned out to be a knowledge of its own origin?

CHAPTER 2

Children Think with Whole Brains: Myth and Reality

Jerre Levy

I have often been astonished to learn of the ideas about human brain organization that surface in educational journals, teachers' newsletters, the popular press, *New Yorker* cartoons, and even advertisements for cars. These notions include:

- Rationality and logic are the sole province of the left hemisphere.
- Intuition and creativity are the sole province of the right hemisphere.
- Standard school curricula educate only the left side of the brain.
- Music and art are reflections of right-hemisphere processes.
- Modern technological civilizations depend on left-hemisphere functions and do not engage right-hemisphere functions; therefore, people with potentially high right-hemisphere capacities are the victims of discrimination in modern, advanced cultures.
- When engaged in any particular activity, people think with only one hemisphere at a time, either the left or right, depending on the activity.
- Some people think only with the left hemisphere; others think only with the right hemisphere.
- Scientists who study brain asymmetry now have all the answers regarding how children should be educated.

These assertions are either known to be false by neuropsychologists or are totally lacking in any supportive scientific evidence. Yet they have been accepted by many in the educational community, and inferences derived from them are currently having an impact on educational practice. Further, certain of these myths contain a strong strain of anti-rationalism in their suggestion that: 1. rationality only characterizes half the human brain and, 2. logical reasoning and creativity are polar opposites. Additional implications are that western concepts of intelligence refer solely to left-hemisphere processes, that standard intelligence tests measure only left-hemisphere competencies, and that any real creative insights derive from the right hemisphere.

The realization that the whole brain is actively participating in perception, encoding of information, organization of representations, memory, arousal, planning, thinking, understanding, and all other mental operations whether it be a social interaction, painting a picture, playing the piano, doing mathematics, writing a story, attending a lecture, or seeing a movie, seems to have escaped many, if not most, popular writers.

Only through misapprehension could some endeavors be attributed to left-hemisphere processes, and others to right-hemisphere processes. The two sides of the brain *do* differ, and they differ in quite important ways. The nature of these differences has little connection with the popularized picture, however, and the implications for human cognition and emotion are not what has been propagated.

Information About Hemispheric Differences

Language

Split-brain investigations and studies of patients with damage to one side of the brain demonstrate that speech is almost entirely confined to the left hemisphere in the vast majority of right-handers. There is some evidence that the right hemisphere may occasionally be able to generate spoken words, particularly if these are stimulated by strong emotion, but ordinary language production can be assumed to be almost always under control of the left side of the brain.

Other aspects of language are not nearly so asymmetrically organized as speech. The isolated right hemisphere of split-brain patients understands a great deal of what is said to it, has a comprehension vocabulary equal to that of a normal 12-year-old, and can read at least simple words. Its mechanisms of comprehension almost certainly differ from those of the left hemisphere, since it appears to have little or no comprehension of syntax and grammar, is unable to follow complex verbal instructions if these place too great a burden on short-term verbal memory, and seems to have no capacity for analyzing phonetics and deriving the sound images of words it reads. It knows that the word "cat" refers to a particular creature depicted in a drawing, but it does not know that the word "mat" rhymes with the name of the creature shown in the drawing.

Tachistoscopic investigations of brain asymmetry in normal people reveal that the two hemispheres are equally competent at reading concrete nouns and adjectives, but that the left hemisphere controls processing of verbs, abstract nouns, and adjectives. These findings suggest that when word meanings are susceptible to image or representation, there is little difference between the two sides in their abilities to recognize the word. When an imagistic representation is difficult or impossible, however, an asymmetry in favor of the left hemisphere emerges. A full appreciation of the meaning of concepts, of course, includes elaborate sets of verbal associations as well as sensory and experiential associations. When a normal person hears the word "dog," he or she does not merely derive the dictionary definition, but also generates images of dogs in various postures and activities, recalls the sounds of barks and howling, and, probably, recreates the emotions that real dogs elicit. This rich and full meaning of "dog" is derived by an intimate, collaborative integration of the processes of both sides of the brain.

That representations of meaning are incomplete and distorted for each separate hemisphere is apparent from observations of split-brain patients. One of the patients, N. G., asked me one day, "How is Professor Sperry? I haven't seen him for some time." Immediately after being assured that Sperry was well, N. G. passed him in the hallway. Sperry nodded, as did N. G., but neither spoke. When we had returned to the laboratory, she whispered to me, "Who was that man? He looked kind of familiar."

One would think that N. G. possessed a clear representation of who Sperry was, yet her failure to recognize him by visual cues shows that the left hemisphere's representation of the concept "Professor Sperry" did not include how he looked, or at the least, included only a vague and ill-defined image. This image was sufficient for generating a sense of familiarity, but insufficient to permit recognition. Fluent language usage can often mislead the listener into believing that complete and accurate concepts underlie the words and sentences.

Other evidence of the role of the right hemisphere in structuring meaning comes from findings that when patients with right-hemisphere damage are asked to provide a synopsis of stories read to them, they selectively omit emotional and humorous content. Obviously, the left hemisphere's memory structure for verbally presented material is incomplete, and the attentional system is biased to respond to only a subset of the information presented. In speech production, the grammar and vocabulary of these patients is normal, but frequently they are unable to convey emotional intonation. Since, in verbal interactions, tone of voice and speech modulation are important sources of communication, far less meaning is conveyed to the listener than would otherwise be the case. If someone tells us in a completely deadpan tone, "He killed the bear," we do not have the foggiest notion whether the person is elated by this fact, shocked, grieved, angry, proud, or surprised. We know a fact, but we do not know its implications, or how we should respond.

Right-hemisphere processes are very important for the apprehension of full meaning from oral or written communications and for the expression of full meaning.

Both hemispheres not only play critical roles in the purposes of language, but also in organizing the perceptual and cognitive processes that are prerequisite to understanding. Although reading disorders occur more frequently with left-hemisphere than with right-hemisphere damage, complete alexia (inability to read) can also occur when damage is restricted to the right side of the brain. I once examined a right-handed patient with massive damage to the right hemisphere whose speech and speech comprehension were fully intact. This patient had no damage to the left hemisphere, but developed a dense alexia; only after months of training was he able to read single letters, and with great difficulty, single words. He could decode one word at a time if all other words in the sentence were covered with his hands. He could "read" an entire sentence if he moved his hands so as to progressively uncover each subsequent word, but upon completion of the sentence, he was unable to report its meaning.

The patient showed similar difficulties with arithmetic. He could add and subtract single-digit numbers, but made many errors with double-digit numbers as well as with single-digit multiplication. Double-digit multiplication was impossible for him since he was utterly unable to align numbers on the page in a rational manner. When asked to multiply 7 times 8, he said, "Fifty-eight? Thirty-seven? I can't get an image of what it is." That he was suffering from a rather severe perceptual organizing disorder was affirmed by the observation that his verbal I.Q. was a normal 110, but his performance I.Q. was a severely retarded 35, yielding a full-scale I.Q. of 77. (This demonstrates quite clearly the fallacy of believing that I.Q. tests assess only left-hemisphere processes.)

Reading and arithmetic are not merely linguistic activities; they depend on perceptual organizing functions and imagistic memory. Research has demonstrated that a normal person's *right* hemisphere actually predominates in initial letter processing or instances when the writing is complex. Longitudinal studies of children reveal that those who prove to be good readers by the time they enter fourth or fifth grade displayed a right-hemisphere superiority at letter and word recognition in first grade that gradually shifted to a left-hemisphere superiority as the recognition process became automatized. These differential superiorities do *not* mean that the other hemisphere plays no role in reading; they merely reflect the relative predominance of one hemisphere or the other at various stages of reading fluency.

This brief review of the roles of the two hemispheres in various aspects of language should be sufficient to demonstrate that in the normal child or adult, both hemispheres contribute important and critical processing operations. The final level of understanding or output cannot be allocated to one hemisphere or the other. As the child learns to read, communicate orally, learn history, or engage in any other so-called "verbal" activity, both sides of his or her brain are learning, being educated, participating in the growth of understanding. The child's appreciation of literature depends on his or her ability to synthesize letters into words, words into sentences, sentences into meaning and thought. It depends on the ability to apprehend and respond to the rhythm of language; to imagine and feel the scenes and moods; to empathize with the characters and understand their emotions, values, and personalities; and to integrate all this into a rich and full meaning with structure, configuration, and detail. Such a process cannot be accomplished by either side of the brain alone, but represents so intimate an integrative activity that, in the end, we cannot say which side of the brain contributed what.

Art and Music

Disorders of music and artistic production regularly occur with damage to *either* side of the brain. The composer Ravel suffered a left-hemisphere stroke in mid-career and never produced another piece of music for the rest of his life. If music and creativity were the province of the right hemisphere, unfairly suppressed by an uncreative left hemisphere, one might have expected that once Ravel's left hemisphere was destroyed, he would have produced his best and most creative music.

The fact is that the left hemisphere is critically important in discriminating and in producing temporally ordered sequences. Patients with left-hemisphere damage have grave difficulty saying which of two tones occurred earlier in time—an ability unaffected by damage to the right hemisphere. Clearly, an understanding, appreciation, and expression of music depends on an ability to discriminate time relationships. If such discrimination is disrupted by left-hemisphere damage, it is not surprising to find correlated disruptions in musical ability. Studies of normal people have confirmed that it is the left hemisphere that orders events in time, even when the sensory cues are initially presented to the right hemisphere.

Normative studies show that discrimination and memory for single musical chords is superior in the right hemisphere. This finding is consistent with its general advantage for memorizing sensory experiences that are resistant to verbal, analytical description. Hemispheric asymmetries in the recall of melodies depends on whether temporal, rhythmic elements or chordal tones are of greater importance. Musical training is also a factor. For the musically untrained and unskilled, melodies tend to be perceived as single global configurations—a right-hemisphere predilection—but for the musically trained and skilled, the components of melodies are apparent, a left-hemisphere function.

Music involves sounds, their ordering in time, their loudness and softness, and their form and rhythm. It engages its listeners at the sensory, emotional, and intellectual levels. Neither hemisphere alone possesses all the specializations of music; neither alone can create or appreciate the magnificent compositions of our great composers. No basis exists for believing that music is a specialty of one hemisphere or the other—only overwhelming evidence that both hemispheres are essential for its creation and appreciation.

What of art? Damage to either side of the brain produces disabilities in drawing. With left-side damage, overall configuration continues to be adequate, but detail is radically impoverished. With right-side damage, rich details remain, but overall form is inadequate. We love a Rembrandt painting because of its beauty of color and form, the perfection of a hand, the tiny sparkle in an eye, the fact that every detail is perfectly depicted and part of a whole that is more than itself. It elicits memories, creates imaginations, and has meaning that makes contact with our own experiences. It causes us to think, to reason, to feel.

It is possible to sketch a head, having no eyes, mouth, nose, or ears, yet clearly recognizable as such. Similarly, it is possible to draw features, clearly representative of a human face, but with no unifying outline or form. Real art is neither pure configuration nor pure detail; it is a brilliant synthesis of the two together. A barely discriminable change in the line of a mouth makes a Mona Lisa or not. Art is no more a right-hemisphere process than it is a left-hemisphere process. When it achieves lasting value it is an intimate synthesis of both. It is intellect and feeling; perfection of detail and perfection of form; color that calls up multiple associations and color that calls attention to itself alone.

Studies of perception show that for memory for faces, deciding whether an array of dots is aligned in columns or in rows as defined by relative dot distances, locating a briefly exposed dot in space, discriminating line orientation, or matching arcs with circles of the same diameter, the right hemisphere surpasses the left. This is not true for matching two identical arcs or two identical circles, discriminating depth from binocular cues, mentally folding drawings into their three-dimensional forms, or remembering random shapes that have no verbal labels. These perceptual memory and organizing capacities are obviously important in art, but they certainly do not point to any special "creative" capacity of the right hemisphere. One might as well say that the absolute superiority of the left hemisphere at phonetic analysis, understanding rhymes, and deriving meaning from syntactical construction of sentences is indicative of a special "creative" ability of the left hemisphere!

These and other studies demonstrate that the two hemispheres differ in their perceptual roles, but none supply any evidence that one side is more "creative" than the other, more responsible for music and art, more capable of a truly creative act, more "intuitive."

Logic and Mathematics

Very little data is available about hemispheric asymmetries in mathematical and logical function, although arithmetical disorders can occur with either right-side or left-side damage. The right hemisphere of split-brain patients can do simple single-digit addition, subtraction, and multiplication and it surpasses the left at discriminating line orientation, orientation of other objects in space, and at discriminating the direction in which a point moves. These capacities, as well as the spatial-perceptual superiorities noted earlier, are of major importance in geometric understanding, which, itself, is necessary for a real understanding of algebraic relationships.

Given the left hemisphere's superiority in extracting meaning from syntactical structure, it might be expected to surpass the right hemisphere in derivation of meaning from algebraic structure and manipulation and reordering of algebraic symbols, but we have no direct evidence of this. The indirect evidence inferred from greatly superior symbol manipulation is so strong that I would be extremely surprised if the prediction were not borne out. Algebraic ability in manipulating symbols is not, of course, the defining characteristic of logic. Logical operations emerge in many endeavors—some involving mathematics, others involving verbal and symbolic manipulation.

In geometric reasoning, the right hemisphere is clearly superior, greatly surpassing the left hemisphere in operations such as viewing an "opened-up" drawing of an unfolded shape and mentally folding the drawing into a three-dimensional object. This mental manipulation of spatial relationships involves not only visualization abilities, but a rule-governed plan of transformation. I would call such rule-governed transformations highly *logical.* An even more striking example of right-hemisphere reasoning comes from split-brain studies showing that the right hemisphere can inspect a set of geometric shapes, extract the defining characteristic property of the set, and identify the shape within the set that does not belong. The right hemisphere does this at a far better level than the left. Given any reasonable definitions, this right-hemisphere ability reflects abstraction, generalization, and logic.

Patients with right-hemisphere damage very often show severe deficits in appreciating their current states, in integrating the various aspects of their lives, and in deriving reasonable expectations for their futures. They often deny that anything is the matter with them, that they are paralyzed, and they confabulate reasons why they are in wheelchairs. In a word, they behave illogically. Former Supreme Court Justice Douglas suffered a right-hemisphere stroke and returned to the Court in a wheelchair. When asked how he was doing, he responded, "Great! I'm just great. Everything's wonderful, and there's nothing the matter with me!" Taken aback, the reporter noted that Douglas was in a wheelchair. Douglas laughed. "The wheelchair? Oh, well, I tripped in the garden this morning and hurt my leg. It'll be well in a few days." If logic were the sole province of the left hemisphere, we would expect *not* to see such disorders with right-hemisphere brain damage.

Lest you think that the mythology is backwards, note that logical disorders also occur with left-hemisphere damage. Even in patients who have not lost speech, verbal reasoning is quite diminished. The ability to interpret proverbs, to recognize verbal analogies, to identify how two things are alike, and to perform other verbal reasoning tasks shows clear disorder. Patients tend to become overly concrete and less capable of drawing abstract generalizations.

The direct implication of these observations is that both hemispheres are involved in thinking, logic, and reasoning, each from its own perspective and in its particular domains of activity. Thinking and logic in the normal person derive from the specialized processes of both sides. Each hemisphere appears to have a limited and biased perspective and a restricted set of competencies that may allow adequate (but not excellent) performance in a highly restricted cognitive domain, but not a deep grasp of or insight into language, music, mathematics, or any other field of human endeavor. The creations of human culture derive from the fully integrated actions of the whole brain, and any further advances will require an intimate and brilliant collaborative synthesis of the special skills of both sides of the brain. All of the available data point to the validity of this conclusion; none supports the idea that normal people function like split-brain patients, using only one hemisphere at a time.

Interhemispheric Integration

What is the direct evidence that two hemispheres working together are better than either alone or even the sum of the capacities of the two sides? In contrast to normal people, the two hemispheres of split-brain patients cannot be simultaneously active. Only one hemisphere at a time is capable of attending to the sensory world. With bilateral sensory input, half the sensory world is missed. It is simply not perceived. This implies that the severed *corpus callosum,* the massive bridge of fibers interconnecting the two hemispheres, normally plays a highly important role in facilitating arousal of *both* hemispheres, in making it possible for both hemispheres to process information and to derive perceptions at the same time. Why would the brain be built this way if the *corpus callosum* did not also serve to integrate the cognitive activities of the two simultaneously thinking hemispheres?

Split-brain studies lead to a prediction of normal brain function. If dual tasks require interhemispheric communication, the imposition of a dual task in normal people should increase bilateral hemispheric engagement, even if both tasks are specialized to a single hemisphere. Further, if increased hemispheric engagement promotes optimal functioning of the brain, then subjects should be able to perform the dual task as well as a single task, perhaps even better, if the dual task requirements do not place too great a burden on operating capacities.

Joseph Hellige of the University of Southern California and his associates have shown that as task complexity increases, bilateral hemispheric engagement increases, and performance is, consequently, enhanced. Interestingly, it appears that even split-brain patients attempt to engage both hemispheres as task complexity increases. When two different colors are presented—one to each side of the brain—and patients are asked to match the color they see from among a set of choices in free vision, a single hemisphere controls the match through all trials. For some patients this is the left hemisphere, for others, the right, but the dominating hemisphere retains control of processing throughout all stimulus presentations. If colors are presented in varying geometric shapes, with the shapes irrelevant to the color-match required, unihemispheric dominance decays. It is as if a single hemisphere is unable to retain dominance with the increase in task complexity—a change that, in normal people, might be reflected as an increase in bilateral hemispheric engagement.

These observations suggest that normal brains are built to be challenged, that they only operate at optimal levels when cognitive processing requirements are of sufficient complexity to activate both sides of the brain and provide a mutual facilitation between hemispheres as they integrate their simultaneous activities. When tasks are at a very simple level, bilateral activation may be at a low level, with reliance on a single hemisphere that receives only weak facilitation from the other side. Generalizing from the split-brain findings, this would mean that attentional capacity would be low. The capacity to sustain attention for more than the briefest periods would be greatly diminished. Psychologically, this would be manifested as boredom and poor attention. Educationally, it would mean that simple, repetitive, and uninteresting problems would be poorly learned, with little benefit for either side of the brain.

Considerable evidence now suggests that the right hemisphere plays a special role in emotion and in general activation and arousal functions. If this is so, if a student can be emotionally engaged, aroused, and alerted, both sides of the brain will participate in the educational process regardless of subject matter. With maximum facilitation of both hemispheres, the result will be an integrative synthesis of the specialized abilities of the left and right into a full, rich, and deep understanding that is different from and more than the biased and limited perspectives of either side of the brain.

Implications for Learning Styles and Educational Practice

What does all this have to say regarding individual differences in learning styles? The evidence strongly disputes the idea that students learn with only one side of the brain, but, we do have evidence that there are individual differences among people to the extent that one hemisphere is more differentially aroused than the other. Gur and Reivich, for example, have found that people differ in the asymmetry of blood flow to the two sides of the brain, and that those having an asymmetric flow in favor of the right hemisphere perform better on perceptual completion tasks (thought to be right-hemisphere specialized). Individual differences exist in the extent to which people show a biased attention to the left or right side of space. Persons with a leftward bias tend to perform better on face-recognition tasks; those with a rightward bias, on phonetic analysis of nonsense syllables.

These differences suggest that whole-brain learning may be better accomplished for different people with different methods. In other words, the child with a biased arousal of the left hemisphere may gain reading skills more easily through a phonetic, analytic method, while the child with a biased arousal of the right hemisphere may learn to read better by the sight method. I am suggesting only that the *gateway* into whole-brain learning may differ for different children, *not* that one hemisphere or the other should be the object of education. Ultimately, our aim should be to assure that the child who learns to read through phonics will develop a fluent skill in sight reading, and that one who learns through the whole-word method will develop excellent skills at phonetic analysis so that any new word can be decoded.

Similarly, some children may better gain mathematical understanding if they are first taught the structure of algebraic equations and the methods of symbol manipulation. In the end, however, we want these children to appreciate the geometric, spatial functions specified by equations. We want them to understand *why* we say an equation of the form, $X = A + BY$ is called "linear," while one of the form, $X = A + BY + CY^2$ is called "quadratic." We want them to visualize a straight line defining the function between X and Y for the linear equation, and a quadratic curve defining the function between X and Y for the quadratic equation. Other children better understand if they are first taught the visual, geometric relationships, but, ultimately, we also want them to be able to specify these geometric forms in a symbolic equation.

From this perspective, "learning styles" refer to the method of introducing material, not to the type of understanding we ultimately want the child to gain, nor to the hemisphere we seek to educate. Standard school curricula, in contrast to some prevailing mythology, are *not* biased in favor of the left hemisphere. Reading, writing, grammar, literature, history, science, mathematics, music, and art all equally depend on both hemispheres and on the synthesis of their specialized abilities. Advanced societies and their technological and cultural accomplishments are reflections of brilliant syntheses of the partial perspectives of each hemisphere. Great men and women of history did not merely have superior intellectual capacities within each hemisphere, but phenomenal levels of emotional commitment, motivation, attentional capacities, and abilities for long-sustained interest in their particular areas of endeavor—all of which reflect the highly integrated brain in action.

The research is not yet available to demonstrate conclusively what all this means for educational practice, but at least certain inferences seem to me to follow directly from current research. Since these are merely inferences, without direct data for corroboration, I may be wrong. Educators are cautioned to use their own experiences and wisdom to check the validity of my conjectures. They should also be aware that my interpretations may not be accepted by all researchers, and that future research within a classroom setting may yield a different picture. Nevertheless, I feel some obligation to communicate the educational implications as I see them at the present time.

First, the popular 1960s idea that the educational experience should, under all circumstances, be "nonthreatening" to the child often meant that the educational experience should be nonchallenging, that children should not be confronted with material that stretched the limits of their capacities. This viewpoint indicated that the child should be prevented at all costs from gaining any notion of his or her abilities relative to others. To learn of his or her own special weaknesses or special skills supposedly generated either a poor self-concept or produced an unappealing arrogance. Yet challenges are what appear to engage the whole brain, to generate excitement and interest and attention, to provide the substrate for optimal learning.

Indeed, in spite of the best efforts of teachers and parents to hide the truth, children are remarkably adept in discovering where they stand with respect to other children, in understanding their own special skills and recognizing their own special difficulties. Students select fields of endeavor in accordance with their self-recognized abilities, tending to go into areas where their skills are high and avoiding areas where their skills are low. If students are so aware of their differential abilities in different areas, what might be the psychological/emotional consequences of trying to hide their strengths and weaknesses from them? We might unintentionally communicate to them that there is something shameful in being more or less apt than others in certain areas. How much better and healthier it would be to be truthful with children, to let them know that people are highly diverse in their skills and abilities, and that this diversity is what makes societies possible at all. They should be grateful for and appreciate the special skills that others have while acknowledging their own personal skills as gifts to be developed to their highest level.

Even small children can and should understand something about human brains. They can understand that the two hemispheres differ, that within each side there are many different processes, that all children use whole brains but use them in different ways, so that some people understand how cars work, while others find them very confusing. They can understand that some can write stories that everybody loves to hear, while others find writing a difficult chore. The child *needs* to learn how he or she thinks. The child *needs* to learn what constitutes a challenge in each area of endeavor, and *needs* to take comfort in the fact he or she lives in a world where an individual need not be perfect in all things because other people who have different ways of thinking will contribute to his or her life, just as he or she contributes to theirs. The child *needs* to appreciate people who are different, not resent that they may be better in some things or be ashamed at his or her particular weaknesses. The child *needs* to know where he or she is especially good and can achieve satisfaction and accomplishment, not only for the sake of his or her own emotional well-being, but for the sake of the world.

Formal education is only the beginning; if it is good, it teaches people how to educate themselves throughout their entire lives. And for this continuing self-education, individuals need to learn their own special pathways to learning, the ways they organize their thinking and identify their interests. They need to learn those things that engage their emotions, that are seen as thrilling challenges to understanding, that capture their attention, and that hold through years of effort. They need, in other words, to learn how to engage their whole brains in feeling, thinking, understanding, and achieving satisfaction.

So, in brief, the first of my inferences from current brain research is that challenges are not threats. Recognizing diversities does not lead to shame or arrogance; human brains are built to be challenged and built to understand themselves. In the classroom, I believe that children will learn best if their limits are stretched, if their emotions are engaged, and if they are helped to understand themselves and their own special ways of thinking and seeing the world.

A second inference that I draw is that all subject matters necessarily engage the specialties of both sides of the brain, and that the aim of education is to guide the child toward a deep synthesis of these differing perspectives. Regardless of how the subject matter may be best introduced for a given child, whether through left or right-hemisphere processes, this is only the initial step, a gateway into the whole brain. The synthesis we seek is not merely the sum of understanding of each side. This would yield merely two biased and incomplete representations of reality. We seek something that is more than and different from a simple addition, that is the real power of the human mind. How is such a synthesis to be achieved? We do not yet know. The research has not been done. Yet knowing the goal, perhaps it will be possible for teachers with sensitivity to find a way long before scientists can supply specific recommendations.

References

Dimond, S. J., and Beaumont, J. G., eds. *Hemispheric Function in the Human Brain.* New York: John Wiley & Sons, 1974.

"Hemispheric Specialization and Interaction." In *The Neurosciences: Third Study Program,* edited by F. O. Schmitt and F. G. Worden. Cambridge, Mass.: The MIT Press, 1974.

Segalowitz, S. J., and Gruber, F. A., eds. *Language Development and Neurological Theory.* New York: Academic Press, 1977.

Vinken, P. J., and Bruyn, G. W., eds. *Disorders of Speech, Perception, and Symbolic Behaviour.* Handbook of Clinical Neurology, vol. 4. Amsterdam: North-Holland Publishing Co.; New York: John Wiley & Sons, 1969.

Wittrock, M. C., ed. *The Brain and Psychology.* New York: Academic Press, 1980.

CHAPTER 3

Brain Behavior Research

Thomas R. Blakeslee

The Nobel Prize in medicine was awarded recently to Roger Sperry of the California Institute of Technology for his work in unraveling the secrets of the two hemispheres of the human brain. In the words of the Nobel committee, Sperry developed "an entirely new dimension in our comprehension of the higher functions of the brain."

This new understanding is of extreme interest to educators because it indicates that we have been ignoring and misunderstanding the important contributions of the nonverbal half of the brain. Sperry showed that when the two halves of the human brain are surgically separated, they can each have separate thoughts, knowledge, and emotions. Though the right half of the brain is superior to the left in some important abilities, the split-brain patient's conversation ignores and even denies the thoughts, knowledge, and emotions of the right brain.

The Split-Brain Experiments

When you look at a human brain (Fig. 1), it is difficult to see how people could ever have thought of it as the physical basis of a singular "mind." The human brain is clearly a double organ consisting of *two identical-looking hemispheres* joined together by several bundles of nerve fibers.

Sperry's first experiments were done on animals.[1] He showed that if the connections between the hemispheres were cut, it was possible to train each hemisphere separately so that the right side of the animal would learn one response while the left side could be taught a contradictory response. The right paw, for example, could be trained to push a lever when the animal saw an "X" on the right, while the left paw (and left visual field) would ignore the "X" and respond only to an "O." Since each hemisphere has nerve and visual connections only to the opposite side of the body, each side of the body was controlled by a different hemisphere (Fig. 2).

The "split-brain" operation has now been done on dozens of humans for relief of epileptic seizures. Though *all nerve connections between the two hemispheres (Fig. 1) are cut,* the patients seem surprisingly normal after the operation. Akeletis,[2] in 1944, reported on 25 split-brain operations without noticing any significant change in the patients' mental abilities!

---

1. Thomas R. Blakeslee, *The Right Brain* (New York: Doubleday, 1980), p. 117. (Includes glossary and extensive bibliography); R. W. Sperry, "The Great Cerebral Commissure," *Scientific American,* January 1964, pp. 42–52.

2. A. J. Akelaitis, "A Study of Gnosis, Praxis, and Language Following Section of the Corpus Callosum and Anterior Commissure," *Journal of Neurosurgery* 1(1944): 94–102.

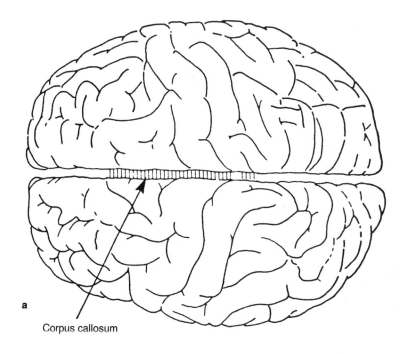

Corpus callosum

a

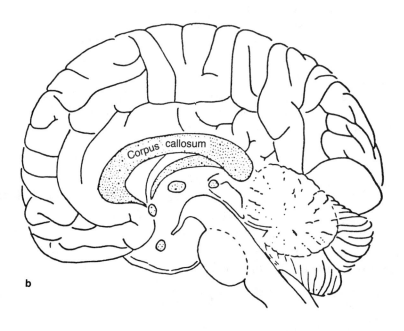

Corpus callosum

b

Figure 1.

In 1962, Sperry began testing a new series of human split-brain patients. By using techniques similar to the ones he developed in animal experiments, he was able to demonstrate that the patients indeed had "two minds." To quote Sperry:

> . . . in the split-brain syndrome we deal with two separate spheres of conscious awareness, i.e., two separate conscious entities or minds running in parallel in the same cranium, each with its own sensations, perceptions, cognitive processes, learning experiences, memories, and so on.[3]

Since the split-brain patients appear so normal after their surgery, much of what we consider normal behavior is possible without any interaction between the hemispheres whatsoever.

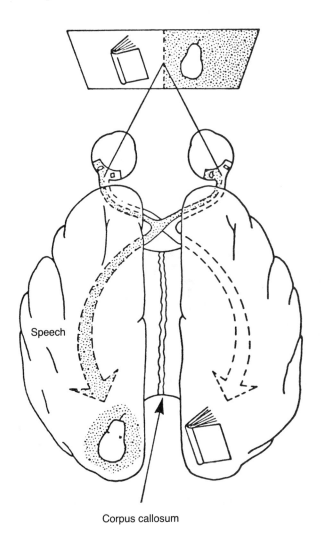

Corpus callosum

Figure 2.

3. R. W. Sperry, "Mental Unity Following Surgical Disconnection of the Cerebral Hemispheres," Harvey Lectures, Series 2 (New York: Academic Press, 1968), p. 318.

Even Sperry was amazed at how normal the split-brain patients appear to the casual observer. To quote again:

> ... (L. B.), a boy of thirteen, was talking fluently on the morning following the surgery and was able to recite the tongue twister, "Peter Piper picked a peck of pickled peppers ... etc." He also had recovered already his former personality and sense of humor and was passing off facetious quips to the doctors and nurses on the ward about having such a "splitting headache" that morning. ... He has been able to return to public school after having lost one year, and is reported to be doing passable work even though he had long been only a D student before surgery.[4]

Using special apparatus (Fig. 3), Sperry and his assistants, Levy and Gazzaniga, were able to separately test the abilities of the two hemispheres. They found that the seemingly "normal" conversation of split-brain patients was coming from the patient's left hemisphere. The right hemisphere showed a superior ability at nonverbal problems and would indeed take over control when appropriate, but all verbal or written responses were strictly from the left hemisphere (Fig. 3). If the word "pencil" were flashed on the left (to the right brain), the patient's left hand could pick out a pencil from a group of objects. If the patient were asked what he picked, he would answer that he did not know because indeed the left brain, which was doing the talking, saw and felt nothing. When asked why he selected the pencil, he would answer with something like "Well, I must have done it unconsciously."[5] This tendency of the left brain to rationalize and take credit for actions that we know to be under control of the right brain is very common. Since it appears to be an

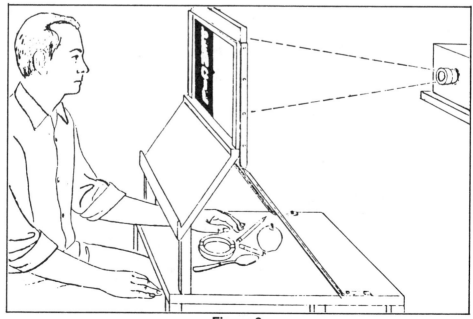

Figure 3.

4. Ibid., p. 302.
5. R. W. Sperry, "Hemisphere Disconnection and Unity in Conscious Awareness," *American Psychologist* 23(1968): 723–33; Blakeslee. p. 14.

already ingrained habit immediately after the split-brain operation, it is likely that the normal brain has the same habit.

Our Distorted View of Consciousness

Most of our knowledge of education and psychology is attained through discussions, articles, and tests based on the left brain's language processing. Since the left brain constructs an imaginary world in which it rationalizes and takes credit for actions of the right brain, it is not surprising that education has tended to ignore the functioning of the right brain.

Brain surgery gives us a spectacular demonstration of the distorted view of consciousness we get from verbal introspection. Since the brain is insensitive to pain, brain surgery is usually done with a local (scalp) anesthetic. This procedure makes it possible for the doctor to talk to the patient during the operation. In four cases of complete removal of the right hemisphere (hemispherectomy), Austin reported "Conversation with the patients was carried on throughout the operation without any significant change in conscious state."[6]

Our verbal reporting of consciousness is so one-sided that complete removal of the right hemisphere goes unnoticed, though it does cause serious losses in objective consciousness and performance. Often the patient ignores the left side of his body and visual space, yet rationalizes by claiming, for example, that his left hand is "somebody else's." Emotional response and voice is flat and nonmusical. Words are understood only in their literal meaning with metaphor and tone of voice totally missed. Simple spatial tasks like putting a shirt on right side up or finding the way back from the bathroom are impossible.[7]

Removal of the left hemisphere is much less common because it virtually eliminates verbal abilities. Several cases have been recorded, however, where a serious tumor threatened the person's life. These patients all retained their nonverbal personalities and emotional responses—an important kind of consciousness that is ignored by the left brain. One patient who had his left brain removed at the age of 47 was found five months after his operation to have a Wechsler performance I.Q. of 110. This placed him in the top 25th percentile of the population in nonverbal reasoning ability, even though his verbal I.Q. fell to zero.[8]

Split-brain patients have given us a unique opportunity to separately test the abilities of the two halves of the brain. When all of the studies are taken together, a clear pattern emerges (first observed by Jerre Levy). It appears that since the kind of brain organization needed for language is not compatible with many other important tasks, the human brain tends to organize as two specialized hemispheres. The left hemisphere organizes for sequential,

6. G. Austin, W. Hayward, and S. Rouhe, "A Note on the Problem of Conscious Man and Cerebral Disconnection by Hemispherectomy," in *Hemispheric Disconnection and Cerebral Function*, edited by M. Kinsbourne and A. Smith (Springfield, Ill.: Charles C. Thomas, 1974), p. 103.

7. Howard Gardner, *The Shattered Mind* (New York: Vintage Books, 1976), p. 296; Blakeslee, p. 140.

8. Aaron Smith, "Speech and Other Functions After Left (Dominant) Hemispherectomy," *Journal of Neurology, Neurosurgery, and Psychiatry* 29(1966): 467–71; Blakeslee, p. 153.

logical things as required by language, while the right hemisphere seems to think more directly in sensory or visual images—without the abstractions of words.

Thus we have the best of both worlds because we have language and logic, yet we can recognize a face in a crowd at one glance. We have teamwork between intuitive and logical thinking that is extremely powerful. This teamwork has been recognized by the great creative thinkers from Aristotle to Einstein.

Two Kinds of Knowledge

Verbal and nonverbal knowledge are quite distinct and basically incompatible. Take, for example, our memory of a person's face: We can remember verbally that he has "a black moustache and glasses" and then we try to find the face in a crowd by examining each face for those features. This is basically how a computer achieves recognition; it is cumbersome, and totally ineffective if the moustache is shaved off.

The nonverbal approach to the same task involves remembering the face as a complete image—without words. This method is so effective that we can often recognize a friend's face at a glance in a childhood class picture, taken before a moustache is possible. Sometimes "a picture is worth a thousand words." Old vacation photos can be recognized years later with no effort, even though they are just a small subset of the millions of scenes from the vacation and since that time. The visual memory has no problem with recognizing things that are upside-down, backward, partially obscured, or otherwise altered.

The visual memory is a direct record of a sensory image just as a muscular image in dancing or sports is directly remembered. It is possible to know something in a nonverbal way, yet not know it verbally (and vice versa). One can have a "feel" for throwing a ball which involves many subtle, intuitive corrections for movement of the receiver, wind, sloping terrain, etc. This is possible without any verbal or analytical knowledge of the equations or principles involved. On the other hand, a mathematician who programs gunnery computers may be an expert in the left brain knowledge of trajectory—yet have no "feel" whatsoever for throwing a ball. Essentially, they are two different approaches to the same knowledge. Each has its own strengths: The equations are too slow to use in a ball game, while the "feel" ceases to work when the projectile must strike its target in another continent or planet.

Verbal and nonverbal knowledge each have their areas of proper application. Unfortunately, education has tended to give a very unbalanced emphasis to the left brain, verbal approach. Many graduating engineers, scientists, and even artists have learned the equations but not the "feel." This is a natural result of exposure to teachers who are unaware of the nonverbal side of their own minds.

To improve education, we must first improve the teacher's understanding of his or her own thought processes. The one-sided picture of our consciousness provided by verbal introspection must be replaced by a consciousness which also includes awareness of our nonverbal perceptions. Unfortunately, this requires changing mental habits which have taken a lifetime to form. Scientific evidence has taught us to see the earth as a sphere, in spite of the fact that it looks flat. Likewise, the evidence of mental duality can help us to reinterpret our mental experience for a deeper understanding.

The educational process must be approached as a dual one which produces both verbal and nonverbal understanding. To do this, we must engage and exercise both the verbal and nonverbal side of the student's mind. The ability to use these two processes *together* must be exercised. The basis of the creative process is an interplay of intuition and logic. This interplay can only be developed by practice.

Though several of the split-brain patients returned to school and did average work, they had exceptional difficulty with geometry. Franco and Sperry[9] studied these students and concluded that the separation of the hemispheres prevented the right brain's visual insights from being communicated to the left brain for logical proof and verbalization. Geometry, therefore, is an excellent exercise of this important interaction in normal students.

A Danger in the Learning Styles Approach

One of the important lessons of the split-brain studies is that verbal and nonverbal modes of thought each have their place. Sports, dance, and art are best approached with the verbal channel virtually shut down. Most creative thought, however, requires a kind of teamwork between verbal and nonverbal processing. One of the biggest dangers in the "learning styles" concept is the possibility of one-sided development. Because a student tends to favor a left or right-brain approach does not mean we should develop only the favored approach. To do so is to reinforce habit. The ideal would be to develop *both* halves of the brain and their ability to work together.

The organization of the hemispheres is almost entirely a matter of training. Mental habits established in school can strongly help or harm a student's creative capacity. If the left hemisphere of the brain is surgically removed before the age of five, normal speech will develop in the *right* hemisphere. This incredible plasticity of the infant brain shows just how much education can influence effective brain organization. If one side of the brain is overlooked, the student will never realize his full potential.

Keep in mind the notion of *balance.* If a student tends to respond only to a left or right-brain approach, do not reinforce the habit by catering to it. Do not classify students as right-brain or left-brain types, allowing the weaker mode to atrophy. To realize the marvelous potential of the human brain, *both* modes of thinking must be developed. Even more important, they must be developed interactively; the true basis of creativity is in the interplay of intuition and logic.

9. L. Franco and R. W. Sperry, "Hemisphere Lateralization for Cognitive Processing of Geometry," *Neuropsychologia* 15(1977): 107–14.

CHAPTER 4

Education and the Left Hemisphere

Robert Zenhausern

Neuroeducation is a term that can be applied to that aspect of education that focuses on the interaction of the brain and behavior in learning systems. Within this framework an indictment has arisen: Education is too left hemisphere oriented.

Any discussion of an overly emphasized left hemisphere orientation must flow from an understanding of the contribution of each hemisphere of the brain and its integration into observable behavior. All too often, the hemispheres are described in terms of product: verbal or logical for the left hemisphere, emotional or intuitive for the right hemisphere. The emphasis, however, must be on process, not product, if we are to maximize strengths by tailoring our teaching to the unique style of each student.

For the most part, the two hemispheres do the same things, but they do them differently. What differentiates the two hemispheres is their processing style: sequential for the left hemisphere and parallel for the right hemisphere (Bradshaw and Nettleton, 1981).

Consider these two situations: 1) You are given a verbal description of someone and then must identify that person; 2) You are shown a picture of a person and then must select her. The first task demands the sequential style of the left hemisphere—the words descriptive of the various facial features are read in sequence and must be combined into an overall perception. The second situation reflects the parallel style of the right hemisphere—the picture is seen as a whole and various facial features can be extracted. It is clear that the right hemispheric approach is more efficient for this task. The picture is seen all at once (in parallel) while the verbal description must be processed sequentially. Language by its very nature is *sequential*. Word order and syntax, essential to meaning, cannot be easily processed in parallel. Hence, the left hemisphere has been labeled the "verbal" hemisphere because its sequential processing style is compatible with the sequential nature of language, just as the parallel processing style of the right hemisphere is compatible with the demands of spatial tasks. From this point of view, cerebral asymmetry is related to a compatibility between the processing style of a hemisphere and the type of processing required for a task.

For the most part, cerebral asymmetries in processing reflect *relative efficiency* rather than a "can do-can't do" dichotomy. There seems to be one exception to this relative rather than absolute difference between the hemispheres: in most persons, only the left hemisphere is capable of speech and of phonetic representation (Levy, 1974). The right hemisphere cannot tell whether the two words "though" and "blow" rhyme, since the task demands that the written word (grapheme) be converted to an auditory form (phoneme). Only the left hemisphere has this capability.

For other tasks, even if the processing style of either hemisphere is compatible with the task, one hemisphere is clearly superior. In the example of facial recognition, right hemisphere/parallel processing is superior, even though the task could be accomplished by left hemisphere/sequential processing. Other tasks can be done equally well by either hemisphere. A list of concrete words, for example, could be learned by converting and storing them as visual (right hemisphere) representations or in an auditory/verbal (left hemisphere) form.

The most common misconception about brain functioning stems from an exaggeration of the importance of functional cerebral asymmetry. In an intact individual, no task can be accomplished without the integrated functioning of both hemispheres. On the other hand, integration does not mean equality, and as tasks change, the relative importance of the two hemispheres changes. Thus, the left hemisphere is relatively more activated when a verbal response is required and the right hemisphere when a visual or spatial response is required. The tasks that can be completed in the processing style of either hemisphere (e.g., remembering words) are most pertinent to learning styles analysis. People do not process tasks in the same way. The goal of instruction based on learning styles must be to make the teaching strategies of the teacher compatible with the learning styles of the students.

Dyslexia and mathematics learning offer examples of areas which may be considered in light of neuroeducation and learning styles.

Dyslexia

There is a cognitive style variable based on the more or less consistent tendency to use the processing style of one hemisphere more frequently than the processing style of the other (left vs. right activation—Gur and Gur, 1981). I have developed a questionnaire that classifies individuals into these right or left orientations.[1] Using this questionnaire, Zenhausern et al. (1981) found that the seven learning style elements scores that differentiated rights and lefts were identical to those that Dunn and Dunn (1977) found differentiated good and poor readers. Oexle and Zenhausern (1981) found that while good readers split almost evenly between rights and lefts, 17 of 20 poor readers were rights. This finding was replicated by Golden (1981).

Given the importance of the left hemisphere to the verbal skills involved in reading, it seems likely that an individual who tends to be a right would have a problem in left hemisphere processing. Since half the good readers in our study scored right, a right hemisphere style is not the cause of poor reading, although it is a related factor. Golden (1981) was able to specify one problem very clearly. While good and poor readers did not differ in process-

---

1. Available from the author.

ing semantic information, the poor readers were quite inferior in both speed and accuracy on a rhyming task. The semantic task involved determining whether two visually presented words had the same meaning; the rhyme task involved determining whether two visually presented words rhymed. Since the rhyming words were not orthographically similar (though/blow) auditory processing (left hemisphere) was necessary. In the semantic task, the meaning of the words did not depend on hearing them. These results seem to indicate that many poor readers do not have a problem with meaning, but with *converting a written word to its auditory equivalent.*

Traditionally, we teach reading by associating a word with a sound, and from that sound derive meaning. For some, this is a classic mismatch that arises when individual differences are ignored. Reading aloud, word for word, is difficult for someone who is slow in converting a written word to its auditory equivalent. Suppose this same individual could look at a paragraph, quickly explain the basic meaning, and answer questions about what was read. Shoud we say this person cannot read? Phonetic decoding is an important skill in reading, but *comprehension* is the goal. The two skills can be taught separately so that difficulty with phonics does not interfere with comprehension. Education *is* too left hemisphere oriented if phonetic decoding is considered the only evidence of reading ability.

Mathematics Learning

There is an interesting parallel in mathematics to this dual skill approach in reading. Children who have not learned the basic arithmetic operations obviously cannot solve word or more complex problems even though they may understand the logic involved. Although these basic skills must be mastered, the use of a calculator to solve the more complex problems would permit the skills involved to be taught separately from the basic arithmetic processes. Too much emphasis on the "correct" way can handicap a child. Consider a student who consistently gives fairly correct answers to mathematics problems but who shows no work of the process employed. Do we say that the student has not learned the subject? Or do we try to find out how he or she solved the problems so we can teach other students who think the same way?

The indictment that education is too left brained may reflect the fact that only certain answers are considered evidence of learning. Education will never be too left brain oriented if teaching is tailored to the individual strengths of students.

References

Bradshaw, J., and Nettleton, N. "The Nature of Hemispheric Specialization in Man." *The Behavioral and Brain Sciences* 4(1981): 51–91.

Dunn, R., and Dunn, K. *Teaching Students Through Their Individual Learning Styles: A Practical Approach.* Reston, Va.: Reston Publishing Co., 1978.

Golden, M. "Grapheme to Phoneme Deficit in Dyslexia." Doctoral dissertation, St. John's University, 1981.

Gur, R. C., and Gur, R. E. "Handedness and Individual Differences in Hemispheric Activation." In *Neuropsychology of Left-Handedness,* edited by J. Herron. New York: Academic Press, 1980.

Levy, J. "Psychological Implications of Bilateral Asymmetry." In *Hemispheric Function in the Human Brain,* edited by S. Dimond and J. Beaumont. New York: John Wiley & Sons, 1974.

Oexle, J., and Zenhausern, R. "Differential Hemispheric Activation in Good and Poor Readers." *International Journal of Neuroscience,* 15 (1981):31–36.

Zenhausern, R.; Dunn, R.; Cavanaugh, D.; and Eberle, B. "Do Left and Right Brained Students Learn Differently." *Roeper Review* 4(1981): 36–39.

CHAPTER 5

Brain-Compatible Education

Leslie A. Hart

I propose to discuss what I view as the most important development in all the history of education. In fact, I submit that the topic can fairly be called the most important and pervasively valuable advance in the entire history and prehistory of humans.

We can think of that history as being some four million years or more — depending on how we define "human" — or we can consider only the 100,000 or 200,000 years that *homo sapiens,* or "Modern Man," has been on earth. Or we might take the 10,000 years, as round number, that we say civilization has existed. No matter; I am suggesting that what is happening now has never happened before. We are entering wholly new ground.

In the introduction to his book, *Broca's Brain,* Carl Sagan says:

> We live in an extraordinary age.... By far the most exciting, satisfying and exhilarating time to be alive is the time in which we pass from ignorance to knowledge . . . the age where we begin in wonder and end in understanding. . . . There is only one generation privileged to live through that unique transitional moment and that generation is ours.

Of course, there is no way we can be prepared for rare, stupendous transitions. Change of this scope sneaks up on us. We tend to be occupied with details. Most of us, for instance, have lived through all or most of the "computer revolution." Yet it may be hard to say when we individually became conscious of what was happening and its major implications. To many people, "computer" is still a word that intimidates and causes uneasiness, even though virtually everything happening around us is affected by, or dependent on, computer use.

But I suggest that this computer revolution is trivial compared to what I will call simply the coming of the Brain Age.

Until perhaps 25 years ago, humans operated without a substantial understanding of the brain that is our "chief executive" or "head office." I dare to predict that within 15 or 20 years we will be operating on almost all fronts with the basis of the new understandings now available and developing.

We are familiar with the cliché that we have been making sensational progress in technologies, but few advances in human affairs—perhaps even slipping back in some places. Learning improvement; elimination of poverty and crime; racial and ethnic conflict; marital, family, and child-rearing difficulties; alienation; drug abuse; social planning; personal emotional handi-caps . . . these are a few of the problem areas in which we seem to make little progress. I am suggesting that these are areas in which understanding of the brain, the *human* brain, is essential, that with the new understanding now available we can begin to make progress on exponential growth curves that characterize our advances in technical areas.

Those who are not much interested in brain matters may, I realize, regard this kind of talk as grandiose and not helpful. But those who have begun to think in "brain" terms may well glimpse what lies ahead and see current developments as helpful and promising in the extreme—nowhere more so than in education.

A Fresh Approach

Why is the brain approach essentially new?

First of all, we have all been in the grip of the behavioral psychologists who have dominated that field in this country, and indeed still do. The early behaviorists made it a firm policy to steer away from the brain about which little was known. That avoidance is only now slowly breaking down. Schools, of course, were set in their present class-and-grade form about 140 years ago, before there even existed a field called "psychology." School people had no interest in or knowledge of the brain.

Secondly, we have only recently accumulated and organized enough knowledge about the human brain to have a "critical mass" that can be applied and that permits building a theory of learning. Most of these new findings are no older than 30 years; some are much more recent.

The Proster Theory that I first advanced about nine years ago, drawing from many disciplines, was published in 1975. It appears to be the first comprehensive, brain-based theory of *human learning*. Quite possibly others now exist or are being developed.

Education has never had a viable, coherent, useful theory. We have little experience in applying a theory to practice. Our primitive trial and error methods have kept us wallowing in failure, going around in circles as we "rediscover" old approaches that did not work and spinning our wheels with fads and buzzwords. Imagine someone giving you a large box of parts that could be used to build a television receiver. You could try for a lifetime, or many lifetimes, to build a set, but without theoretical understanding it would be hopeless. Theory guides what you are doing and suggests better ways to do it.

A theory is not a recipe. It does not tell you what to do Monday. But with theory we can build, and keep building. We can both design and construct educational settings that will work enormously better to produce more effec-tive learning.

Where Learning Happens

We must realize first that *the brain is the organ for learning.* Unlike "mind," which is a vague term, the brain is real, specific, tissue. "Brain" means unification, centralized control. Most creatures don't have brains. Insects, for example, have an assortment of ganglia that are not unified. The moth cannot learn not to fly toward the candle.

The brain usually weighs 3 pounds (1,500 grams) or a bit more. It is not by any means a gelatinous all-purpose mass; on the contrary it has a most complex architecture, with structures for various purposes, all intricately interrelated. Protected in its box of bone, the brain handles (in health and for practical purposes) all learning, all emotions, and almost all behavior.

Most of the brain's functions can be listed under four headings:

1. *Housekeeping.* The brain controls the many subsystems of the body that keep us alive, such as blood pressure, digestion, salt level, temperature, etc., as well as balance and muscle coordination.
2. *Adjustment.* The brain adjusts these systems to meet conditions and needs. The major adjustments involve what we call "emotions." The prime concerns here are individual and species survival.
3. The brain receives and processes *informational input* and *extracts patterns* from it. So to speak, it "recognizes what is happening."
4. The brain *builds and stores programs* for all kinds of activities.

This listing can be particularly valuable for educators. We should understand that we cannot take the often brilliant achievements of brain research and simply pass them over directly to schooling. The neuroscientists work mainly in the microworld of detail. They do not yet know how "learning" is somehow stored in the brain, but if they found out tomorrow, it would not likely help much in education. Educators would still have the problem of organizing for learning and making it happen.

In general, educators do not have to understand the detailed electro-chemical workings of the brain. Rather, we need a macro or molar approach: *to grasp what the brain is for, how, in broad, it evolved, how it keeps the species alive, and how its major portions work in respect to our ordinary daily living and learning.* (Most scientists have studied disease and trauma rather than normal brains in normal use).

The Brain's Overwhelming Numbers

We can generate more respect for the brain—even that of a "stupid" child—if we consider the numbers involved. In the retina of one eye, for example, there are more than 100 million receptors! The key cells of the brain, neurons, number at least 30 *billion,* and some may have at least 10,000 connections with other neurons. As we perceive the possible combinations beyond the trillions, we can begin to grasp why the brain can be so subtle— and why each brain is so different from any other.

Years ago it was supposed the brain was a sort of telephone switchboard: the incoming (afferent) signals were connected so that "response" (efferent) signals were sent to the muscles. Today the old, simple stimulus-response notion appears ridiculous. The entire afferent/efferent network accounts for less than 5 percent of the nervous system.

Much is known about how the brain evolved over some 400 million years or more. We can explain, for instance, why the eyes, in the front, partially process what is seen, send information to a way-station in the center of the brain, which in turn sends to the occipital lobes at the very rear of the head where the visual areas determine the pattern of what was viewed.

The brain is not "logical" in design; it expresses changing survival needs over a very long time. The brain we use today is probably exactly like that of humans tens of thousands of years ago. The brain a child brings to school was not developed for formal schooling but for surviving in a changing world long ago—and particularly for hunting. To expect that brain to be comfortable with typical schooling obviously is absurd. We need *brain-compatible* schools that accept the brain as it is.

Today, we can understand to a large degree the implications of this view. We can also grasp the startling idea that sequential or linear logic was invented only about 4,000 years ago. Our much older human brain took its shape long before that time so *no part of the brain is "naturally" logical.* It resists efforts to make it function logically; yet great efforts are made to teach logically, often with dismal results!

The Three-Level Brain

Paul MacLean, one of the world's leading researchers in brain evolution, has made us aware of the "triune" nature of our brains. A very old (reptilian) brain forms the core, managing basic functions and making some simple, broad decisions. It is a rigid, conservative brain that clings to ancient ways. Over and around it has formed a newer, much larger brain (old mammalian) that today handles many aspects of emotion. Over and around this, in turn, is the huge cerebrum (new mammalian), a brain that in evolutionary time was "born yesterday." The cerebrum is a distinctively human brain in size and complexity, accounting for about five-sixths of the whole brain. While it is adventurous, eager for new input, its size makes it slow to arrive at decisions. Under "threat" it downshifts, Proster Theory holds, letting the older brains have more influence. Teachers see this happening when a child "freezes."

The cerebrum or newest brain handles language and all we think of as "education." But if we want students to learn, they must be in non-threatening settings. Threat and learning are opposed. (An exception is pure rote learning which can proceed under moderate threat.) The conventional classroom, however, is in every sense a high-threat situation for most students, one that inhibits learning beyond rote, severely and constantly.

The learning theory that educators study has long been criticized as fragmentary, and of little practical use. The great bulk of it was derived from study of rats and other animals in laboratory boxes. *But the rat and other small animals have only a trace of the cerebrum or new brain!* A rat brain is about 600 times smaller and a million times less complex than a human brain. We could study the rat brain for centuries and never learn much about the cerebrum, much as we could study wagons and find out little about gasoline engines. "Rat psychology" has given us a lot of misleading answers.

Further, there are plainly two kinds of "learning": 1.) what we can call "species wisdom" that is passed on with the genes (a bird can build its nest without instruction, without ever seeing another nest built), and 2.) "new learning," acquired after birth. The simpler a creature is, the more it depends on the built-in species wisdom. Even rats, fairly high up the scale, rely much more on genetically transmitted behaviors than on learning after birth. Humans, of course, do most learning after birth, over a period of many years. (Not that genetic factors are unimportant; they likely have more effect than we commonly realize.)

Learning as Programs

Brain authorities agree that humans operate by *programs*. A program is simply a fixed sequence of steps toward a foreseen goal. The bird has a program for building its nest. A washing machine works by a mechanical program of step after step. If we look at our behavior, we can readily detect the programs. Count, for example, the steps you go through to enter your car and start it up, to cook a meal, or to play a piece on the piano.

Proster Theory defines learning as *the acquisition of programs useful to the learner.* This is a helpful definition, one that can turn us away from asking questions simply to see if a student can answer, to watching instead whether the students *has* and *uses* a suitable program at the right time.

In our first 20 years we acquire programs in the hundreds of thousands. We need a program, for instance, to recognize a word, another to utter it, still others to write, print, or type it. We need a huge brain to store these countless programs.

We learn programs in groups of alternatives, or variations. To eat with a spoon, we need a whole set of programs for different spoons and different foods. (The term "proster," a compression of "program structure," means such a set.) To illustrate, we learn to open doors by pushing, pulling, stepping on a pad, turning a knob, using a key, pressing on a bar, etc. To operate in the "real world," we have to build and store a "proster" for door-opening. When we encounter a particular door, we have to select the right program for the need.

The Role of Patterns

To choose the proper program, one has to *evaluate* the situation at hand. The program selected is then put into use, and either achieves the goal or aborts. When our chosen programs work, our confidence grows; if too many failures occur, we lose ground—as we can see in any typical school.

Evaluation rests primarily on *pattern-detection*. Because accurate and sensitive pattern recognition has been vital to human survival, we have developed brains for which this is a natural function. In part, brains are *designed* for pattern detection as lungs are for gas exchange and the heart for pumping blood. The brain does not have to be *taught* pattern detection; indeed, that effort may interfere and inhibit.

Young children readily know the pattern "chair" and distinguish chairs from stools, benches, sofas, etc. even though chairs come in a huge variety of forms. A four-year-old will say "Tommy hitted me and I falled down," showing a grasp of the past tense "ed" pattern. Learners can recognize the letter "a" or a question mark, even though these symbols are found in many styles, sizes, or colors. One recognizes the *pattern,* not a specific shape. Amazingly, we can quickly spot a person we know among 500 strangers.

To detect patterns, however, we need a huge amount of *input.* To recognize dogs, we must see many dogs and non-dogs, and receive some feedback on which is which. Input is the raw material from which we form a sense of pattern. We can define the *process* of learning as *the extraction of meaningful patterns from confusion.*

Schools usually try to present patterns in neat, "logical," unconfused settings that miss the point: the pattern has to be extracted from all the ambient noise, irrelevancies, and accidental elements. The brain will do this, brilliantly and effortlessly, if threat is low, input high, and the situation "real," i.e., complex and confused. This ability is inborn, and cannot be taught, but conditions can be created (high input with feedback) that foster a range of pattern recognition.

One of the most valuable aspects of a brain-based theory is a focus on patterns. What we often call "insight" or "concept" is nothing more than pattern recognition.

As patterns are learned, finer and finer discriminations can be made. The brain is marvelously adept at using *clues.* As brain researchers have long agreed, *probability,* not "logic," is the key to discrimination. We recognize a friend by clues that add up to "Harry"; a dog by fur, color, size, and motion clues that indicate the probability of "dog" (and are subtly different than those of "cat").

From childhood, we have been conditioned to accept that Greek-type "logic" is the ideal and even most noble form of thinking. But we need only look around us at human achievements to see that very little has stemmed from sequential logic. Even in the sciences, advances typically come from hunches, transfer, accidents, and serendipity. Most technological progress comes from a slow bit-by-bit accretion.

The jigsaw puzzle presents a good illustration of how humans work. If 20 people are given identical puzzles to put together, likely no two will do it the same way—but all will complete it. We cannot understand what "individual" means until we recognize that each brain will use what *it* has stored from experience to interpret what it is now dealing with. No two brains see the same "outside" world.

With Proster or other brain-based theory, we can now enter fresh ground. We can finally design instruction instead of using obsolete models based on class-and-grade. Schools can be *brain-compatible,* created to fit the human brain, with teaching focused on *programs* and *patterns.*

Much work has been done on methods and materials, so that we can at once, if there is the will, begin applying the new theory. Learning outcomes should be far superior, and schools far happier places.

References

"Educational Implications of Recent Brain Research," (Symposium with Sylvester, Chall, Wittrock). *Educational Leadership* 10(1981).

Hart, Leslie A. *How the Brain Works.* New York: Basic Books, 1975.

Sagan, Carl. *Broca's Brain.* New York: Random House, 1979.

CHAPTER 6

Learning Literacy in Nonverbal Style

Richard Sinatra

Historically, instruction in written literacy has been almost exclusively dominated by analysis and learning of the verbal coding system. Most people believe that mature reading and writing cannot occur until complete mastery of the written symbol system takes place. Mastery of letters, sounds, and words has led many educators and parents to an intense preoccupation with what they conceive of as the "basics." For many youngsters, particularly those who have not learned these basics the first time around, phonics, word attack skills, and sentence analysis exercises occur year after year after year.

Three "Basics" Concerns

Three concerns arise about what is "basic" in written literacy instruction. First of all, are there not ways to teach the verbal coding systems without constant repetition of more-of-the-same, an approach that is hardly suitable to all learners' learning or cognitive styles? Chall and Mirsky (1978) recommend that students needing remedial reading training should be taught through right-brain processing modes in which they may excel to give them an opportunity for success and increase in self-worth.

Secondly, what really are the basics? Is interpretation of written symbols from which reading and writing gain their genesis more basic than either oral language or nonverbal experience itself?

Finally, what are the implications of brain frontier research for written literacy instruction? One of the great by-products of recent inquiries into the differing processing modes of each brain hemisphere in learning and literacy may well be the impact made on school curricula, especially in the language arts.

The Holistic View to Literacy Instruction

We already see leading educational theorists and researchers in the field of literacy instruction such as James Moffett (1968), Ken Goodman (1979), Frank Smith (1979), and Roger Shuy (1981) espousing a holistic, meaning-oriented, top-down view to written literacy instruction. Top-down advocates feel that language must be studied in the natural context of its use and that language arts instruction should proceed from whole to part. They criticize the piecemeal, part-to-whole, bottom-up approach to written literacy instruction exemplified in skills management and subskill approaches as unnatural, restraining, and fragmentary.

Essentially, when written literacy is continually dissected and analyzed in these approaches, the relative significance of the pieces to the whole are altered. Fredricksen (1976) adds that an over-reliance on a part-to-whole processing style for young readers predisposes them not to apply the powerful top-down strategies and cognitive schema relevant to their own life experiences. Like the others, Goodman (1979) feels that written literacy must be regarded as an extension of natural development and learned in the same way the oral language is learned. Literacy must involve real, natural, and relevant tasks. Translated to the classroom this means that teachers must engage youngsters in real functional use of written language—to label, to chart, to inform, to stimulate imagination, and to develop story sense.

The Nonverbal Core to Literacy Learning

While many conceptual models of the language arts clearly indicate that the oral and written language systems have their roots in nonverbal experience, few educators seem to acknowledge or capitalize on this implication in presenting nonverbal forms and structures to language-deficient students who could benefit from their use. Scholars feel that the content of messages, whether oral or written, is based on nonverbal experience. Before one can code an experience into any particular message form such as speech, writing, drawings, sign language, or even graph and flow charts, one has to focus on the raw experience he or she wishes to present and organize it in the mind, probably without the use of words. This focusing is conceptualization or incubation of idea which is conceived holistically, all-at-a-time. If words are not used to prompt the idea, conceptualization occurs as a flash of insight, an intuition, a grasp of a whole relationship. This is the gift of the right brain. Once the insight is analyzed and broken down into logical parts so that it can be discussed or written about, the left brain assumes the commanding role.

Moffett and Wagner (1976) remind educators and parents that since each level of coding is basic to the next, it is erroneous to think of reading and writing as "basic skills." Reading and writing may lay the foundation for all subsequent *book* learning but they really depend on the learning acquired through two prior levels of coding—nonverbal experience and the oral language. These authors maintain that the real basics are conceptualization and speaking, not the symbol system preoccupied with mechanics, spelling, and word recognition.

In two separate programs, I was able to apply these models by using nonverbal experience to increase reading vocabulary and comprehension for learners with long-standing deficits in reading (Sinatra, 1975, 1977). In one summer program (1975), more than a thousand black youngsters participated in an outdoor camping program that became the experiential base for their reading and writing instruction. They learned to read a significant number of new vocabulary words associated with the outdoor, physical experience.

In the second summer program (1977), 44 remedial reading youngsters completing grades one through five learned a significant number of new vocabulary words holistically, through experiential contexts. During the regular school year these youngsters were taught reading through a part-to-whole, synthetic phonics approach. Abandoning that approach in favor of one that stressed involvement in meaningful activities prior to reading and writing, the students participated in such activities as drama, science, arts and crafts, Indian lore, rhythm, and dance and heard new vocabulary words used by specialists to describe what was happening in these experiences. Students made visual-verbal experiential connections with the new words during reading and writing activities that followed.

The Learning Style of Right-Brain Preferents

It is my contention that we really cannot begin to consider holistic views of written literacy instruction unless we acknowledge the conceptual strength of the nonverbal, visuospatial, affective brain and the implication of right-brain strength for the learning style of the "whole" learner.

Learning styles emanate from the processing capabilities of *both* brain hemispheres but subcultures within our literate society condition the use of one thinking style more than another. For instance, Ramirez and Castañeda (1974) reported that Mexican American children showed a preference for the field-sensitive (or field-dependent) mode of thinking characterized by behaviors associated with right-brain processing. Using a number of cognitive/learning style instruments, Cohen (1969) found that urban, inner-city children preferred a global, holistic mode of problem solving in contrast to middle-class children who used an analytical, parts-specific thinking style. Thus, children who use a relational thinking style in which orientation toward reality is self-centered and attention is focused on the global characteristics of stimuli are discriminated against in many standardized tests of intelligence and achievement which assess an analytic cognitive style.

Perrone and Pulvino (1977), synthesizing the research of others, pointed out that different cultures do educate their youth in differential ways—some focusing on one hemisphere processing style more than the other—but the development of the diverse potential of both brain hemispheres is preferable to development of one hemisphere only. They conclude it is highly important to assess an individual's cognitive/learning style, discovering representational systems and learning preferences which would allow appropriate educational offerings to be designed that enhance strengths while aiding weaknesses.

Over the years, however, the school has focused on activities that cater to one part of the brain—the left hemisphere, much to the dismay of some renowned neuroscientists (Sperry 1973; Bogen, 1977). Educators undoubtedly took their cues from the findings made in the mid-1800s that two regions in the left hemisphere were primarily responsible for the production and comprehension of speech in humans (Geschwind, 1979). Then, zealous to ensure the exact mastery of reading and writing skills, schools focused on the use of narrowly prescribed strategies to written literacy found in skills management and decoding approaches.

Research on analysis of behavior of epileptic patients after brain surgery, conducted in the 1960s, changed the view of brain functioning forever. Joseph Bogen, neurosurgeon, and Roger Sperry, psychobiologist and one of the 1981 recipients of the Nobel Prize in medicine for his split-brain research, were the primary investigators of patients whose nerve connections between the right and left hemispheres had been severed. They found that the human brain was a composite of two interacting systems—the left and right hemispheres—each capable of its own processing approach and mode of memory functioning.

Through the 1970s more and more research appeared confirming that the right brain does make significant contributions to learning. For some youngsters, especially the gifted, the talented, and even the retarded, right hemisphere functioning may dominate their overall cognitive/learning styles in reading and writing. We now know that right hemisphere involvement is important in language learning and overall conceptual development. Yet school language arts instruction is almost all left-hemisphere bound, prompting one school principal to think of school as being "left-brained" (Hunter, 1976). Even so, the right hemisphere could be considered a silent partner in the school establishment; students need it to survive holistically despite language arts methodologies and curriculum approaches that detract from its optimal functioning.

The Nonverbal Style for the Disabled

Nonverbal, right-brain involvement in literacy learning appears to be especially important for the reading and learning disabled who experience traditional deficits in the storage and organization of verbal material (Bauer, 1977; Wong, 1978; Maier, 1980). Vellutino et al. (1975) and Vellutino, Smith, and Karman (1975) found significant differences between the severely learning disabled (dyslexics) and normals on verbal but not on nonverbal tasks. In two studies comparing good and poor readers (Marcel, Katz, and Smith, 1974; Marcel and Rajan, 1975), poor readers correctly identified more words and almost twice the number of letters presented to the right hemisphere than did the good readers, although good readers correctly identified more words tachistoscopically presented to the left hemisphere. Using a paper and pencil test designed to differentiate between left and right hemisphere preferents with 20 good and 20 poor readers, Oexle and Zenhausern (1981) found that the good readers activated both brain hemispheres almost equally (9 right and 11 left); but 17 of the 20 poor readers indicated a preference for right brain activation.

Both Guyer and Friedman (1975) and Witelson (1976, 1977) showed that learning disabled children, particularly males, have overriding right hemisphere spatial and holistic processing abilities. Witelson proposed that the learning disabled have atypical hemispheric specialization for language and for spatial processing. Her results suggest that in the learning disabled, spatial functions are found in both hemispheres in contrast to normal specialization in the right hemisphere. She proposed that two neural correlates operate for the learning disabled: 1.) a deficiency in the verbal, sequential, analytic mode of information processing, and 2.) an intact or overdeveloped use of the spatial, parallel, holistic mode representative of nonverbal types of communication. In this regard, Bannatyne (1971) felt that learning disabled males have a visuospatial organized brain in which left hemisphere language functions subserve the more dominant spatial functioning of the right hemisphere.

In a very illuminating study, Symmes and Rapaport (1972) reported that 54 disabled readers with a mean WISC intelligence score of 114 were considered a group of "unexpected reading failures" in which physical, emotional, and academic factors were ruled out. Selected from a larger group of 108 disabled readers, each of these 54 learners performed at a superior level in six spatial visualization tasks. The parents of these children also reported that they had excellent skills at model building and visual classification. When Suiter and Potter (1978) found that learning disabled children recalled significantly more material organized visually through picture arrangements, they suggested that verbal recall could be facilitated by utilizing visual materials to teach learning disabled children.

The Nonverbal Mode in Literacy Learning

In recent years, I have proposed in a number of contexts that holistic, visuospatial strategies could be used with remedial readers and writers, learning disabled students, and normal learners to develop their written literacy skills. With Blau (1981), I suggested that tracing and kinesthetic movement in word learning for those with verbal memory deficits focuses attention on the configuration of the whole word while the separate features of the word are touched and traced. With Spiridakis (1981), I showed how visuospatial cues could be used to increase the sentence proficiency of children with limited English proficiency. Later (1982b) I showed how pictures, sentence configurations, and function words could be visually presented to older remedial students to increase their ability in producing more linguistically mature sentences.

In other sources (1979, 1980, February 1981, and Winter 1981), I have shown how visual compositions (picture stories arranged to infer nonverbal stories) can be used to increase reading and writing proficiency at the paragraph or whole composition level. Visual composition allows the nonverbal to contact and organize the verbal. Finally, for young children, I have outlined a number of specific strategies which capitalize on the use of pictures, realia, drama and movement, configurational maps and designs, graphs, and imagery to involve the nonverbal processing mode of the right brain in learning to read (February 1982).

Based upon this work and the suggestions of others (Fox, 1979; Kane and Kane, 1979), the following outline shows how each brain hemisphere contributes verbal and nonverbal processing to the learning of reading and writing.

Contribution of Each Brain Hemisphere to Reading and Writing

Left Hemisphere Verbal Mediation	*Right Hemisphere* Nonverbal Mediation
• Phonemic discrimination; grapheme to phoneme correspondence; analytic processing of parts to name word	• Grapheme array perceived in gestalt; deriving meaning directly from spoken or printed word; image produced
• Learning rules of syllabification and identification of word parts (structural analysis) such as prefixes and suffixes; applying rules to lists of words	• Learning new words holistically, in "natural" content areas such as music, gym, shop, the arts, and some sciences; associating real experience with word meaning
• Memorizing words of songs such as with the "Star Spangled Banner"	• Feeling memory of melody patterns through chanting, jingling, and singing to induce words
• Using nonsense syllables and nonsense words to teach word attack skills	• Teaching concrete, image producing words and building associative webs (synonym, antonym, classification) amongst word meanings
• Naming and describing objects and parts of space through verbal mode	• Finding way in space; tracing route, touching and holding objects to label and describe; arousing associations with object
• Identifying and naming words using denotative meanings such as dictionary definitions	• Identifying and naming words using connotative, associative, image producing strategies through figures of speech, metaphor, simile, and analogy; using the context to arrive at an intelligent guess of a word's meaning
• Sequencing events or numbering in order; arranging from part to whole	• Relating events to a whole theme; associating ideas to central image which may or may not have sequence orientation
• Locating the main idea sentence in a paragraph and constructing an outline of parts	• Forming key image of a paragraph (or theme) and visualizing details in relationship to central image
• Reading and following verbal directions	• Looking at a plan, blueprint, map, or picture; tracing route, internally verbalizing, and then reading or writing directions
• Reading and writing exercises which emphasize denotative language and literal comprehension such as getting the facts, "locating the answer," etc.	• Obtaining meaning from the visual (pictorial), and structural (webs and semantic maps); personalized, affective associations (emotion) made with theme and ideas in passage
• Subskill approach to reading and writing development such as occurs in skills management systems, criterion reference systems, diagnostic-prescriptive programs, etc.	• Whole discourse mode or whole language approach; presenting schema or nonverbal representation of whole discourse scope, such as semantic mapping; arousing personalized association to theme

- Attention to mechanics of writing, i.e., spelling, punctuation, and agreement
- Analyzing and labeling parts of speech, finding subjects and predicates, telling functional use of sentence parts

- Analyzing literary works, separating parts and passages to isolate content or intent of author
- Writing compositions from lists of facts and information given on a topic; constructing outlines following teacher prearranged format
- Writing answers to specific questions or topics where information is generally given in text and needs to be located and copied; summarizing a work; adding to existing information

- Attention to the gestalt of writing coherent sentences in meaningful sequences
- Composing and writing sentences through intermediary steps such as sentence combining or through whole composition involvement in prewriting (composing), writing, editing, and refining.
- Literary synthesizing by discovering relationship between two or more disparate themes, events, characters, etc.
- Writing from visual compositions, which are sequences of pictures arranged to *infer* a story or stories
- Synthesizing several works or passages to relate meaning in a novel way; creating new ideas not there before

Remember that both brain hemispheres cooperate in most learning tasks, that successful reading and writing require both analysis and synthesis, and that written literacy itself, based on the nature of the alphabetic coding system, is a process of verbal mediation in the left hemispheres of most learners. The intent of the chart above is to point out that different strategies and activities will tend to involve one hemisphere more than the other. After initial involvement in one brain processing approach, learners could be introduced to a parallel processing approach. A reading selection in social studies about the Lewis and Clark exploration will probably emphasize verbal processing. Yet students could be asked to form a key or central image of that selection and visualize the different events in relation to the key images they hold in their separate minds. This visualizing will help them recall the significant events of what they have read. The left and right processing strategies complement each other and expand learning.

If teachers and curriculum developers look down the left-hemisphere column of the chart, they will undoubtedly note many favorite language arts activities they have been using for years. By shifting to the right column, however, they can also devise and implement powerful strategies that utilize *nonverbal* schema to organize *verbal* material. By engaging the right hemisphere and activating its processing style in the acquisition of reading and writing skills, teachers can make learning environments more meaningful, holistic, and memorable while better meeting the learning style preferences of learners.

References

Bannatyne, Alexander. *Language, Reading and Learning Disabilities.* Springfield, Ill.: Charles E. Thomas, 1971.

Bauer, Richard. "Memory Processes in Children with Learning Disabilities: Evidence for Deficient Rehearsal." *Journal of Experimental Child Psychology* 24 (1977): 415-30.

Blau, Harold, and Sinatra, Richard. "Word Learning: Using the Right Brain." *Academic Therapy,* September 1981, pp. 69-75.

Bogen, Joseph. "Some Educational Implications of Hemispheric Specialization." In *The Human Brain,* edited by M. C. Wittrock, pp. 133-52. Englewood Cliffs, N.J.: Prentice-Hall, 1977.

Chall, Jeanne, and Mirsky, Allan. "The Implications for Education." In *Education and the Brain,* edited by Jeanne Chall and Allan Mirsky. Chicago, Ill.: University of Chicago Press, 1978.

Cohen, Rosalie. "Conceptual Styles, Culture Conflict, and Non-Verbal Tests of Intelligence." *American Anthropologist,* October 1969, pp. 828-56.

Dale, Edgar. *Audiovisual Methods in Teaching.* New York: Holt, Rinehart and Winston, 1969.

Fox, Patricia. "Reading as a Whole Brain Function." *The Reading Teacher,* October 1979, pp. 7-14.

Fredricksen, C. H. *Discourse Comprehension and Early Reading.* Paper presented at the conference on theory and practice of beginning reading instruction. University of Pittsburgh Learning Research and Development Center, Pittsburgh, 1976. ED 155 622.

Geschwind, Norman. "Specialization of the Human Brain." *Scientific American,* September 1979, pp. 180-97.

Goodman, Kenneth. "The Know-More and the Know-Nothing Movement in Reading: A Personal Response." *Language Arts,* November 1979, pp. 657-63.

Haley-James, Shirley. "Twentieth-Century Perspectives on Writing in Grades One Through Eight." In *Perspectives on Writing in Grades 1-8,* edited by Shirley Haley-James, pp. 3-18. Urbana, Ill.: National Council of Teachers of English, 1981.

Hunter, Madeline. "Right-Brained Kids in Left-Brained Schools." *Today's Education,* November/December 1976, pp. 45-48.

Kane, Nancy, and Kane, Martin. "Comparison of Right and Left Hemisphere Functions." *The Gifted Child Quarterly,* Spring 1979, pp. 157-67.

Kellogg, Ralph. "Listening." In *Guiding Children's Language Learning,* edited by Pose Lamb, p. 128. Dubuque, Iowa: William C. Brown, 1967.

Maier, Arlee. "The Effect of Focusing on the Cognitive Processes of Learning Disabled Children." *Journal of Learning Disabilities,* March 1980, pp. 34-38.

Marcel, T., and Rajan, P. "Lateral Specialization for Recognition of Words and Faces in Good and Poor Readers." *Neuropsychologia* 13 (1975): 489-97.

Marcel, T.; Katz, L.; and Smith, M. "Laterality and Reading Proficiency." *Neurospychologia* 12 (1974): 131-39.

Moffett, James. *Teaching the Universe of Discourse.* Boston, Mass.: Houghton Mifflin, 1968.

Moffett, James, and Wagner, Betty Jane. *Student-Centered Language Arts and Reading, K-13.* Boston, Mass.: Houghton Mifflin, 1976.

Oexle, J., and Zenhausern, J. "Differential Hemispheric Activation in Good and Poor Readers." *International Journal of Neuroscience* 15 (1981): 31-36.

Perrone, Philip, and Pulvino, Charles. "New Directions in the Guidance of the Gifted and Talented." *The Gifted Child Quarterly,* Fall 1977, pp. 326-40.

Ramirez, Manuel, and Castañeda, Alfred. *Cultural Democracy, Bicognitive Development and Education.* New York: Academic Press, 1974.

Shuy, Roger. "A Holistic View of Language." *Research in the Teaching of English* 15 (1981): 101-11.

Sinatra, Richard. "Language Experience in Title I Summer Camping Programs." *Reading Improvement,* Fall 1975, pp. 148-56.

————. "The Cloze Technique for Reading Comprehension and Vocabulary Development." *Reading Improvement,* Summer 1977, pp. 86-92.

————. "Using Visuals in the Composing Process." In ERIC *Resources in Education,* ED 189 601.

_____. "Visual Literacy: A Concrete Language for the Learning Disabled." In *Learning Disabilities: An Audio Journal of Continuing Education,* edited by Marvin Gottlieb and Larry Bradford. New York: Grune & Stratton, 1980.

_____. "A Visual/Spatial Approach to Sentence Development." Paper presented at 8th Plains Regional Conference of International Reading Association, September 1980.

_____. "Using Visuals to Help the Second Language Learner." *Reading Teacher,* February 1981, pp. 539-46.

_____. "Visual Compositions and Language Development." *Technology and Mediated Instruction,* Winter 1981, pp. 16-23.

_____. "Learning Style and Brain Processing in Reading." *Early Years,* February 1982.

Sinatra, Richard, and Spiridakis, John. "A Visual Approach to Sentence Combining for the Limited English Proficient Student." *Bilingual Resources* 4 (1981).

Smith, Frank. "The Language Arts and the Learner's Mind." *Language Arts,* February 1979, pp. 118-25 and 145.

Sperry, R. W. "Lateral Specialization of Cerebral Function in the Surgically Separated Hemispheres." In *The Psychophysiology of Thinking,* edited by F. J. McGuigan. New York: Academic Press, 1973.

Suiter, M., and Potter, R. "The Effects of Paradigmatic Organization on Verbal Recall." *Journal of Learning Disabilities,* April 1978, pp. 63-66.

Symmes, Jean, and Rapaport, Judith. "Unexpected Reading Failure." *American Journal of Orthopsychiatry,* January 1972, pp. 82-91.

Vellutino, Frank; Harding, C.; Stazer, J.; and Phillips, F. "Differential Transfer in Poor and Normal Readers." *Journal of Genetic Psychology* 126 (1975): 3-18.

Vellutino, Frank; Smith, H.; and Karman, M. "Reading Disability: Age Differences and the Perceptual-Deficit Hypothesis." *Child Development* 46 (1975): 487-93.

Witelson, Sandra. "Abnormal Right Hemisphere Functional Specialization in Developmental Dyslexia." In *The Neuropsychology of Learning Disorders: Theoretical Approaches,* edited by R. Knights and D. Bakker, pp. 233-55. Baltimore, Md.: University Park Press, 1976.

_____. "Developmental Dyslexia: Two Right Hemispheres and None Left." *Science* 195 (1977): 309-11.

Wong, Bernice. "The Effects of Directive Cues on the Organization of Memory and Recall in Good and Poor Readers." *Journal of Educational Research,* September/October 1978, pp. 32-38.

CHAPTER 7

Teaching to the Whole Brain

Patricia K. Brennan

P reliminary evidence suggests that left-preferenced people learn analytically and right-preferenced people learn globally.

A recent study conducted by Zenhausern, Dunn, Cavanaugh, and Eberle with 353 high school students in Ohio disclosed the following:

Left-Preferenced Students	Right-Preferenced Students
N=116	N=231
• Require formal design	• Require low light
• Are teacher motivated	• Need warm environment
• Are persistent	• Are relatively less motivated
• Are responsible	• Prefer to learn with one peer
• Prefer to learn alone	• Have tactile preferences
• Do not need mobility	• Need mobility

The literature on analytic-global learners describes left-preferenced individuals and analytic learners similarly. They both learn sequentially (step-by-step), are inductive (going from the parts to the whole), emphasize the importance of language and verbal ability, and tend to be reflectives. Similarly, the right-brained and global literature describes holistic learners who are deductive (going from the whole to the parts), emphasize spatial relationships and emotions as characteristic, and tend to be impulsive.

I believe that in any given classroom, there are probably an approximately equal number of analytic and global learners. But our school system has traditionally geared education to the left-brained analytic learner. We present all the parts of a given lesson and expect children to be able to piece the puzzle together and "get the picture." Have you ever been asked the question, "Do you get the picture"? Chances are it was a global person who asked the question. Global learners thrive on getting the whole picture and then discovering the elements necessary to make up that picture.

To reach all students in a typical classroom, we must teach in both directions. If you start a lesson by teaching inductively, turn the whole thing around and teach deductively. Mathematics is a useful case in point. When I am teaching the Pythagorean theorem, I start by teaching it inductively, (chiefly because I am a left-preferenced, analytic learner and I am most comfortable teaching in that mode). I could stop there and feel that I had taught a pretty good lesson. I presented logically and sequentially every step needed to solve the theorem: $a^2 + b^2 = c^2$. If one leg of the right triangle is 3 cm and one leg is 4 cm, $3^2 + 4^2 = c^2$ or $9 + 16 = 25$. Find the square root of c^2 and you will know the length of the hypotenuse. We learn to solve for c today, tomorrow for a, and the next day for b. On Friday we have a test. Sound familiar? If this were the only method for teaching this concept, I can assure you that I would not be the only one frustrated by the results. But, if after teaching inductively you also teach deductively, your joy will be as evident as the other half of your class.

One deductive method for teaching the Pythagorean theorem is as follows: Draw a right triangle whose sides are 3 cm and 4 cm and whose hypotenuse is 5 cm. If you draw a square on each side of your triangle, what can you tell from your measurements? Side a is 9 sq. cm, side b is 16 sq. cm, and side c is 25 sq. cm.

Therefore: $\quad 9 + 16 = 25$
or $3^2 + 4^2 = 5^2$
$a^2 + b^2 = c^2$

In geometry you *can* "see" the whole picture and then discover how the parts fit to make up the whole. The next time someone says to you, "I hate math, I've always hated math," ask them if they liked geometry. About 75 percent will say that they liked geometry but hated math. The reason? In geometry, you can "get the picture." The sooner we begin to pictorialize other math concepts, the sooner we will have fewer math haters.

Young children are all global learners until about the age of seven and will "get a better picture" of a number concept if it is presented globally. In teaching addition, for example, you might start with a picturesque story of a birthday party to which they are allowed to invite 10 friends. Use actual people; keep it real. They are very excited; the big day is finally here. Who arrived first? *name* Who came second? *name* Now how many people are there? *2* How many presents do you have so far? *2* How do you know you have 2? *Kathy brought one and Maria brought one so now I have two.* Let's open the presents and see what's inside. One doll and one paint set. $1 + 1 = 2$. Someone else is coming. And so forth. . . . The typical child will learn far more about the concept of addition from this kind of presentation or a similar life experience than being told $1 + 1 = 2$, or shown $\Delta + \Delta = \Delta\Delta$

Teaching math or any analytical subject can be done globally once the teacher is aware that he or she can and should teach in both directions. Similarly, a very global subject such as social studies can be taught analytically. Take any lesson you have prepared and teach it analytically or globally. About half the class will "see" it. Then turn that lesson around and start from the other perspective. The other half of your class will likely react: "I see what you're saying now. I get the picture!"

Part Four

Next Steps

Next Steps

Scott D. Thomson

Forecasting is an imperfect art, at best. The failed predictions of economists and meteorologists alike confirm a healthy, common sense skepticism that people have about anyone who offers visions of the future, even when those visions are based comfortably upon quantitative data.

"The future," however, will continue to arrive at our doorstep day by day, having its greatest impact upon the young. The alertness of educators to new knowledge about the learning process, therefore, will materially affect a student's opportunity for immediate growth. More importantly, this knowledge will play an important part in fulfilling long-term potential.

The first step to take for the benefit of our students is to recognize the modest but real successes made to date in the field of brain/mind behavior. Recent research findings on learning styles and brain behavior provide a significant new framework for understanding the ways students process information. The early applications of this knowledge in a school setting mark the solid beginnings of major new methodologies for instructing students, as well. The possibilities are genuinely exciting to those persons engaged in this research and practice.

The research community during the past five years has seen a spectacular increase in the number of studies reported on brain/mind behavior. Among practitioners, the first pioneers in a handful of schools have been joined by almost 40 school districts that are now engaged in utilizing information on student learning styles and cognitive processing in the diagnosis, advising, and instruction of their students. The growth has been over a relatively short time.

As late as 1978, the NASSP found it difficult to attract even 20 educators to attend a meeting on student learning styles. Gradually, however, through the dedicated work of Rita Dunn, David Cavanaugh, and Gerald Kusler, interest had grown by 1980 so that 30 or 35 participants would attend. Now, we see nearly 500 informed and enthusiastic persons at this national conference in New Orleans. By any measure, significant progress has been achieved for us all.

At this point, however, enthusiasm must be muted by the reality of the distance still to be covered. We still lack an integrated theory of learning. While we acknowledge the major contributions made by the behavioral, cognitive, and developmental schools of learning theory, great pockets of these theories still don't fit neatly side by side, and so they continue to flap about unattached to one another. Also, it appears that we do not yet fully comprehend the contributions that social psychology may make to an integrated theory of learning, although the social context appears important to a number of learner attributes, including motivation.

Fortunately, enough has been learned to avoid some well-intentioned but naive proposals of the past. For example, the concept that all students should be instructed by a single formula involving large group instruction, small group discussion, and independent study violates our current understanding of student learning style. Some students may indeed prosper under such an instructional mix, but others would be much better off spending most of their time in a self-contained classroom with a directive teacher. Other students would prosper best being assigned primarily to small discussion groups. Yet others would achieve more prodigiously by individual study, or by an emphasis on tactile, "hands-on" learning experiences. Certain students consciously need to focus upon developing their linear, logical thinking powers. Others need to develop more "right brained" imagery so as to balance brain hemispheric dominance and thus strengthen forecasting capabilities. All of these individual pieces about the information processing model can help to build a better schoolhouse.

We can now say with reasonable assurance that instruction should begin with an analysis of the ways a particular student processes information and then build from that point. This insight provides the practitioner with a more substantive framework for planning than did earlier "single approach" proposals for teaching all students. A multiple approach to organizing instruction for students becomes, then, the basic rationale for individualizing student learning opportunities. The methodology by which material is presented should depend on the particular way a student processes information. Students with similar learning profiles can be clustered together for instruction. This strategy would replace old concepts of individualization which depended too heavily upon "independent study," a format that disadvantages some students and advantages other students.

Recognition also should be offered to the "boot-strap" nature of much research and most practical application in the field of learning style and brain behavior. At the research level, precious little foundation or federal assistance has been available to conduct this important work. The Spencer Foundation has supported the investigations of Julian Stanley and Jerre Levy, and some government grants assisted the seminal studies developed by Roger Sperry. Much of the research and all of the practical, school-site applications, however, have been achieved by a combination of local funding and true grit and determination. Imagination, most fortunately, is not necessarily limited by a restricted dollar flow from outside sources.

Next Steps

Given the modest but encouraging progress to date, what should be our next steps? What research projects and practical applications will likely be of greatest value to our understanding of learning style and brain behavior? What is reasonably attainable from our present perspective?

I suggest six "next steps" for the consideration of persons interested in extending our understanding of the field. The proposals are not modest. Neither are they unattainable. They include:

1. Maintaining the vision that schools can become better places for students to learn than they are now.
2. Improving the preparation of teachers.
3. Continuing to build a solid base of research on mind/brain functions.
4. Developing a science of application of mind/brain research in school settings.
5. Creating comprehensive, cohesive, and uncomplicated instruments to assist in identifying the ways students process information.
6. Expanding information networks so that researchers and practitioners can be in close communication with one another.

Schools as Better Places To Learn

Better conditions for learning than ordinarily exist can be developed in a school setting. Our current knowledge about learning style and brain behavior, although limited, provides a sufficient base for improving the learning environment for students.

The methodology of teaching has been at a "patent medicine" level for much too long. We frequently dispense educational aspirins, treating symptoms rather than root causes. A student faces difficulties in algebra? Transfer him to general math! Another student cannot draw well? Send her to drafting classes. Still another student reads slowly? Send him to a lower group or to remedial classes. Some students can't understand the verbal explanation of an experiment? Read it again! And so it goes, symptom after symptom, with schools never overcoming the initial challenge but rather redirecting the student to easier, "second choice" goals. The psychological impact, not to mention the knowledge unattained, can be devastating to a young person.

But there can be a better way, using our current knowledge about the ways students process information. Both halves of the brain need to be stimulated by teachers using visual and holistic illustrations as well as linear and logical examples. Student learning styles can be diagnosed and profiled so that a kinesthetic learner is not constantly bombarded with verbal messages and so that an auditory learner is not inundated with tactile projects and games.

Ultimately, the *vision* of an improved school remains all-important because it is this vision that motivates principals and teachers to drop old routines and to apply new insights about learning to the students they serve.

Improving Teacher Education

It is fashionable today to criticize teachers for lacking sufficient preparation in the various subject fields, particularly math and science. Also, it has become popular for states to require that teacher candidates establish competence through minimum tests of writing and speaking. While these concerns must be properly addressed, they are insufficient to prepare teachers adequately for the classrooms of the next decade.

Teaching must begin with the student, for the student is the focus of the activity. In the past, some attention was directed to the developmental and social dimensions of the student's individuality. Little attention, however, was focused on the individualities of information processing. All students, it was assumed, would benefit by a benign mixture of visuals, activity projects, oral lessons, and written work.

Given our current knowledge about learning style and brain behavior, this traditional approach is insufficient. What is the student's diagnosed preference for a learning environment? What is his or her intellectual approach to adopting and assimilating information? What are his or her underlying strengths for the cognitive processing of information quite apart from environment?

It is this realm of knowledge that must be included in teacher education programs today if tomorrow's students are to be adequately instructed. Teacher educators must move to a higher level of understanding about student information processing, and must develop with teacher candidates appropriate techniques to utilize this information with their students. To do less will cause failure where success is possible, and will result in blocking many young people from their potential.

The competent teachers will in the future be as comfortable with assessing the learning styles of their students and adapting the learning environment to the processing preferences of their students as they are discussing adolescent growth and development or reviewing interesting details about their own subject field. It requires the entire package to enter the classroom as a fully professional teacher.

Enlarging the Research Base

More than 50 studies currently exist which report data on student learning styles. At least that same number can be found in the areas of brain behavior or hemispheric dominance and their relationship to information processing. The majority of these studies reflect a reasonable research base and convey significant information about learning style or cognitive style or brain behavior and learning outcomes. When positive results are found, they generally indicate that student learning and achievement can be improved by tailoring instructional methodology wherever possible to each student's style.

Much, however, remains to be accomplished. We must continue to build a solid research base for a fuller understanding of mind/brain functioning. We must continue to unlock the elusive secrets that explain the organizing elements of the mind. Some discoveries may not affect the learning process, but surely most will have some impact on perception and on the retention and integration of information.

Research should be pursued vigorously at all levels: physiological, metaphysical, and intellectual. "The mind" is not synonymous with the human brain; our perceptions, feelings, and intuitions transcend the mechanisms of the brain. Mankind's goal since Socrates has been to fathom this relationship.

Less lofty goals, however, will serve educators. We are most immediately concerned with certain specific questions: How does the mind develop ordering processes, or habits, or associations? What enhances insight and divergent thinking? What stimulates memory or the acquisition of tactile skills? These understandings, as a sample, are important so that educators can work with, not against, the proclivities of students, individual by individual.

Given the broadened interest today in mind/brain research by numerous influential groups ranging from medical educators to the armed services, it is likely that data on some of the important questions about learning will accumulate at an accelerated pace during the next decade. Some of this knowledge will be of value to teachers, principals, and college instructors as they work to improve the learning environment.

Developing a Science of Application

Given the active, growing research base in the field, some caution might be considered appropriate before classroom applications are designed and implemented. Perhaps this advice would be beneficial if our current methodologies were adequate. Unfortunately, however, much pedagogy still operates at the "voodoo" level. Many classrooms are conducted on a trial-and-error basis, even by experienced teachers. Intuition and raw-boned experience cover major gaps in the methodology that teachers bring from their professional training to the classroom.

"Everyone knows" that the tough subjects like mathematics should be taught to all students in the morning. "Everyone knows" that all bright students are verbal rather than kinesthetic learners. "Everyone knows" that slow students profit from films. And so the myths continue, not based on research, but resting on folklore or tradition. Clearly this is not good enough, even for the interim.

A sufficient research base exists, even now, to begin to identify the learning proclivities of students and to differentiate learning environments according to student style. Instructional modalities should not continue to be identical for every student, nor should variety be introduced simply for the sake of providing novelty. Rather, variety should follow the nature of the learner—in response to each student's particular approach to adapting and assimilating information.

We know that this information processing is affected both by cognitive and environmental factors, and that some of the cognitive dimension is independent of environmental factors. We also know that the instruments currently available to diagnose cognitive and environmental preferences are too technical or lack comprehensiveness, among other deficiencies.

These shortcomings, however, should not preclude the application of current levels of knowledge for two reasons: (1) Sufficient data exist at the applications level to assure that the diagnostic instruments now available do provide valuable guidance to teachers, particularly with students who are not achieving as expected; and (2) Valuable insight results from the feedback that practitioners provide to the research community. Some of the most useful gains made in the profession of education have come from this researcher/practitioner partnership as both groups work in a common area, and as information flows in both directions.

We do not, it must be admitted, currently possess a solid set of organizing principles of pedagogy with which to teach students. Part of our profession's proclivity for faddishness reflects this lack of an organizing framework. Prudent applications of our new knowledge about learning style and brain behavior, however, can strengthen the framework. We can begin to place students in a learning environment that reinforces their learning tendencies instead of violating them. Particularly, we can remove obstacles to learning, such as when students' styles are at odds with their environment. We can advance methodology significantly if we use our current knowledge. This step will move us toward the long-range goal of achieving a holistic understanding of the student and methodology and curriculum in a mutually supportive, complementary relationship.

Comprehensive and Practical Instrumentation

A multiplicity of specialized instruments currently exist to probe cognitive and environmental factors in learning. Many of these tests have contributed significantly to the development of a research base. Other instruments have been used by practitioners with students to attempt to identify proclivities for learning. In all, more than 30 instruments have been developed in the field. Most are currently available for use.

A major need now exists to consolidate and simplify this instrumentation so that it can be applied in school settings.

Priority should be given to the development of a comprehensive yet practical instrument, one that encompasses the cognitive, environmental, and affective factors important to an understanding of the ways that individuals process information. Key elements of the best existing tests should be consolidated to contribute to this new second or third-generation vehicle.

The proposed instrument should reflect a sophisticated pragmatism. It will need to probe an individual's learning patterns, yet must be easily administered to students. A complicated, clinically oriented test will fall short of the requirement.

Currently, the lack of a single instrument that incorporates the cognitive, environmental, and affective dimensions of thinking constitutes a major hurdle to widespread application by practitioners of contemporary knowledge about learning style and brain behavior. It is essential, therefore, that a major effort be mounted to create this instrumentation. Such a development also is essential to prevent giving educators an opinion that the field is too complicated to be of practical use to most schools. The classic instrument for assessing style and cognition, when completed, will be profound but usable.

Expanding the Information Network

The Learning Styles Network, founded and managed by the NASSP and St. John's University, provides a strong base for the interchange of information about learning style and brain behavior. The Network, in addition to publishing three newsletters a year reporting the recent developments in research and practice, also acts as a monitoring body for all related research. It offers other services such as filmstrips, printed bibliographies, and consultant support.

Further monitoring and reporting of the field is needed. The flurry of activity by schools of medicine in Canada and the United States, for example, often fails to reach beyond medical circles. The private sector and Defense Department both have begun to explore the field. The information network, therefore, must be expanded beyond the realm of psychology and professional education to encompass developments in these other areas throughout the United States and overseas.

Some obvious steps are in order, to include: (1) formal sectional meetings at the annual convention of the AERA, (2) founding a journal to incorporate research and practice from all active sources, (3) initiating annual national conferences on learning styles and brain behavior, and (4) creating a computer-generated data base. Other steps can be taken as the field expands, not the least of which is incorporating knowledge about learning styles and brain behavior in textbooks on educational psychology.

Conclusion

For generations, educators have been stymied in their attempt to understand the ways that students perceive and process information. This void contributed to some unhappy consequences, including the faddishness and insecurities of a profession without an adequate data base.

Certainly we still have a long way to go before we fully comprehend the wellsprings of human thinking. But investigators are beginning to tap some fertile strata. More importantly, the strata already tapped offer some useful guidelines for teachers and administrators interested in improving student learning opportunities.

The possibilities are even more promising if psychologists, professional educators, and interested colleagues from related fields pursue actively the opportunities at hand. The ultimate reward could be magnificent: the formulation of an integrated theory of learning together with a supportive instructional methodology. Only when education reaches that point will it become a confident and mature profession.

Appendix

Student Learning Style†

Cognitive Styles

Reception Styles
* Perceptual modality preferences
* Field independence vs. dependence
  Scanning
  Constricted vs. flexible control
  Tolerance for incongruous or unrealistic
    experiences
  Strong vs. weak automatization
  Conceptual vs. perceptual-motor
    dominance

Concept Formation and Retention Styles
* Conceptual tempo
  Conceptualizing styles
  Breadth of categorizing
  Cognitive complexity vs. simplicity
* Leveling vs. sharpening

Affective Styles

Attention Styles
* Conceptual level
  Curiosity
  Persistence or perseverance
  Level of anxiety
  Frustration tolerance

Expectancy and Incentive Styles
* Locus of control
* Achievement motivation
  Self-actualization
  Imitation
  Risk taking vs. cautiousness
  Competition vs. cooperation
  Level of aspiration
  Reaction to reinforcement
* Social motivation
  Personal interests

Physiological Styles
* Masculine-feminine behavior
  Health-related behavior
  Body rhythms
  Need for mobility
  Environmental elements

†Student Learning Style Model: James W. Keefe, 1979.
* Styles with the greatest implication for improving the learning process.

An Annotated Bibliography of Selected Learning Styles Instrumentation*

General

Cognitive Style Interest Inventory by Seldon D. Strother in *The Way We Learn: Educational Cognitive Style,* Athens, Ohio: Ohio University, 1975.

A self-report inventory based on the Oakland Community College model of "educational sciences" (Bloomfield Hills, Michigan) allowing the student to represent his/her preferred way of obtaining meaning from the environment. The Inventory is self-scoring.

Cognitive Style Mapping, a Modified Hill Model, utilized by Mountain View College in Dallas, Texas, Harryette B. Ehrhardt, Coordinator.

Computer-generated cognitive style maps and class diagnostic records are available.

Cognitive Style Mapping Inventory, compiled and revised by East Lansing High School, East Lansing, Michigan 48823, 1975.

Similar to the Strother *Interest Inventory* but arranged for computer scoring.

Learning Style Inventory (students, 1978) and *Productivity Environmental Preference Survey* (adults, 1977) by Rita Dunn, Kenneth Dunn, and Gary E. Price. Price Systems, Box 3271, Lawrence, Kansas 66044.

Self-report questionnaires yielding information about how a given student learns. There are 36 subscales covering 18 elements in four areas: Environmental, Emotional, Sociological, and Physical (computer scored).

Learning Style Inventory: Primary Version by Janet Perrin, St. John's University, Jamaica, New York 11439, 1981.

Based on the Learning Style Inventory of Dunn, Dunn, and Price and designed for young children. The questionnaire consists of 12 charts, each containing a series of pictures and questions that assess a different element of learning style. The inventory is individually administered and scored on a student profile form (about 20 minutes).

Learning Styles Inventory and *Instructional Styles Inventory* by Albert A. Canfield and Judith S. Canfield, 1976. Humanics Media, Liberty Drawer 7970, Ann Arbor, Michigan 48107.

Short inventories of learning and teaching styles used to date primarily at the college level. Administration time is about 15 minutes.

Cognitive and Affective Styles

Child Rating Form by Manuel Ramirez and Alfred Castañeda, in *Cultural Democracy, Bicognitive Development, and Education.* New York: Academic Press, 1974.

A direct observation checklist yielding frequency of behavior scales on field independence/sensitivity and cultural differences. Teacher completes for younger students; older students can rate themselves. Administration time varies. A revised version will soon appear in *New Frontiers* to be published by Pergamon Press, Inc.

Learning Style Identification Scale by Paul Malcom, William Lutz, Mary Gerken, and Gary Hoeltke, Publishers Test Service (CTB/McGraw-Hill), 2500 Garden Road, Monterey, California 93940, 1981.

A short (24 item) self-scored rating scale based on the concept of learning style as the "method students use to solve any problem that they encounter in their educational

*No attempt has been made to include all available learning style instruments in this selected bibliography, but only those that are more recent, widely accessible, or in the public domain.

experiences." Five styles are identified based on classification of information reception and use, cognitive development, and self-concept.

Myers-Briggs Type Indicator by Isabel Briggs Myers and Katherine C. Briggs, 1976. Consulting Psychologists Press, Inc., 577 College Avenue, Palo Alto, California 94306.

A measure of personality dispositions and interests based on Jung's theory of types, suitable for early adolescents through adults. Provides four bipolar scales which can be reported as continuous scores or reduced to types.

Student Learning Styles Questionnaire by Anthony F. Grasha and Sheryl W. Riechmann, Institute for Research and Training in Higher Education, University of Cincinnati, Cincinnati, Ohio 45221, 1974.

A hand-scored, self-report inventory of 90 items designed to elicit student attitudes toward the courses taken in college or high school and to identify related learning style. Six styles are described: Independent, Avoidant, Collaborative, Dependent, Competitive, and Participant.

Cognitive Styles

Cognitive Profiles by Charles A. Letteri in *Cognitive Profile: Basic Determinant of Academic Achievement.* Burlington, Vermont: Center for Cognitive Studies, 1980.

Seven tests of cognitive style that in combination predict student achievement level as measured by standardized achievement test scores. The seven dimensions are: 1) Field Independence/Dependence, 2) Scanning/Focusing, 3) Breadth of Categorization, 4) Cognitive Complexity/Simplicity, 5) Reflectiveness/Impulsiveness, 6) Leveling/Sharpening, and 7) Tolerant/Intolerant.

Inventory of Learning Processes by Ronald R. Schmeck, Fred Ribich, and Nerella Ramanaiah in "Development of a Self-Report Inventory for Assessing Individual Differences in Learning Processes," *Applied Psychological Measurement,* Vol. 1, 1977, pp. 413–31.

A 62-item, true-false inventory grouped by factor analysis into dimensions of synthesis/analysis, study methods, fact retention, and elaborative processing, reflecting a continuum of student information processing preferences from deep and elaborative to shallow and repetitive (20 minutes).

Learning Style Inventory by David Kolb in "Disciplinary Inquiry Norms and Student Learning Styles: Diverse Pathways for Growth," *The Modern American College,* edited by Arthur Chickering. San Francisco: Jossey-Bass, 1981.

A 5–10 minute self-report inventory calling for a rank ordering of four words in each of nine different sets. Each word represents one of four learning modes: feeling (Concrete Experience), watching (Reflective Observation), thinking (Abstract Conceptualization), and doing (Active Experimentation). The 4-MAT System of Bernice McCarthy elaborates on this model to provide a teaching-learning process geared to four learning types.

Gregorc Style Delineator by Anthony F. Gregorc, Doubleday Road, Columbia, Connecticut 06237.

A self-report instrument based on a rank ordering of four words in each of 10 sets revealing four combinations of learning preference dualities: 1) Abstract Sequential, 2) Abstract Random, 3) Concrete Sequential, and 4) Concrete Random. Administration time is approximately five minutes (observation and interviews are suggested for corroboration).

Hemispheric Dominance

Differential Hemispheric Activation Instrument by Robert Zenhausern, Department of Psychology, St. John's University, Grand Central Parkway, Jamaica, New York 11439, 1979.

A 26-item paper and pencil test of hemispheric dominance. Subjects rate themselves on behavioral correlates of hemispheric specialization by indicating their relative preferences for right brain (spatial/visual) or left brain (verbal) tasks. This style is related to other learning characteristics such as thinking style, memory recall, and maze learning capability.

Your Style of Learning and Thinking (SOLAT) by E. P. Torrance, C. R. Reynolds, T. R. Riegel, and O. E. Ball, Forms A and B, 1976, 1977, *Gifted Child Quarterly* 21(1977): 563–73.

A 36-item self report, multiple choice questionnaire that classifies subjects according to right, left, and integrated styles of information processing. Each item presents choices for the three modes based on an analysis of the research on brain hemispheric functioning.

Perceptual Modalities

Edmonds Learning Style Identification Exercise by Harry Reinert, in "One Picture Is Worth a Thousand Words? Not Necessarily!", *The Modern Language Journal,* April 1976, 160–68.

ELSIE provides a profile of students' preferred perceptual styles based on patterns of responses to 50 common English words. Four general categories are defined: Visualization, Written Word (reading), Listening, and Activity (kinesthetic).

Field Independence /Dependence

Group Embedded Figures Test (also *Embedded Figures Test* and *Children's Embedded Figures Test)* by Herman A. Witkin et al., 1971. Consulting Psychologists Press, Inc., 577 College Avenue, Palo Alto, California 94306.

EFT was originally designed for research in cognitive functioning and cognitive styles and used extensively to assess analytic ability, social behavior, body concepts, etc. The GEFT is a group version of the test (approx. 15 minutes). Field independence and dependence characterize analytical vs. global styles of information processing.

Hidden Figures Test, Educational Testing Service, Princeton, New Jersey 08540, 1962.

Similar to the Group Embedded Figures Test—from the ETS Kit of Factor-Referenced Cognitive Tests, but available separately.

Scanning /Focusing

Learning Strategies Questionnaire by Norman Kagan and David R. Krathwohl, in *Studies in Human Interaction,* HEW/USOE Bureau of Research, Washington, D.C. 20202, 1967.

A short self-report questionnaire developed for use at the college level to describe learner strategies that either focus on the details of a learning situation (focusers) or attempt to piece together the larger picture (scanners), on a continuum of discrete to global orientation. A scanning strategy is related to field independence and to academic success.

Reflection /Impulsivity (Conceptual Tempo)

Matching Familiar Figures Test by Jerome Kagan, in "Impulsive and Reflective Children," *Learning and the Educational Process,* edited by J. Krumboltz. Chicago: Rand McNally, 1965.

Assesses individual differences in the speed and adequacy of information processing and concept formation on a continuum of reflection vs. impulsivity. The subject is shown 12 pictures (standards) and, in each case, six strikingly similar alternatives, only one of which is correct. Reflectives tend to take longer and to produce more correct solutions than impulsives.

Leveling /Sharpening

Schematizing Test by R. W. Gardner et al., in "Cognitive Control: A Study of Individual Consistencies in Cognitive Behavior." *Psychological Issues,* Vol. 1, No. 4, 1959.

Assesses individual variations in memory processing on a continuum of leveling vs. sharpening. Each subject is asked to judge in inches the sizes of 150 squares successively projected on a screen. The squares range in size from 1–14 inches on a side and are shown in a prescribed order.

Affective Styles

SRI Student Perceiver Interview Guide, Selection Research, Inc., 2546 South 48th, Southeast Plaza, P.O. Box 6438, Lincoln, Nebraska 68506, 1978.

A structured interview process designed to elicit student perceptions grouped under 16 themes that are predominantly affective in nature. Institutes leading to trained certification are held regularly in designated cities.

Conceptual Level

Paragraph Completion Method by David E. Hunt et al., in *Assessing Conceptual Level by the Paragraph Completion Method,* Ontario Institute for Studies in Education, 252 Bloor Street, West, Toronto, Ontario M5S 1V6; 1978.

A semi-projective method to assess the degree of school structure needed by an individual. Conceptual level is the maturity shown in completing six incomplete statements involving conflict or uncertainty. The method requires specialized training.

Locus of Control (Internality/Externality)

People in Society (Internal/External) Scale by Julian B. Rotter in "Generalized Expectations for Internal Versus External Control of Reinforcements." *Psychological Issues,* Vol. 1, No. 4, 1959, pp. 11–12.

A questionnaire to find out how people react to certain important events that they experience in a society. Measures the degree of control a person feels over his/her world.

Intellectual Achievement Responsibility Questionnaire by V. C. Crandall, W. Katkovsky, and V. J. Crandall in "Children's Belief in Their Own Control of Reinforcements in Intellectual-Academic Achievement Situations," *Child Development* 36(1965): 91–109.

The IAR scale is designed to assess internal-external perceptions of the control one exerts specifically in intellectual and academic situations. There are elementary and secondary school versions of the questionnaire.

Locus of Control Inventory for Three Achievement Domains (ages 13+), by Robert H. Bradley, College of Education, University of Arkansas at Little Rock, Center for Child Development and Education, 33rd and University, Little Rock, Arkansas 72204, 1976.

Measures locus of control in three performance areas: physical, social, and intellectual.

Physiological Styles

Questionnaire on Time by Rita and Kenneth Dunn, St. John's University, School of Education and Human Services, Grand Central Parkway, Jamaica, New York 11439.

Simple checklist enabling the student to determine preferred working times during the day. Scales are early morning, late morning, afternoon, and evening.

The National Network on Learning Styles

cosponsored by

National Association of Secondary School Principals
and
St. John's University, New York

Why a Network?

Research Activity together with the Practical Application of Student Learning Style in School Settings has created the need to establish a national network.

This network provides subscribers with information about developments in the field of learning style and teaching style.

The services include:

- three newsletters annually providing summaries of the latest research, practical applications, and experimental programs
- information about conferences, institutes, and inservice workshops for teachers and administrators
- descriptions of publications and dissertations in the field
- identification of resource personnel and exemplary school sites
- updated bibliography of publications and films
- response to written or telephone requests for information.

For more information, contact NASSP or St. John's University, Grand Central Parkway, Jamaica, New York 11439.